By Agnes de Mille

Speak to Me, Dance with Me

Agnes de Mille, November 1933
(Photo by Janet Jevous)

AGNES DE MILLE

Speak to Me, Dance with Me

An Atlantic Monthly Press Book
LITTLE, BROWN AND COMPANY • BOSTON • TORONTO

Second Printing

T 04/73

Library of Congress Cataloging in Publication Data

De Mille, Agnes.
　Speak to me, dance with me.

　"An Atlantic Monthly Press book."
　I.　Title.
GV1785.D36A37　　　　792.8'2'0924　　　72-10732
ISBN 0-316-18038-6

ATLANTIC—LITTLE, BROWN BOOKS
ARE PUBLISHED BY
LITTLE, BROWN AND COMPANY
IN ASSOCIATION WITH
THE ATLANTIC MONTHLY PRESS

Published simultaneously in Canada
by Little, Brown & Company (Canada) Limited

PRINTED IN THE UNITED STATES OF AMERICA

To my sister
Margaret de Mille Doughman
who lived through this

They love dancing well that dance barefoot upon thorns.
                    Thomas Fuller (1608–1661),
                        Gnomologia

The glory of his nostrils is terrible.
He paweth in the valley, and rejoiceth in his strength;
he goeth on to meet the armed men.
He mocketh at fear and is not affrighted;
neither turneth he back from the sword.
. . . . .
He swalloweth the ground with fierceness and rage.
. . . . .
He saith among the trumpets, Ha, ha.
                        Book of Job 39:20–25

Author's Note

I KEPT a full-length diary up to the age of twenty; thereafter, nothing except memoranda on dances. But I did write letters, long, journallike accounts, especially to my mother, and she preserved every word.

These letters have been altered only to the extent of organizing scattered material; and of eliminating family business and allusions to persons not bearing on the main story. My letters were, I find on rereading, larded with requests for services regarding ballet slippers and costumes, storage rentals, bank overdrafts, publicity, and managers, all very dull matter to the unconcerned, and embarrassing to me now in its revelation of the extent to which I used my mother. In some instances, people whom she had met are described as though she had not for the benefit of the reader. Also, for purely literary reasons sequences of events have been changed; life is so daily and so unclimactic as to become exhausting in the detailed telling. Finally, certain private remarks have been deleted by my editor as libelous. I was never discreet, nor particularly kindly, and Mother loved gossip as well as anyone. All conversations are quoted exactly. In my first book, *Dance to the Piper*, I telescoped my various visits to London for the sake of brevity. They are here listed with correct dates.

I wish to thank Edward Weeks of the Atlantic Monthly

Press for being patient, for being careful, for being stern, for being, on occasion, daringly permissive, but for being under all circumstances encouraging.

I wish to thank the Dance Archives of the Library of Performing Arts, Lincoln Center, New York, for helping in research and in the obtaining of pictures; the Smith College Library for providing me with copies of my letters to Mother; Thérèse Horner and Marie Rambert for the donation of the Ballet Club photographs; William Berenson of London for tireless legwork in tracking down lost friends; the dance critic Joseph Gale for initial enthusiasm; and Walter Prude for finding me a title.

                                                        Agnes de Mille

Merriewold

Speak to Me,
Dance with Me

I was born in New York City, where my father was a successful playwright. He went to Hollywood at the urging of his younger brother, Cecil, when I was very young, and I grew up there, acquiring a sound, even excellent, schooling. Since I loved the life and the environs and my family, I had a happy childhood.

Many people have written about Hollywood, but very few natives, and very few who like it. The writers, usually those who went out to make a quick financial killing, and did or did not succeed, invariably regretted that the atmosphere found was not that of their college libraries.

My family lived quietly and apart, but the values maintained in my father's business, which was moving pictures, did have a shaping influence on all our lives. It was my home, after all, and although I later went far away and tried for other goals, I used the yardstick I had grown up with to measure my failures. The Hollywood point of view was that one must be a success, successful in worldly terms, that is: recognized universally and paid largely. There was no other kind of success. My father was an educated man, and my mother was the daughter of Henry George, one of America's greatest economists and philosophers, who died poor. My parents tried to counteract and modify the local attitude, but we lived in Hollywood and we lived by Hollywood, and success was success.

In Hollywood one put on a tremendous front; one associated with the powerful; if a woman, one was pretty and sexy. This was not only helpful, this was obligatory. Other attributes were not essential: talent, for instance. Not in those days. This was why Hollywood was so attractive; the untalented and vulgar need not be disqualified. People the world over recognized the opportunity and for this reason there was magic there, the magic of pure luck. It became almost a mystic quality.

Hollywood, in terms of the movies, is now no more than a ruined capital; nevertheless, every time the plane circles down over the vast stretches of look-alike cottages, one recognizes, almost as an odor, the latent power. It trembles in the air. It is there, present as it is in baseball arenas or racetracks or gambling casinos, or for that matter, in Kremlin Square, life-and-death attention by adult men and women to something that concerns them nearly, without diversion, without alloy, without consideration for any other value or interest, something to kill for. In the case of Hollywood, it was and is — money. One had the feeling that the gardens of Hollywood reached to Moscow. One had the sense that Hollywood could buy the world, and often did.

The artistic market was centered in London, Paris and New York, but Hollywood was the ultimate reward.

Behind the writing of every play, every song, every acting or dancing lesson, was the dream of a Hollywood contract. It was not so expressed. Quite the contrary. The more sophisticated the artist, the greater the proclaimed contempt. But artists came, and a lot stayed, and they lived very well, better than they could elsewhere. The ones that failed, and this includes some immortals, were bitterly scornful.

We natives knew that the city contained more colleges and universities than any other place of comparable population in the West. We were acquainted with the academic faculties and we knew librarians and doctors and architects in vine-covered cottages on hillsides with home-tended gardens and rare books and choice cuisines. We knew that conversation could be quite as good as anywhere else and the music nearly as good. So we didn't mind the scorn. Whether the transients sat around in expensive Moroccan villas with whirling sprinklers on the vast uneventful lawns, luxuriating in the prostitution of their gifts, made not a whit of difference beside the fact that after all they were there. It was a worldwide compulsion.

They had come, and mostly they grumbled because they were not immune to being sent away again. If under the system it was possible for quite mediocre people to live like dukes, it was equally possible for them to have their status reversed without warning. Only the producers who owned controlling shares of stock were impervious — and Charlie Chaplin.

At the forefront of this strange and potent community there had marched since 1913 my Uncle, Cecil Blount de Mille. He rode the fluctuating business deeps as on a surfboard, with gaiety and bravado. If he had any doubts as to his own ability or scope, he never expressed them. He had doubts about his colleagues; he expected the worst in business dealings and was always ready. He was himself a phenomenally shrewd man who augmented an instinct for popular taste with bold and astonishing business coups. His success was a world success, and he enjoyed every minute of it, and it lasted. He kept sex, sadism, patriotism, real estate, religion and public relations dancing in midair like jugglers' balls for fifty years.

He was particularly known for his dicta on the beauty of women. If he found a young woman attractive, she might very well turn out to be Gloria Swanson. If he found her unattractive, she had a long, long road to go before she could again approach a camera. Styles have changed since, but C.B.'s dream of beauty set the standard in early Hollywood. None of his family women looked like his dream. It mattered to none but me. His daughter, Cecilia, very handsome, but not pretty, chose to raise horses, an eminently wise decision, however expensive. She has been for fourteen years the only woman on the Board of the California Thoroughbred Breeders' Association (the largest in North America) and the only woman president, 1963–66.

He was the most glamorous figure of my youth and probably the most powerful. I did not always admire Cecil's later pictures, but I never got over wondering what he would think of me. He was a kind of monarch, and although a younger son, he was the head of the clan.

Not as famous, but perhaps more subtly influential, was his older brother, my father, William de Mille, whose forte was gentle domestic drama which foreshadowed the present school of English comedy and French genre. He concerned himself with domestic relations and character revelation. Cecil thought all this rather dull and commonplace. It was as common as humanity and it was not dull. But it did not, like Cecil's style, appeal to the Arabs and the Chinese. It did not set every little shopgirl to doing her hair differently. In fact, Pop's pictures were often about shopgirls, which was no news to them. Pop's co-workers have said they thought he was years ahead of his time. He wrote and directed over fifty pictures.

I considered my father a very great artist and I adored him. He was all that meant excitement and reaffirmation in my life. His praise was everything I sought and his disapproval was a dimming of my sun. Therefore, any conflict of will became an agony. That I had a will of my own I consider rather surprising, my infatuation was so deep and so dependent.

Both men were rich, Cecil very rich. Father considered himself moderately paid, but in the 1920's he earned a steady four thousand a week with almost no taxes the year around until he had to take the dreadful adjustment of a renewed contract and was reduced to two thousand. Mother maintained a comfortable but restrained household and saved out of her housekeeping budget ($200 per week), against the day which she felt must surely arrive when all this affluence would cease. Why she felt this I do not know. Perhaps she wished it. She feared and disliked the atmosphere of the studios and wanted Pop to return to the East and to playwriting without financial guarantees. This had been the background of their early marriage when they had been happy. Those household savings of my mother were what was to give me a career.

Both men wanted boys. Their wives gave them nothing but girls. We were a family of women, with spinster aunts and dependent widows. The men never expressly said they wanted sons, but Cecil determined to name his only child after himself and was stopped at the fount by his mother, who persuaded him to let the baby be baptized Cecilia and give it some sex. (He later adopted two boys as well as a girl, Katherine.) My sister and I were named quite femininely, Agnes and Margaret, after members of the de Mille clan, but Pop referred to us for the first eight years of our lives as "the boys." "How are my fellers?" he wrote Mother; "How are the boys doing? Kiss my boys good-night." Sometimes he addressed my beautiful little sister as "old man." He wished me to become a tennis champion. He wanted me to learn fencing and boxing. He took me fishing. He taught me photography. Above all, he wanted me to write plays. He wrote my mother from New York: "Incidentally, I showed him [John Erskine] Agnes's sonnet and the Miracle Play and he was really delighted. Of course, he had some criticism — but he thinks the kid really has 'It.'

"Don't talk to her too much about it for she is inclined to think her own opinion is nearly always the right one, but I was very much pleased with the effect of her work on John."

I wanted to act. It's all I wanted to do. I was a good actress. Certainly not, he said. Why? Well, first I was gap-toothed, then I was spotty and gawky — no, that I never was. But I developed an unfashionable bosom, aggressive and some-how so unsexy. "Your sister is so dainty and appealing," everyone said. She was flat as a pancake and therefore chic in the clothes of the twenties — and she was neat; I came apart at every seam. Then it turned out I was ugly. No one ever expected this, but they accepted it and proclaimed it. And in time I came reluctantly to believe them. Were the de Milles not expert? Crooked teeth and that awful Jewish nose inherited straight from my Jewish grandmother. If there was one certain thing no Jewish producer in Hollywood would put a camera on, it was a female who looked Jewish. I was doomed. But I was a good actress, I said. That was not the point. Barbra Streisand was to change all that, but so very much later.

So I said I would dance. Uncle Cecil thought this inter-esting. He'd seen some dancers he found attractive and pro-vocative. Father had seen none and was appalled. Tennis, yes. Dancing, no. "You see," said Mother, "your Father knows you will be accepted anywhere if you play fine tennis."

"I can go a lot of places if I dance well," I muttered. So

I was turned back to Chopin, Dumas, my mother's garden and long, long daydreams. I was a very moody girl, sullen in the parlor and mean in school. Mother said I entered any social gathering on the defensive with the expression, "I dare you to like me." My sister was a raving little beauty and sweet-natured, with a string of beaux from the time she was eleven. She flirted outrageously with my father's colleagues — even Walter Wanger. They loved it. I was amazed at her boldness. Mother was shocked. Margaret continued and Father found her amusing — I wasn't amusing; I was rock-passioned.

But, being incapable of any unfilial disloyalty or violence, there was for me no thought of a Duncan-type revolt. All I wanted was to dance beautifully, but unlike Duncan, I wasn't sure I could. Nor did I believe, as she did, that I had been sent to change the world. I was the granddaughter of one who had. I knew that pattern; it was a tough one. People could be responsive enough to emotional vagaries, but not to blueprints; I could not be vague; I had learned to count exactly.

Since it had been established that I wasn't pretty and was no housekeeper, obviously then it was to be my talents which would make men find me adorable, my brilliant, active, successful talents. Ah, me — the learning ahead!

Father wrote in my autograph book:

> *My first-born child you are*
> *But that's nothing.*
> *I'd rather love you*
> *For what you do*
> *Than because you're mine.*
> *So go to it.*

And Mother wrote beneath:

*I who have always been known as the daugh-
ter of my father, and the wife of my husband,
pray that some day I will be known as the
mother of my daughter.*

There are two birth processes. The biological one, which
is so brutal and traumatizing that doctors say certain individuals never recover, and the rupturing of the invisible net
spun around our world by parental prejudices. Fathers are
there to help break through, but some fathers are not patient.
Some fathers abandon us.

Mother and Father got divorced and we moved away. It
was a terrible divorce. Father was never the same man after,
although he remarried and married happily. Mother was
shattered, and I elected not to speak to Father for two years
in an effort to help her reestablish a life.

My dancing career was begun, therefore, totally without
de Mille help. And this imposed a dreadful handicap. There
was not an office, not an agent, not a manager I addressed
who did not ask the simple question, "Why don't your folks
give you a job?" Since they were the fountainheads, the
answer must be obvious.

The affluence did fade. Father's work had entered a period
of long diminuendo and he began having excruciating tax
problems. In fact, his tangled finances, the divorce settlement, and the usual Hollywood dodgings about these matters
grew into a nationally known case which lawyers across the
land followed with grim interest. Cecil faced all the same
problems but came through unscathed. His bookkeeping had
been dazzling and he'd had no divorce to make fiscal complications. Slowly during the years, the government bankrupted
Pop and took away all his savings, every penny. He suffered
a heart attack over the troubles and only his staunch wife

pulled him through. At the beginning of this sad decline the depression hit and Hollywood disintegrated.

When Pop first saw me dance two years after I started, he offered to give me six thousand dollars to further my work. I wanted an appearance in Paris. John Erskine, father's classmate at Columbia and head of the Juilliard School of Music, persuaded him that I was being conned by a European racketeer and the offer was withdrawn. Later, Pop had no six thousand to give me.

At the time of the divorce he made my sister and me very generous allowances because, as he explained, he wanted us to be free. But Mother was in collapse and freedom was out of the question. Not that she lay around or sulked; she was still powerful and active, but her heart, that is, her pride, had been broken. She was a desperate woman.

She married me and as a wedding gift she gave me my career.

My sister, who was an honor student in both history and English, ran away from Barnard to go on the stage. Father and Mother deplored the decision. I, who had learned how jolly a cum laude could make one, cheered her on. Her final interview with Dean Virginia Gildersleeve was brief. "Oh, don't go, my dear," begged the dean, "The last girl to make this dreadful mistake and spoil all her chances was Helen Gahagan!"

Margaret went. Shortly afterwards she married, against Mother's dire warnings, a moving-picture producer, Bernard P. Fineman, then my father's boss. Both men handled this delicate situation with tact.

After several years of tentative theatrical efforts, my mother and I elected to storm Europe and London without Pop's six thousand. It seemed imperative to get away from New York. I had just been fired as choreographer from my

first big job, *Flying Colors*, book and lyrics by Howard
Dietz, music by Arthur Schwartz.

The theater in that period was very rough — particularly
the musical theater; all of the musical producers were tough
and hard, except Winthrop Ames, whom I never met. The
musical theater was controlled mainly by the brothers Shubert, and what the Shuberts and their friends or rather, their
associates, looked for in a young woman was well known. I
didn't have it. The English producers, on the other hand, I'd
heard, were willing to look for something else.

The Shuberts owned thirty theaters in New York City,
and landlorded approximately one hundred and fifty theaters
in key cities right across the continent. In fact, they held
what was virtually a monopoly on the few theaters that had
not been taken over by movies. This made them influential.
They would present anything the law permitted if they
thought there was cash in the project. And in the course of
fifty years and over five hundred productions, they spon-
sored almost everything, including a few very good shows.
It was always difficult, however, to approach them with a
new idea because they bought only what had been proven
salable.

The barrier of cold and calculating appraisal that a young
artist had to pierce was practically impenetrable and if one
were shy, as I was, and uncertain, as I was, it was final. One
time when Uncle Cecil was negotiating with Lee Shubert,
I asked him for a word of help. He explained, as he refused,
that his word would do no good. It would have, of course;
Lee recognized power. What Lee's henchman simply asked
was, "So, why doesn't your uncle give you a job himself?"
Nevertheless, I got to Mr. Lee.

Mr. Lee must have been very old during my Shubert era,
but his appearance defeated calculation. His hair was black,

shiny and flat. He was sunburned to a somber mahogany and so embalmed with unguents and oils that his skin had lost mobility and texture. Indeed, few ever saw an expression of any sort cross his face. He had cultivated the ability to speak without moving his lips. His voice was an old man's, high and querulous, which came oddly from that dark, foreboding mask. His eyes were black and brilliant and burned with watchful steadiness in the gummy skull. He seemed not to hear or take any notice, but no one was fooled. There are animals that sit unmoving in this fashion with unblinking eyes, apparently lost in inner thought until something edible passes. Mr. Lee knew everything that happened in theatrical New York, every click of every cash register in every box office, every complaint of every chorus girl about salary or dressing-room plumbing. He didn't know much about music or manuscript, but that was of no consequence. He could buy taste. He could not buy watchfulness. Not of that sort. This is the dark, primeval, digestive instinct that means survival. This is the shellfish opening and closing in Pleistocene waters. This is the eye in the jungle. I think Mr. Lee would rather have lost a leg than a bargain. There was magic about him. Like any witch doctor, he knew just where the life-blood trickled. And the young and helpless gazed on him as on a fetish or object of powerful taboo. And there was magic about the great maroon car and its liveried chauffeur that waited in Shubert Alley. When that awful receptacle blocked the passage, the taboo, we knew, was inside working. Little girls sweated through their mascara as they passed by.

Today David Merrick attempts the same effect, but he has a sense of humor, and this spoils everything.

The other New York managers may have been physically less spectacular, but they were equally tough, if not as powerful — Ziegfeld, Gordon, Brady. And the agents were the same, but rabid because dependent and frightened. It was from a Gordon production that I had just been fired, but Shubert had fired me, too. New York was dead for me. And, so, of course, was Hollywood. There were no ballet companies. This firing was drastic.

Mother knew about this. What she did not know about was that I had at the same time been jilted. The ordinary experience of being courted, completely won, and then discarded was to me so astonishing, so overwhelming, that my pride could not adjust. I grieved as my mother had and for much the same reason. I failed to understand how people so sincere and charming as we simply wouldn't do. Looking back, it seems easy to grasp, but then, no! I never knew why men didn't want me for a wife. It's plain as a pike staff. I would have been a dreadful wife. I didn't give a rap about a house or domesticity, and very little about anyone else's problems except my own. I was extremely interested in me. Men hanker after something else. It is really not the wife's career they mind. They would accept a career if she would get on with it successfully but unnoticeably while keeping her best attention for the husband's needs and work. I was capable of devoted love. I was not capable of domesticity. And I did not intend household chores to limit my activities. The basic needs of a man or a child would be something else again, but these did not include marketing or sweeping floors.

The artist is a devourer and cannot accommodate. That is why so few creative women can marry, unless it is with a colleague. Passion, character — even love, deep love — do not modify the flaw of divided attention. It's that simple. The only easy solution would have been to be as light in love as a bachelor boy. But I was trained not to be, nor was I inclined to be.

At least I kept my mouth shut. Mother didn't know I'd had a romance.

We went in October 1932 to Europe, Mother and I, quite alone, and we launched a brief season in Paris, Brussels and London without management, public relations, patronage or money, the budget for the season being as I recall (exclusive of passage, board and keep) $1,200. This financed seven public appearances in three foreign capitals. The concerts in London were sufficiently well received to elicit an invitation from Ashley Dukes, the writer, and his wife, Marie Rambert, reinforced by the critic, Arnold Haskell, to repeat the series the following June in the Dukeses' private theater, the Mercury, at Notting Hill Gate.

I was to take classes from Rambert and give my concerts in her theater, which Ashley proposed to rent to me for ten pounds a performance. It was against the Lord Chamberlain's regulations to perform publicly in English theaters on Sunday but various theatrical organizations got around this by forming clubs and selling subscriptions, hence the name "Ballet Club," which catered to a subscribing audience every Sunday night. During the week, Ashley Dukes produced experimental theater pieces, some noteworthy, and on odd nights the theater was let to visiting transients. I was to have one night a week, either a Tuesday or a Thursday.

I was to pay my way on every level, but I was used to paying my way and it would be cheaper than in New York or Los Angeles, where the name de Mille invited exploitation. The name de Mille was not so awfully regarded in London.

Marie Rambert, a nationalized Pole, was trying to establish a repertory ballet theater along the lines of the Diaghilev company. She was trying this in a vestry house on a stage eighteen feet square, where a sigh or heavy breath penetrated to the outer lobby. Her company consisted of dumpy maidens, a few stringy adolescent boy soloists, and kitchen-garden choreographers. Ashley owned a good deal of Notting Hill and Shepherd Bush real estate, because Ashley had eighteenth-century ideas about property, and both he and his wife kept themselves scrounging to pay rates and to maintain the theater mortgages. One day when their two daughters would be grown there would be leisure and affluence, and just very possibly generosity. In the meanwhile, there was cheese paring of the most parsimonious kind and niggling about everything. Mim, as we called her, did this with a kind of passion; every penny saved was one more effect onstage. Ashley followed the habit with historic justification. Land paid off — ergo, buy only land.

Mim had small support from her husband emotionally and little financially. He despised dancing, I think, because he was a bona fide man of letters (playwright and translator of French and German plays), and it was in the tradition of belles lettres to despise the physical or lesser arts. Also, although several of his plays had been produced in London (the most successful was *The Man with the Load of Mischief* starring Fay Compton, which enabled him to buy the church property at Notting Hill), most of his time was relegated to criticism. (He was, among other things, the London editor of *Theater Arts Monthly*.) His success appeared definitely limited, and not likely to expand beyond the measured limits he had set. He began to think in terms of producing. Mim had far more ambitious ideas.

Mim kept on fighting upstream, her guts torn out of her and nothing but her instinct and her taste to guide her. They were enough. Hers was the excitement of discovery, and in her theater was no prejudice against anything except imita-

Marie Rambert explaining a technical point to Arnold Haskell on the stage of the Mercury Theater. Left to right: Robert Stewart, William Chappell, Pearl Argyle, Marie Rambert, Prudence Hyman, Arnold Haskell, Frederick Ashton, Andrée Howard, Diana Gould (Photo by British-Continental Press, Ltd.)

tion and vulgarity. These Mim smelled getting off Bus #52 and barred the door.

The most astonishing aspect of this busy little troupe was its caliber. Among its handful of members were five choreographers who were going to make international names: Frederick Ashton, Antony Tudor, Walter Gore, Andrée Howard, and Frank Staff. Among its dancers were Alicia Markova, Diana Gould, Prudence Hyman, Hugh Laing, Pearl Argyle, William Chappell, Peggy van Praagh, and Maude Lloyd. They worked for pennies, but they worked as hard as any royally endowed company, and their standards were as sound. Mim saw to that.

Sir Frederick Ashton is now rated as history. He was born in Peru of English parents. He worshiped Anna Pavlova when young and studied with her in London, determined on a dancing career, a highly questionable and exotic decision for a young, middle-class Englishman. His first choreographic essays had been duets with Tamara Karsavina (and what gallantry and perspicacity it took for Diaghilev's greatest star and the toast of Europe to appear onstage with a twenty-two-year-old English boy!). He also danced with Rambert. This was in the Camargo Society which lasted a few scattered performances in the Hammersmith Opera House. Then Rambert got busy at Notting Hill and made Freddy chief choreographer in residence. He dished out a new ballet every month, inveigling Alicia Markova to dance the leads. As Diaghilev had just died, she had no suitable place to dance, so why not Notting Hill?

Ten years later, in 1944, John Martin was to proclaim in the *New York Times* that Markova was probably the greatest ballet dancer of all time, a pronouncement impossible to substantiate but certainly indicative of admiration.

Ashton took a class from Mim every morning and composed in the afternoon. He was a languid exquisite with one of the soundest gifts ballet has ever known.

Antony Tudor — ah, that one! Tudor, in my book, is unique. A good part of his style was right then being discovered on the floor of the Ballet Club. But few believed in him outside of Rambert who, no matter what others said, continued to commission and produce new works. It is a good thing she did, because his critics were harsh and one was powerful.

Across the city from Mim, an Irishwoman, Edris Stannus, was struggling equally hard. She worked with more application than Mim, but her taste was less perceiving. She could get along with men, however, and Mim could not, which was to be her undoing. The rival took from Mim whomever she needed and Mim let go, however bitterly, because egocentric as she was, she never stood in the way of a young artist's progress. But there was throughout the seasons a royal scrimmage between them for talent. Stannus thought Antony had none and refused for twenty years to let him near her, and when she did it was to be long after his American success. This was too bad because she was Ninette de Valois and she founded the Royal Ballet.

Both women have made permanent contributions to dance. De Valois organized one of the five ranking companies of the world. Rambert continues to provide the best nursery. Both ladies are now Dames of the British Empire. They were nothing of the sort then, and they gave each other short shrift.

One of their powerful associates was the critic Arnold Haskell, who had been fervent in asking me to return. Haskell was a small, neat, crisp, balletomane of seemingly large fortune. He was dominated by two passions — the sculpture of Jacob Epstein and classic Russian Ballet. He was married to a much larger person, a charming Russian lady, a one-time dancer named Vera. Haskell had much to do with the growth of English ballet and it was my good fortune that he was my patron and enthusiast. He was also a considerate friend. I found some of his tastes finicky, but not his enthusiasm. I also thought he overrated me, but I hastened not to say so and used his quotes liberally.

It was into this prim, ecclesiastical-looking cauldron that I proposed to go, an overwrought pantomimist with four hundred dollars (Mother's) and a talent for acting. The plan was that I was to be only informally attached to Ballet Club, but I was to be in the middle of it. I could never have managed to be in the middle of any state company. I was about to get an education in big style, hard correct Cecchetti technique, hard good rehearsals and public, professional performances.

The family, of course, thought I was running away from failure and consorting with ineffective Bohemians. They thought I was one myself because I couldn't get a job. My relatives always talked of audiences in the millions. Ballet Club seated one hundred and ten, and compared to the West End, New York, or Hollywood, its febrile activity seemed very small, but this, whether we knew it or not, was where the action was — here and in a few barren studios in Greenwich Village, New York.

If I have one sure gift, it is to be at the place where great things happen, or rather, in that wonderful fermenting prelude to greatness wherein movement and power form. Planning has nothing to do with it, nor has foresight, nor intelligence. Unwilling, resentful, and unknowing, simply I am there. This is the story of someone who got not what she wanted, but better than she deserved.

CHAPTER 1

In May 1933 I embarked for London to try my fortunes, for the first time in my life quite alone. Hitherto I had never been away from my mother for more than a few weeks, nor had I ever attempted business negotiations without her advice and support. She gave me four hundred dollars — all she had to spare. My father promised fifty dollars a week; this would be ample for a student but not enough for a theatrical producer. With me went all my costumes, music and press material. My repertory I carried in my head. I was to stay at the English-Speaking Union in Dartmouth House, Mayfair, because it was respectable, inexpensive (tea nicely served in a Grinling Gibbons room for two shillings*) and centrally heated. It was a kind of stylish hostel and although men and women were both registered there, Mother (who had thoroughly cased the joint) knew no hanky-panky would be permitted. It was a long way from Notting Hill, a forty-minute ride involving two buses, but it was elegant, and morally safe.

I had before me on arrival the immediate task of find-

---

* For those who like to figure, the pound sterling was then worth about $2.70, the shilling 17¢.

ing partners, stage manager, wardrobe mistress, members
of corps de ballet, publicity manager. Last winter's pianist,
Norman Franklin, was already engaged.

I hoped to find a lover. Mother suspected this. I hoped
to have a great, immortal love affair while I was resting my
feet. I felt a pressing need for this. I was not being watched,
for once, so I had free choice. The world of men was mine.
It was pretty breathless. Of course, I would have only a
couple of hours a day to give to the pursuit.

My sister Margaret, who seemed to have an unending
succession of love affairs, great and small, gave her whole
attention to the matter; and she said one must do this. I
didn't believe her. In any case, I didn't want a succession,
just one immortal love.

This book is not about my sister, but she appears constantly, if briefly. Lest she be thought to be a mere pretty
cipher, a doll, let me clarify the point. She had beauty, certainly, and was always marvelously groomed and stylish.
But she had biting wit as well, and no small intellect; she
took honors in history and English at Barnard. But above
all she had energy and good humor. It was I who sulked and
went into melancholia; it was Mag who tried not to. She
made a daily effort to be cheerful. And while given to flash
temper and even on occasion cruel and abrupt outbursts, by
and large, she was sympathetic, and she was always amusing
and concerned. She held my mother together in the dreadful
days with unflagging gay attention in a way I could not
approach. She was the least hysterical and most bearable of
any of our family. That's not saying a whole lot, but it is
giving her her due. She was beloved and she was always
successful.

When separated from her daughters, Mother wrote every

day and she expected the same attention in return. Margaret was always obliging, giving her the menu of every dinner and the guest list, also details about clothes. I didn't know what I ate, but always knew what on and with whom, and I supplied a full schedule of the unimportant matters, hoping to reassure her; but about the real turmoils of my life, I did not write. Mother was a worrier and when she worried, she intervened. In times of sickness or family crisis, she was indispensable. In times of ordinary betrayal and despair, she was an added corrosive. So we prevaricated. Pop never asked and never expected to be told. It's possible he didn't want to know. He asked once about intimacies, and I wept and that sealed us off further from one another. Mother wanted to learn my heart because she loved me and was concerned, and because she was living by proxy and was curious. But the scalpel lay right by her caressing hand, or so I thought.

Mother gave a first impression of frivolity; clothes, edibles, social furbelows and arabesques being her delight. She was in reality as high- and serious-minded a woman as I ever met, but disorganized, entertaining moral purpose and inconsequentials to the cancellation of both. A friend once said that Mother's composition was General Booth and Wendy in about equal proportions.

For her goodness, she was revered by young and old, but particularly young men if they were not her daughter's suitors; for her pertness and caprices, she was prized around the world's circle of friends; for her inconsistency and rock stubbornness she was endured with exhaustion by her intimates. Poor lamb, if she could have woven together her loose ends, she would have been a truly great woman. As it was, she was a bewildered and unhappy one. She continued, however, to believe herself infallible, and to give instructions accordingly.

The picture of my mother's character comes through these letters by inference. Her appearance was gentle and charming. She had been a red-haired little beauty. Now, she was ash gray, five-foot, tiny-boned, size-one shoe (her shoes are now in costume museums), with a high, lilting voice and piercing blue eyes. Piercing. Her family quailed before her direct look, and statesmen, policemen, children, and railroad officials paid attention. Her devoted admirers included students ("She taught me how to hope"), blacks ("She treated me with dignity"), cooks ("Sure, and she was lovely to me when my man walked out and I didn't know whether it was a spoon or a plate I was handing her"), merchant seamen ("After my girl was killed in Coventry, she knitted me mufflers and socks"), members of Parliament ("She sent me the Sunday *New York Times* all through the war. She never missed once"), dancers ("When she was in the house we performed more carefully. She would know the difference"), and the director of the Metropolitan Opera ("She never once in all the years I knew her talked of her personal griefs. Intimate as we were she never spoke a word against her husband. Her reticence and dignity were unique in my experience. She had — how shall I say it, she had quality").

A recent friend asked to see her picture. "Well," he remarked, "it's not a face to launch a thousand ships, but it is one to build nations."

On a sunny May morning in 1933, I set sail from Pier 57 on the boat which took Eduard Herriot back from a peace conference in Washington, his diplomatic corps and the best journalists of two continents. There was also an unprece-

Anna George de Mille (Portrait by Penrhyn Stanlaws. Courtesy Henry George School)

dented smattering of performing artists. I traveled tourist, naturally — round trip $125 without time limit.

S.S. *Ile de France*
Wednesday, May 3, 1933

Dearest Mum,

The trip has been heavenly. You can see what the passenger list alone implies: Eduard Herriot, the President of the Philippines, Myra Hess, Paderewski, José Maria Sert, Toscanini, and various theatricals. The assistant purser in *touriste* asked me to sit at his table. You remember him — de Villeneuve — he inspected my ticket on the dock and asked if I were going to sing? I ate only occasionally with him, however, because I was invited up to the first-class dining room frequently, once by M. Villar, the chief commissaire, who sat me beside Myra Hess (charming with delicate wit and a sense of fitness), another time by Mme. Artur, the wife of one of the managers of the line (mother of nine and pregnant with the tenth — returning to Paris for the marriage of her oldest and the birth of her youngest, returning not only out of patriotism but a true French sense of economy because birth in Paris is cheaper). Yesterday for lunch I was the guest of the captain and the president of the line.

Imagine my delight to discover in the tourist smoking room on the first night out Mary Heaton Vorse. I fell on her neck. She is just back from Scotsboro, Alabama, where she covered the rape trial of the young Negro boys. She said the girls were unquestionably common prostitutes, but the girls were white and the boys were not. The girls' word stood. Mrs. Vorse and the journalists introduced to me included William Morris Gilbert — he is head of the NEA in Paris and I gave him the full Single Tax treatment with pamphlets.

This tendency to propagandize at every opportunity was a characteristic Single Tax trait. Mother followed a vow "not to let a single day go by without trying to convert at

least one person." And even my sensible father was bitten
by the bug, working ardently for local reform, buying space
in the *Los Angeles Times* for his brilliant arguments —
"Neighbors, I have big lots on Hollywood Boulevard. You'll
either believe me or support me." My economic onslaught
did not, oddly enough, put Mr. Gilbert off; he spent a good
part of our conversation trying to make me clarify my status
as a virgin. This seemed to be the opening gambit of any
mild flirtation. Boys today generally learn with the offering
of the first cigarette; at that time there was a certain amount
of formal parlaying. In any case, I'd learned the enormous
provocative value of silence. This, of course, was just the
sort of episode Mother had strained every nerve to prevent.
Mother, like all Edwardian women, took for granted the
best, while constantly anticipating the worst. The black
doubts that her pure-minded generation entertained were to
me a never-ending source of surprise. Once when I whispered good-bye to her in floods of tears, I added that I was
breaking off an engagement to a young man of whom she
heartily disapproved. An observant aunt immediately concluded that I was confiding that I had contracted syphilis
and spread the word around the family.

"Virgin" was not a noun one used. It was beyond speech.
The implication being so opposite and so awful.

This was one of the lighter moments of my trip not
relayed in the parental reports.

Mrs. Vorse has offered to act as my official chaperone from
now on. She speaks French, attends all Herriot's press conferences on board, knows nearly everyone. She moved that night
from first to third class (an unprecedented descent) to be near
the writers and so has opened up the ship to her friends, whom
she invited upstairs and down on all occasions. Her wit and in-

sight are remarkable. Herriot has a whole troupe of diplomats
and counselors in tow and there are in addition a large number
of journalists, bearded and beribboned, any number of French
company officials and their wives, diplomats, not of Herriot's
party but traveling back from America with him, French busi-
nessmen, American journalists, musicians and painters of various
nationalities, and only a smattering of what could be termed
regulation American transoceanics.

As a matter of fact, the film stars prove to be almost the most
regulation folks on board. The ship is evenly divided in adora-
tion between Lili Damita (Mrs. Errol Flynn) and Sally Eilers,
with Bebe Daniels bringing up a very poor third, and Ben Lyon
not counting for anything at all. He goes around in berets and
coats that are too large and too brown with enormous leather
buttons and looks just like a cartoon of the rich young college
man and no one pays him the slightest mind. Their child is un-
popular because she won't sit still during the *Guignol* but insists
on dancing and prancing in front of the puppet box throughout
the performance.

Vorse asked me to get in touch with Bebe as she wanted to do
a profile on her for the *New Yorker*. It has taken Bebe three
days to answer my note. They finally got together for an hour
but the material Vorse collected could be used, she said, only for
a caricature.

Damita I have not met at all although I am dying to. She
promenades the decks like a gazelle, an adoring retinue of males
following her or gathering at every corner to await her passing.
Her stride is long and light like a runner's but with a daintier
foot, her smile is rich and radiant, her waist tiny, her poitrine
well in advance, leading the way toward la Patrie.

Sally, by contrast, is sugar-icing American and quite depend-
able and ordinary. She is very sweet and very expensive, but
you would know just what you are likely to get — something
costly and well advertised. With Damita, *qui sait?* As for Bebe —

And right here and now let me say, lest these criticisms of the

American contingent fail to be considered unbiased, that neither Bebe nor Sally made the slightest effort to be nice to me during the trip — no, nor so much as asked me to sit with them while they had tea or drinks in the evening or join in a game of Ping-Pong, barely even nodded to me as they passed through the salons, were just plain rude, in fact. They'd learned I was traveling tourist and notwithstanding they owed their careers to my family, and were personal friends of both de Milles and Mag, who had specifically asked them to look me up, they decided I was in all ways beneath them.

I've done very little except sleep, eat and sit around watching, and no work at all except what was necessary for tonight's ship's concert.

Last evening I stopped by Mme. Artur's cabin (she has been so sweet to me) to ask her something and found her absolutely garlanded with her young, an infant at the breast, while the oldest prepared for the evening's festivities, silver slippers, diamante bandeau, earrings. Mother suckled and gave advice about the coquetries of draping a scarf. "How well she understands her *metier de femme*," said Mrs. Vorse. I suppose she does. I felt as though I'd been looking in a zoo. It's another species; but I must say she looked well content.

Friday May 5: Last night we had weather. The concert took place on extremely rough seas. It was held in the Grand Salon on a small platform erected at one end of the room. The flooring was of uncovered planks replete with nails, cracks, and splinters. I had intended to dance the *Blues*, but hearing the pianist's interpretation of jazz yesterday, I decided to risk *Ballet Class* with a fifteen-minute rehearsal and no lights. It was a wise change. The rest of the program was composed entirely of superb music. The Bach *Gigue* Souquierre played badly also, although I impressed on him that Myra Hess would be present and interested. Poor man, he was too tired and too overworked to care very much.

The dancing of it was, however, something extraordinary. An

hour before the show, the boat began to roll and no amount of slackening speed altered matters. The taps of my shoes started off messily on the rough wood and ended with a silent flip of the ankle in thin air, the boat simply having left my feet, or again in mid-jump I would find the floor pressing firmly against the soles of my slippers with an unpleasant jar on the kneecap and spine. I got through it well enough with only one trip — couldn't help it, the ship lurched and I caught my heel in my gold-lace petticoat. *Ballet Class* made quite a hit. Herriot grabbed my hand as I went through the salon afterwards and complimented me warmly on being *bien intelligente*. Today he repeated the remarks, holding my hand in both of his, and I heard him say beamingly to his staff as I left the dining room, "There goes our little dancer."

After the concert, I had supper with that dazzler, Villar, the chief commissaire. (Villar was decorated last year by his government for promoting international friendship. Did you know?) He also said very enthusiastic things about the Degas. Eilers and Co. never saw fit to allude to the concert in any way. Toscanini stayed in his cabin.

I could not hear Herriot's speech, as I was dressing. It was on the style of Anatole France and I'm told it was superb. Paderewski played exquisitely with a somewhat faded tone and only one moment of the old fire. He looks like a long-legged bird now with a thin bald head and a ruffle of white feathers around his neck. I thought he would faint while he stood to the various national anthems — a-plenty of them last night — and, incidentally, someday get a load of the Philippine hymn; I almost broke into a cancan.

Sunday, May 7: Rambert had my permit sent down to the boat and I boarded the Plymouth tender without a moment's difficulty, a six-week working clause in my passport. The afternoon ride to London was through Paradise — the smooth greens studded and rosetted with clumps of primroses, bachelor's-buttons, deep purple slender hyacinths and magenta bouncing bets, the trees fully leafed out, a clear high sky, and the houses glowing and golden in the slanting sun, and everywhere sheep, and little, little lambs, and cows like toys with slits in their backs for pennies.

Ashley Dukes met me at the train with a nice blue leather automobile. He piled my trunks on a taxi and took me straight to the Ballet Club at the Mercury Theater. We bedded down the costumes in a neighboring bookshop cellar. I saw Rambert only for a fleeting kiss. I always feel when Mim greets me as though I were being readied for use — like a needle being threaded. She is staging a new ballet tomorrow night (*Atlanta of the East* by Antony Tudor) and can't give me a minute until it's over. She was warm, however, and asked after you. Antony Tudor and Hugh Laing were in the big studio painting their backdrop, which lay on the floor. They were graciously welcoming but obviously preoccupied.

Ashley Dukes is about to inaugurate a dramatic season in the Mercury Theater. Before driving me back to the Union, he took me into the auditorium, a vaulted box through which the setting sun streamed. (I'd only seen it in December when it was dark and dank.) He told me excitedly that it was to be called "The Nameless Theater" — and was to exhibit "nameless plays" by "nameless authors" — the actors were to be nameless also (no equity rules about this). One gangling young anonymous author slunk by and was hailed unwillingly and introduced as W. H. Auden, who is, I gather, a poet. He has written a play — *The Ascent of the F6* — which Ashley says is very fine, but which hitherto will be known I suppose as *June 1933 #1* and never again permitted its own picturesque title. Another play soon to be anonymous is *Murder in the Cathedral* — a fresh treatment of the killing of Becket by T. S. Eliot. It comes direct from Canterbury, where it had success. Now, why do you suppose that man has agreed to anonymity?

I mailed my classmate Elliot Morgan's two introductory letters

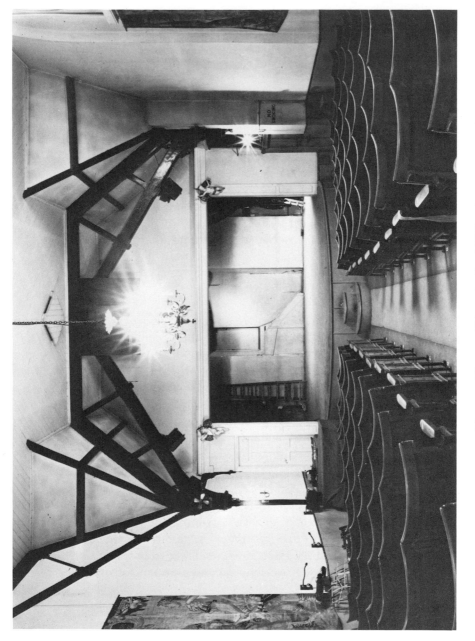

Mercury Theater (Photo by Paul Wilson)

to people he had known in Oxford: one to a writer named Elizabeth Bowen, the other to a Ramon Reed living here. I invited both to tea at the Union. Mrs. Cameron (E. Bowen) couldn't get up to town, but R. Reed phoned — a pleasant clipped voice. He couldn't come. Hadn't Elliot mentioned that he was an invalid? "No," I said. That was odd, said Reed. He couldn't leave his house, but wouldn't I come to him? And so I said yes. After I put down the receiver, I quickly reread Elliot's letter, which I had previously only glanced at. There it was: "A charming young man, unable to walk, paralyzed in the legs."

May 9 — two days later: Mr. Reed lives in Chelsea, way down the King's Road, which is picturesquely called World's End. He has a little flat of two or three good rooms in a modern building with a lift. His household seems to consist of himself, a male nurse, Sharpe, and a huge black tomcat called Solomon.

He is very young — startlingly young — about twenty-two I think, and extraordinarily beautiful. The youth and the beauty grab you by the throat as you see him sitting in his wheelchair. His thinness amounts to emaciation, and in the dead pallor of his face his great dark eyes burn with such intelligence and suffering as to have an almost perfervid quality. His mouth draws down at the corners, but it is still the mouth of a child, even though there is an element of strain and bitterness when he laughs. He laughs as though he were in pain. He has masses of dark brown, wavy hair. His hands are long-fingered and strong. I think he is tall; it is hard to tell. His legs are covered with a heavy lap robe and perfectly motionless. After three cups of tea, I screwed up the courage to ask him what had happened. He said a form of multiple sclerosis. He has been a helpless cripple for five years.

His parlor is charming and cozy with beautiful furniture. The tea was sound (there being some sort of gnome in the kitchen who is able with thin slices of bread and butter, cherry jam and fruitcake). For all of Mr. Reed's fragility, he seems robust enough in mind and spirit, has firm ideas about most subjects, enormous dislikes (which always take energy) and enthusiasm (which takes more), among them Elizabeth Bowen's novels. (He's lent me two — no time to read them yet.) He talks extremely well, even with wit.

I asked him if he could arrange to come to my concert. He said he hadn't been out of his neighborhood in a year, but if the Mercury could arrange to take his chair, he'd get an ambulance and go.

I ought to give him the tickets, but I can't afford to. He'll buy expensive ones, 7/6; I think he's rich.

I asked him if he could arrange to go to the country for a picnic if I could get a car, and he said no, it wasn't feasible. Imagine! All this spring going on outside the city, and he has to stay in his rooms with an occasional push around the square in front of his door.

The critic Arnold Haskell is coming to talk publicity with me tomorrow afternoon. He is enthusiastic and very kind. Afterwards I get down to brass tacks with Rambert. They take things in an alarmingly leisurely way. But I can't rush them, and they know the city and its habits better than I do, so that's that. (They have sent notes to the papers which have been seen by friends.)

I've written a long letter and in detail because I'm not sure when next I shall have time for another. Everyone asks after you, with deepest regret for your absence.

I have a nice room here — "John Bunyan" — specially chosen by the manageress, Miss Ireson, because it is long for dancing, has a full length mirror, and is opposite the closet holding my costumes. She has arranged, against all rules, for me to stay here through the recitals: four weeks.

Tell Mag that the dress and coat she helped me buy have made a sensational hit.

Devoted love,
A.

The English-Speaking Union
Berkeley Square
May 21

Dearest Mum,

Your third letter arrived just before the recital on Thursday. You know how pleased I was!

The sale of tickets had been very bad after the first rush for cheap seats. No one seems to want to pay more than 3/6 and our friends have bought practically nothing. But I simply shut my mind to the situation and went ahead. None of the Single-Taxers, absolutely none, have offered to help in any way. For ten days not a single seat was reserved in a name I could recognize. Isn't that extraordinary? However, we didn't do so badly — £18 the first night with a 7/6 top. The capacity would have been £30. Arthur Schwartz, the Broadway songwriter, came (when he had fired me from *Flying Colors* last summer he had tried so hard to cheer me up: kissed me as I wept and advised me to start troupes of girls in out-of-town nightclubs). Also Basil and Ouida Rathbone bought tickets, and Constance Cummings, the screen actress (in a 5/ seat). The rest were strangers except for the dancers and Haskell.

Not one word of criticism has appeared. There were two West End openings that night, and besides, my small London public has seen me in December. The fact that I had new dances cut no ice whatever. Something of a provincial town after all! Never mind! I danced *Harvest Reel* as I never danced it before, as I've dreamed I could dance. I was good. The dancers in the audience stood up and shouted at the end. Mim said she'd never seen anything like the great tumbling *pas de basques*. Even Mim! Praise from Mim! Ramon Reed was all but out of his chair at the footlights. I gave him a moment of freedom, I know it. If I never do anything else, that's something. "*49*" I did badly, through nerves, but the audience responded so violently it didn't seem to make any difference, laughing, calling, and clapping in an absolute storm of amusement. Rambert and Haskell say I danced both

Degas and *Tryout* better than before (Arthur Schwartz shrieked during the latter) and the Bach *Gigue* I know I did well. The Gershwin group number is generally conceded to be fine in design as well as in execution on my part, but hopeless as far as the English girls go.

Ramon Reed waited in his wheelchair until the auditorium was cleared and then I went out and talked to him. He was highly enthusiastic and begged me to come to tea soon so that he could discuss all in detail. Then the ambulance attendants came to help Sharpe, the nurse, get the chair down the steps at the back of the theater. Sharpe had been very restive through all our talk, saying they would be charged extra if there was further delay. He's a rawboned New Zealander with a manner both hearty and sullen and he switches from one to the other back and forth in a dreadfully trying way. But there's no question that he's the one in charge.

I expect to sell out the next two shows and maybe entice a critic or two to come. Charles Cochran, the manager, I've let strictly alone. I can't go on nagging. It doesn't do any good and I'll lose my morale. My job is to dance and dance and dance and if the big shots never come to me, I'll have done my work at least. But they will — someday — when I don't need them. Arthur Schwartz, I think, will do something. He was surprised at how effective I can be. He was really surprised.

The next show will go off better. I'll have the costume changes shorter. Before this concert we hadn't a moment to rehearse the dressers. The changes are two and a half minutes now, including tights and shoes. I think I can get them to one and a half, but how will I catch my breath and get bare feet into points? The dancers don't know how I do it. The points, I mean. They breathe all right. They're stunned at my procedure. Their point shoes are first carefully warmed up and eased onto readied feet, and nothing goes on bare feet later except adhesive tapes.

Next day — May 22: Now I learn that two of my Gershwin girls are off excitedly to Paris tomorrow to join Balanchine's

Harvest Reel, *1932. This is the quality that Marie Rambert called "Dionysian"*

ballet. Mim is kind of extraordinary in not standing in young artists' ways, but the result of her generosity is that I will have to train two other girls, and it's like teaching deaf-mutes to talk. I'd have to have their costumes altered (the costumes are knockouts) and buy new shoes, and I simply can't attempt all this before the next show, so it's out for Tuesday.

Rambert is nerve-racking but marvelous — a fine critic for me and a staunch believer.

Mim was at the same time precise and deep-cutting. Her daily candor about knees, shoulders, feet, hairdos and deportment was so spontaneous that she restrained it not at all about conduct, good looks, relationships, speech and personal taste. Occasionally, a girl came to pieces in her hands, like an egg, and went all runny with woe. Mim was sometimes checked, but not chagrined. When one of the boys snapped back, however, she reacted like a treed cat and if really baited, called on Ashley and her muse for help.

Hugh Laing was the one who snapped back with the most ferocious energy. Their voices rose like cats, hers in resourceful European English, his in Barbadan. But he had gestures, and long dancer's legs to which he took when overwrought. At the climax of one terrible verbal joust, he rushed up the stairs at the back of the stage and out onto the little dressing-room balcony, slamming the door behind him. The glass shattered with a great deal of noise. Ashley Dukes, two blocks away in Notting Hill High Street, heard the crash and cried out, "My God, Hugh's got Mim!" and ran as hard as he could to save her.

The rehearsals and classes were, of course, in shreds after these spats, but the work continued and the performance got on. The basic impression Mim gave was of nervous tension, because, I think, she felt responsible for all and that if she tried harder she could run the world. Her mouth, which was

Marie Rambert as I knew her

expressive and feminine, was tight and the fine brow lined; the head held rigid as an insect's. Her beautiful eyes shown fiercely in all directions. She darted and skittered and swooped like a swallow, in for the quick attack and away. It was deadly certain and you couldn't get back. Nor out of range of her tongue. She spoke Russian, French, German, Italian, and of course, her native Polish. Her English was fluent, even eloquent, but vinegary and staccato with accent. Her r's were like a snare drum sounding the alert. She was quoted, I believe, more than anyone in theatrical England — except Noel Coward and George Bernard Shaw.

May 23: I had tea with Ramon Reed the day after the concert. He is half-mad with enthusiasm and is planning, if his health permits, to go to all the concerts. He criticized in detail with an extraordinary grasp of technique and style and intent. He may prove a real help. I could use someone beside Mim, you know.

Maybe I should have gone into a ballet company in Europe and worked in the corps and learned something, but I am too old. And I've established myself as a comedian. I don't mind addressing envelopes. Don't fret about this — it's a wonderful release to nerves, really. But since I have also to do all the public relations and business, I am nearly always late for class *pliés*. But in truth, I hate *pliés* and do them rottenly. What stumps the class and Mim are my sixty-four *fouettée pirouettes* on spot. These come at the end of class and I am always there and I always do them and do them well amid cheers and groans from the sidelines.

Oddly enough, Alicia Markova can't do them. Mim brought her in from her rehearsal with Ashton to see. She was astonished. What this means is that I have a strong ankle and can do sixty-four *fouettée pirouettes*. It does not mean that I am a better dancer than Alicia Markova.

I have so much to learn — so very much. I can run and walk beautifully. Most ballet dancers can't. I have a good foot and a hot bounce. I am a jumper, quick off the ground and into the air. (My *entre-chats-sixes* are getting as neat as scissors.) My foot is iron (yesterday Mim gave us in point work the *cygnette pas de quatre* from *Swan Lake*, and I kept up just dandy. That's why I can do sixty-four *fouettées:* My rhythm is, as you know, infallible. But, and this is vital, I have no line, and my gestures are never lyrically accomplished ("No back," says Mim); furthermore they are limited, governed by the impulse toward acting, which is realistic imitation. I must change. My God, if I could do one good pure arabesque! I'm rump-heavy and too short between knee and ankle and who will teach me a cure for this?

I take whatever classes I can. The other morning, a Lady Violet Bonham-Carter distinguished herself in my eyes: on visiting the babies' class and seeing me dance hand-in-hand with eight-year-olds, she said to Mim, "But surely this girl is older than the others!"

I'll write all the personal gossip tomorrow —

Devoted love,
A.

One morning after class I heard music in the auditorium and stepped in. There were four or five of Mim's "lumpy, woolly" girls on the floor of the stage undulating, lifting, settling arms and legs. "It is the Adriatic," said Mim. "It is *Mercure* by Ashton." And by God, it was the Adriatic. "Watch," said Mim. "Venus will rise from the sea." And Venus did, in a yard-square space. Venus was Alicia Markova, the stringiest girl I ever saw, a darling little skeleton, with the great eyes of a moth at the top, and a butterfly blur at the bottom where normally feet would be, and in between shocks and flashes of electricity. When she paused there was the most beautifully surprising line I had ever looked at.

She was twenty, although she looked much older because she was so thin. She didn't look any age when she moved. She became a delicate natural force. Ashton, who was lounging about, gave clipped instructions in his lazy voice. "Mim," I said, "this is extraordinary!" Mim was contemptuous.

"Eggie, Eggie — everrrybody knows Ashton is grrreatly gifted."

I saw his *Capriole Suite* at the next concert, to music by Peter Warlock — just three dancers. Ashton in his best Elizabethan pout, Diana Gould, and Billy Chappell. This was not a reconstruction as I would have done, but a fine translation of the Elizabethan point of view, a poetic and witty evocation, rich as plum cake, not an expected gesture, not a remembered phrase, but all immediately recognizable as something experienced before, if in another form.

"I think Billy's characterization is marvelous!" I said. "The slightly decayed, self-indulgent ferocity of the Elizabethan child."

"Oh, Eggie," squealed Mim. "that never crossed his mind! That expression is just Billy being himself, pretty and difficult — as for Freddie," here she sighed deeply, "he should do so much more, such gifts! But he is not only lazy, he is passionately lazy." Then she ran around the foyer and greeted a countess. "What would he do without me — without my prodding?" she resumed as she passed me en route to the daughter of a beer baron in the basement class. "Ashton would not stir."

Indeed, what? He would probably have got a paying job. She gave him £1 a minute for these lovely ballets, and 10/6 a performance. She paid Markova 10/6 a performance, too. (At that, these were the highest salaries paid.) They, too, had a royal row one night. Mme. Marks, as the kids call her, demanding 3/ for taxi fare home at midnight as she was young, female and unescorted. Mim said sairtainly not, she could very well take the bus like anyone else which would cost 9d and be close enough. Alicia in her tiny tender way got very firm; turned nasty, in fact. Mim capitulated. "But to no one else," she shrieked. No one else had even considered asking.

In order to eat, Freddy, from time to time, did in fact take jobs in a West End variety house, six shows a day. He said he was learning a lot! How to get numbers on, for instance, when promised; how to redo on the spot during orchestra rehearsal; how to hold very restless people's attention; oh, a lot that would come in handy someday. His taste would be corrupted, said Mim. It would not, said Freddy. And in the meantime he'd like to eat.

Another person she thought lazy was Antony Tudor. "Both boys (Antony and Hugh) bone lazy, but *so* gifted. Now, Eggie, you're not lazy — if they had your industry, and you — their . . ." She burst out in her hellish laughter and skipped away. The unfinished sentence hung in the hideous void — "And you had their gifts!" She came back a minute later, having done something final behind one of the partitions, and said in passing, "I do believe in you, Eggie — else you wouldn't be here."

The boys, of course, were not lazy. Hugh danced all day long. Hugh took the beginners' class at ten, the professional class eleven to twelve-thirty, double work with Prudence Hyman until one, then snatched a sandwich with Antony and Liza, the Beautiful Secretary, in the office. From two until three-thirty there was intermediate class, from four-thirty to six double work with Mim and finally home to his digs in Warwick Square, frequently falling asleep on the bus top and waking up in Vauxhall. It helped when he moved into Holland Park Mews with Tudor and could walk

Capriol Suite: *F. Ashton, S. Morfield, W. Chappell*
(*Photo by General Photography Agency*)

home — next door. Mim, of course, taught all these classes unless spelled in the beginners' group by Antony, and Antony as student took the lot, taught or accompanied, while doing all the stage chores, cutting the gelatins (Hugh helping) focusing lights, and so on. When everyone was inconveniently onstage in full flight, there was a cross-eyed handyman dragooned into pulling the curtain.

Everyone did everything at the "B Club," and Ada Rede, the frowsty housekeeper, in the midst of passing tea trays and fixing hot soups, found herself in odd situations, last-minute costume fittings. There was one memorable fitting (three new works), with girls and boys standing around in the basement indiscriminately naked and clamoring amidst distraught sewing women. Ada Rede slammed down the tea tray and exclaimed with true cockney respectability, "I've been married three times and not once has a husband, I'm proud to say, seen me without a nightgown."

Ashley skirted all this hubbub fastidiously, mixing in nothing and devoting half-hours (after a morning of wine-tasting or shopping for Chinese antiques) to rising up and down on his toes in front of the anthracite iron stove in the office while pronouncing pompously on art and sex for the benefit of the laughing and lovely Liza.

He seldom pronounced enthusiastically on Mim's work. Yet, I believe Mim adored him, and would rather have had his approbation than anyone's. She deferred to him on so many matters she herself knew better about. He remained pompous, aloof and amused. And she yearned. She yearned without respite even while she snapped at him. Even while her dancers paid the bills.

Masking the awful importance of her instinct, the very real dignity of her taste, there was the outrageous impudence of Mim's behavior. She was a true showoff, like a

On the Mercury stage. Left to right: Andrée Howard, Diana Gould, Frederick Ashton, Marie Rambert, Robert Stuart, William Chappell, Prudence Hyman, Pearl Argyle (Photo by British-Continental Press, Ltd.)

spoiled child — and her tactlessness and sharpness were a hallmark. She turned cartwheels in Piccadilly at night about once a month.

Ashley was slow, large, ruddy. He looked exactly like any eighteenth-century portrait of a gentleman except that so many of them were stupid. Ashley was far from stupid, just aggravating. He and Mim both had humor, but of different kinds. They seldom laughed at one another's jokes but they enjoyed each other very much, even while maddening each other, almost without pity, except when there was a common threat and then they drew up side by side like any embattled English couple. They were always wandering around among the partitions and small rooms of the school barking back and forth. Next minute they would have their feet on the hob, drinking tea and chuckling. "Oh, Dicken," squealed Mim, "that's rrrridiculous!"

"That preposterous little popinjay!" said Dukes. "He wants his bottom thrashed!"

"God forbid," said Mim. "I'm having trouble enough with his *pliés*." Her eyes are now gentle and beaming.

Mim intended their elder daughter, Angela Dukes, to be a ballerina, something she herself never achieved. "She has the soul of a dancer, the heart and understanding of a dancer, but Eggie," here her eyes would fill with tears and run over. "Only not the body."

"Maybe she should do something else? I hear she's a brilliant mathematician. How about that? Science?"

"Oh, no!" moaned Mim.

"Ashley would like it."

"But Angela wishes to be a ballerina. Only that."

And Mim would blow her nose and look away to where Ashley was firmly closing a door. "Leave that open, Dicken. There is no air!"

Ashley Dukes sitting on edge of Mercury stage (Photo by Howard Coster)

I believe she thought herself wise and kind and very tactful, and a subtle and effective diplomat capable of being the wife of the ambassador to France. She had a truly warm heart and only occasionally meant to be cruel, and then naturally for the victim's good.

> English-Speaking Union
> May 26

Dearest Mum,

People always ask after you. Do I tell you? I mean to. And I want to thank you for the enormous constant effort of your letters. They are a lifeline; you know that I can't write every day, but when I do sit down I can't seem to stop; I get interested.

Now — about Mim . . . I know she means to be kind — and I do believe in her faith and need it, but there's that ten pounds rent every week and daily tuition fees. The Dukes have no endowment; the theater must carry itself. Mim exploits Antony as well as Ashton. She gives him £2 a week, for which he teaches children's classes, accompanies on the piano, does a good bit of janitor work, and stage-manages every performance, even those he dances in. For his ballets he gets nothing and no royalty. But, and this is the heart of the matter, she is putting a stage under his feet, several crafts in his hands, and a company, a production, and an audience at his disposal, and to bolster his spirit, her unswerving faith. She considers the ballets created under these circumstances hers permanently by right. "If only he'd work —"

Hugh got 2/6 per performance until he was graduated to lead roles. He now gets 5/ a night. No one at all is paid for rehearsals, but as Hugh says, "She makes me use my brain. No one else ever has. She is the first to do that."

She teaches the straight Cecchetti (teacher of Pavlova, Karsavina, Nijinsky) curriculum. For every day of the week there is a special set of exercises and Tuesday's may not be given on Friday. The children memorize the schedule like multiplication tables. Mind you, there is no progressive logic to them; they are set in arbitrary sequence. There is a certain amount of ennui in the routines, but they are designed to build thighs and ankles that would support the Brooklyn Bridge and vary the tensions and stretchings so no muscles bulge unduly and the body relaxes and recovers between stresses. "Now, John," raps out Mim, "what is the adage for Wednesday?" God help him if he names Thursday's. When one knows the correct order, one can teach Cecchetti and earn money. Not much, of course. Teaching dancing is something else again. They don't trouble about this in class. One moves for that next door into the auditorium where Mim demands *à haute voix* dancing. Where are they to pick this up? By osmosis leavened with terror.

More soon. I've looked up all your friends and phoned or written everybody I haven't seen. (Details later.) I've been absolutely perfect. Hoping you are the same, I remain, Madame, your obedient daughter,

Agnes.

I had heard that Karsavina was teaching at a more convenient hour than Mim, so I thought I might try her classes for a change. (I discreetly did not discuss this with Mim.) She held her classes in the ballroom of an old Victorian hotel in Bayswater. A scattering of pupils attended, led by Lydia Kyasht, who had been Karsavina's classmate at the Maryinsky School and was the first Russian ballerina in London, enjoying quite a vogue before Pavlova and Karsavina followed.

That day, I took fifth position before history. Across the room sat the great lady, the toast of Europe, the greatest beauty of the Russian Ballet.

She was the only female star Diaghilev ever cherished because she had been able with her personal magic to transform several outright failures into successes. Her qualities as actress and her dancing style were immaculate. Geraldine

Farrar always said she and not Pavlova was the greatest ballet dancer she'd ever seen. When I saw her in 1929 in *Petrouchka* there was, alas, nothing left. I could not understand the legend. Liza Hewitt, secretary at the Ballet Club, explained that she'd been in an auto accident some months before and that she never recovered her fire, that the light dimmed forever. It was she and no one else who created the leads in *Scheherazade, Thamar, Firebird, Pavillon d'Armide, Petrouchka, Sylphides, Spectre de la Rose, Carnival, Daphnis and Chloë;* in short, the standard repertory of this century's ballet dancing. She was to ballet what Bernhardt was to the French theater.

How did she look now? She was small and wiry and thin. She sat at class with knees well turned out in second position, forward on her chair, her British lady's tweed skirt riding up past the tops of her stockings, revealing pink cotton bloomers of the cheapest kind. Her blouse was mussed and not entirely clean, the knotty calved legs were in lisle stockings, the insteps of her feet sprang up out of the hideous buttoned walking shoes of the English matron. Her teacher's cane lay across her lap, but she seldom used it because her hands were occupied with rubbing hair tonic into her scalp. When she had finished massaging, she set combs in a wave and bound up the whole in a dingy veil. All the while she more or less gave instructions about exercises. Her voice had the dark metallic vibrancy peculiar to many Russian women. It is exciting to our ears, I think, because it has a slightly animal quality that has been refined out of the well-bred English chirping and the whining of the American drawl. Crooners use a similar sound, but theirs is synthetic. With the Russian women it is the real sexy thing and your hair stands on your head to hear them. She spoke always wisely, always briefly, often with wit. She was completely unselfconscious, casual, even careless — remarkable traits in a famous beauty.

Was she indeed a beauty? Her skin was dark ivory and the lids of her eyes almost brown. Her lips were dark, too. But the details of her features were not important. Her achievement had been so very great, it moved like an aura about her. She could do anything she goddam chose — rub her head while she paid no heed to her classes, sit with her knees out in wrinkled stockings, demonstrate an awkwardly devised *enchainement* in a too-tight skirt. When she looked you in the eye you were done for. She turned her extraordinary noble little head, she opened her enormous, heavy dark eyes — yes, she was beautiful. She took it for granted.

She began one day after class to reminisce about the premiere of *Firebird* in Paris in 1908. Fokine (who was in love with her, according to Adolf Bolm) made her do the entire role three times running without rest at dress rehearsal. She looked in the mirror in her little stage dressing room and saw gouts of blood in her eyes. "My father, the soloist, Karsavin, told me one could really weep tears of blood!"

She was, I hate to say it, a poor teacher, and after three frustrating tries, I went back to Mim and her scolding. And I didn't tell Mim where I'd been. "Eggie, you must come every day — with your shoulders and your neck and your great bum. You are a dancer only from the ankles down — five inches — not enough!"

CHAPTER 2

English-Speaking Union, London
May 28

Dearest Mum,

If I can't send letters as frequently as you like — "Short ones," you say, "even two lines, but often" — you must remember that you've forbidden me to use German and Italian boats for political reasons and that leaves the French and English. And they do not go oftener than weekly. Short frequent communications are out — long gossipy ones are what you'll get. I'll write them like a diary. Now to catch up on the events I didn't have time to recount in the last letter, everything as it happened —

Monday, May 15: With Arthur Schwartz to MacQueen Pope's, the journalist, for an interview. Arthur is being extremely attentive and kind. I thought he might — like all theater people — not wish to be around his casualty, but he's being staunch, probably due to friendship with Mag. No matter why, he's dandy, and I'm grateful. MacQueen Pope had been to Plymouth to meet Bebe Daniels *et al.*, had stood beside me on the tender, but had not recognized me, nor I him, since Daniels, as is her wont, did no introducing. I missed the publicity break of coming with them to London.

Rehearsals all afternoon.

Tea with Ramon. Home to work and bed early. David Walker

phoning me frantically to ask if I'd lost the way. Not the way, but my mind. It seems I'd agreed to go to dinner at his house that night. I had absolutely no recollection of the invitation. I dressed and was right back again in Chelsea an hour late. You see the state I'm in.

Tuesday, May 16: Light rehearsal until midnight. Antony Tudor stage-managed and lit. Threw out Haydn, five costumes and all. It stank. Home to a bad case of stage fright and loneliness.

Wednesday, May 17: Work all day and night. Every day except Sunday begins with a class at Ballet Club — 11–12:30. I'm usually late — too much business on the telephone and Bus #52 takes forty minutes from Marble Arch. I'll not mention it again, but class always happens, and is always followed after lunch by rehearsals for three or four hours in whatever room is free.

Arnold Haskell gave me a big press tea at his art gallery. Everybody came. My photographs, beautifully mounted and hung all over. Bed early.

Thursday, May 18: My first concert. (Results already written about.) Rambert took me home before the performance to supper and bed at her house. She said the important thing was to get flat between sheets even for twenty minutes.

Who do you think came backstage afterwards to see me? Tamara Karsavina! "Thamar" herself! She wore a black silk redingote with pale pink chiffon roses in the bosom, a high gauze Cossack's hat on her iron-gray curls. There were diamonds at her throat. Thamar, blazing and noble, had come to pay me compliments. She was at this moment the most beautiful woman I had ever seen. And she was gracious. My God, she is a lovely, lovely lady!

After Ramon Reed had gone away in his ambulance, Ashley Dukes brought us ice cream and cake, which Mim and he and I

"49": *Agnes de Mille (Photo by Sunami)*

ate chummily sitting on the footlights in the empty theater, Antony having tidied up and gone home.

Ashley drove me back to the Union. He's very pleasant, amusing and sympathetic when he's away from dancing classes and Mim's fussing. But I must say he was cozy and dear last night even in the theater.

Friday, May 19: Missed class because of 11:30 interview on Hollywood with a reporter from a low-down tabloid syndicate who was interested in my love life only. Tea with Ramon Reed — hysterical with delight over my performance. He seems to have a real sense of style. Talked about every dance in all details with penetrating intelligence and he's coming again. This means a big effort — ambulance and all. Dinner —

Saturday and Sunday, May 20 and 21: Except for writing you I worked nonstop. Diana Gould helped address envelopes for hours very sweetly.

I met Diana at Lubov Egorova's studio in Paris — (it was at Egorova's studio that Zelda Fitzgerald studied — you remember?) Diana works hard every day beside me in class. Mim says she talks too much, and indeed she rarely lets anything go by without a quip. She seems to be always short of pocket money and borrows 4/ or 5/ from me to tide her over to the end of the week. She asked to give out programs at my concert so she could attend without buying a ticket (lowest price: 3/6). I spoke to Mim, suggesting that possibly a scholarship would help her. Mim fairly yelped. "Deeana, my dear, is an heiress. She has a fortune. She lives in a mansion in Chelsea with butlers and maids and chauffeurs. She is due to inherit an enormous lot of money."

"But why then — ?"

"The English, my dear! She is an English gentlewoman."

And it is perfectly true — tea in the nursery, chaperones, ballet classes all day, and for treats, grand balls with the emeralds taken out of the bank vault. Between times, buses, two-shilling lunches, and begging from Aggie, who is a rich American and throws her money around. She always pays back; she never treats.

She is a real beauty, eighteenth-century style, with gorgeous shoulders and bosom, snapping, dark, intelligent eyes, and luminous skin. She must look heavenly dressed up. She looks pretty good in her black woolens, pouring sweat, the heat bringing a strawberry flush faintly through her creamy cheeks.

I've been to her house since; it's next door to Mr. Reed's and she knows I spend some time in the neighborhood and am much alone. Mim was right, it's a great house, with a name, Mulberry House, The Vale, Chelsea, with Bechsteins on every floor and maids running all over in starched caps and aprons. We ate supper — will you believe this? — in the nursery before the grate (real coals — not shillings in the meter). Mama and Step-papa ate in the dining room, but naturally, I was not asked there: I was a dancing companion and an American.

Diana has had the education of all girls of her kind; that is, almost nothing save languages, English history, and parlor talk. Anything more academic stopped for ballet. She is being educated to marry wealth and run a house. I don't know just where the dancing fits. That can't be considered in any way a parlor grace, as Pop used to point out so clearly to me. She has a sister, Griselda ("Gris dear"), equally lovely, but blond, and a brother, mysteriously absent. I'm not sure he's not dead. I gather the money was Gould's (divorced or dead?) and that it's huge. Diana is to be presented next season.

Diana's mama, Mrs. Harcourt, holds Sunday salons, and I'm invited — as next Sunday — if I pass watercress sandwiches. There is music. I'm told the young, of which I'm happily to be a member, sit on the floor; the grown-ups, who include the interesting and musical elite of London, sit on chairs. Mrs. Harcourt pours, and then sometimes goes to the Bechstein and plays four-handed; at the twin Bechstein sits, on special occasions, Artur Schnabel, her friend and colleague, and Mrs. Harcourt keeps up very nicely, thank you. For, it seems, she was a pupil of Leschetizky

Diana Gould in Good Humored Ladies (*Photo by Hughes*)

and very serious about her music, and making quite a name in England until she met Gould, who persuaded her to forego her career for family and fortune. One senses she is not convinced she made the correct choice.

Admiral Harcourt, her present husband, she addresses as *"mon petit marin."* He passes sandwiches, too. Diana recounted all this to me while licking envelopes.

I'll probably go to the Raymond Masseys' for the weekend in the country.

Mum, don't keep writing me to do more socially. I really do all I can. I suppose going to parties does drum up trade. (I know you always wanted me to be asked to a West Point Ball. Sorry about that! And what trade that would have drummed up, I don't like to think.)

The truth is, I like going to parties, though maybe if I were quiet, I would have better breath control. But who knows? I might just blow up with frustration. I can't work this hard and sit home alone nights in John Bunyan. However, you should not encourage me in my vices. There seems to be so much fun not to be missed. And I've never really played.

I wish you were having more fun. Don't keep taking only what Allie called the "woolies" up to Merriewold. Invite someone dashing with low purposes; someone amusing and delightful. There must be someone who doesn't want to save the world. But no, I'm sure you'll have all the faculty of the Henry George School in relays — try not to . . .

Don't fret about me. I'm doing fine.

> Devotedly,
> A.

In Hollywood it was frightening to be poor, because it meant one was a failure or very old; in New York, which seemed to have the best opportunities of the world, it was ignominious and shaming; but in London it could be quite comfortable. The condition was picturesquely historical and not unexpected. It often went unnoticed. Even the duchesses I saw were dowdy, particularly the duchesses. They floundered out of their Rolls Royces in suits no Hollywood extra would have dared expose; the miniver and diamonds were kept in the bank, the town dresses came out of their mother's trunks.

Style was attained only by actresses and parvenues and the little French prostitutes who scampered around Mayfair with the first dusk in their smart little raincoats and tiny rolled umbrellas. My lifelong inclination toward unkemptness took on here the pleasant anonymity of natural coloring and everyone thought at first glance I must be English and forgave me. What was expected of me I could, thanks to Mother, furnish. My diction and manners passed.

Sunday, May 21 (continued): It's hard work, damn hard. The people at the Ballet Club are angels, but everything else I have to do alone and it means steady plodding and my mind on nothing else.

I try to do this every day — plod, I mean. An hour and a half hard class, always late, always hard, though. The other day Mim gave three straight Cecchetti adages in a row, one after the other. Diana beside me looked around cross-eyed — her wet hair plastered on her forehead — and then she said, not wittily, but in a good straightforward English country way — "I'm going to throw up."

Then there's lunch — damp, muggy and thick, and then three or four hours of publicity and costumes, and rehearsing. I can't always do this regularly because of business, but I try.

There are, however, diversions — window-shopping, for instance, down Church Street, Kensington. It would be nice if I had some money; one can pick up Georgian teacups for 3/6 and Victorian chairs or earlier for 10/ but 10/ is a private lesson from Antony Tudor and I don't need teacups. Anyhow, I discovered a wonder bin run by a frowsty old rogue named Kate Kiniar Irwin, who sits in her Dickensian gloom wedged among the bric-a-brac, too fat to move, and attends victims. Only her eyes stir and her incredible Irish tongue. She wears a shapeless, dust-colored garment covering the mountains and meadows of her geographic body, a Carrick McCross fichu pinned with a gnarled Victorian brooch across where the mass shapes into a neck. Her hair sticks out from a tortoiseshell comb like the hair of the drowned, and when she has gathered enough energy, she points with a leg-shaped arm where I am to forage. She offers me tea in George II cups, odd ones, which she also urges me to buy. I don't buy cups. I do buy bits of silk.

I wish I could take Mr. Reed. He'd love it so. But an ambulance to a jumble shop! I have to be content to describe her. He says he'll buy me a teacup. I don't think I'll let him. Besides, what would I do with a teacup? I own nothing I don't use on the stage.

The other day I took Diana Gould and we found ourselves, under Kate's prodding, up in the attic rummaging through trunks of hundred-year-old dresses. I bought two: for £1, a Victorian purple Lyons silk (1855) bound in self-colored satin with fringe of hand-knotted silk — not a crack in the silk nor a button missing; also for £1-10 a sporting costume, three pieces of gray mohair bound in black velvet, just like the dresses of the Guys and Degas ladies at the races. I'm thinking up dances for them.

Opposite the Ballet Club on Ladbrooke Road is a row of two-story eighteenth-century shops, set back from the sidewalk on a crescent of paving. The low windows are Dickensian and in the back of one, a bookstore with gift poems, flower-covered cards and stacks of mystic pamphlets, including a good sampling of Kahlil Gibran, I keep my costumes. Behind the shop is a sort of chapel where people with worn nerves sit to be quiet under a noncommittal stained-glass window which could mean anything, I think, and might just possibly have been designed for a William Morris w.c. There are little cane-bottomed chairs easily pushed aside if I wish to practice, and a small piano.

It was in Mrs. Cancellor's Little Thought Chapel that I had rehearsed prior to my first London concerts the previous winter. Mme. Rambert had burst in upon me unbidden. The fact that I had taken a couple of classes gave her license, she felt, to interrupt my rehearsals. "Let me see you dance," she commanded.

I was so surprised, I complied with the *Gigue*.

"That's very good. That's surprisingly good. Ninette de Valois couldn't put a dance together any better than that. I'll put it on in my Sunday concert."

I recovered my wits. "No, Mme. Rambert, you won't. This dance will be seen first in my own concert before a West End audience. After that we can discuss the matter."

"Hmm," said Mim, and left.

She interrupted again half an hour later. "I've decided not to use your dance." It became clear right then how our future business would be transacted. And the attitude between us never changed throughout our whole relationship.

In the corner of the chapel there is room for my costume trunks. The clothes all have to be carried across the street the day of performance, but Mrs. Kelley, my dresser, does this with the help of her two strong children, girl and boy, pupils of Rambert. I imagine they get their tuition free for slavery to Mim and her theater. Mrs. K is quite somebody. She asked me to tea at her flat and served me in Georgian cups. I sat on early Victorian chairs which Mrs. K said she picked up for 3/6 each on the Portobello Road. I digress. The proprietor of the bookstore is an elderly enormous lady with white hair, a comfortable bosom and elegance of manner. Her thoughts are entirely spiritual and she worries about me when I dash in for a wig. Yesterday she literally grabbed me by the belt and ordered me to sit down. "You're rushing around too much."

"I have to," I murmured.

"Nobody has to. It's not in God's plan. Sit." She seated me and descended herself to rest opposite, the chair creaking in a splintering sound. "Close your eyes. Make your mind blank."

(Has Norman's music come back from the copyists? Was Sue able to match the slipper ribbon? Who the hell is Davis P. who wants eight tickets held until curtain? What shall I do in that ugly, ugly eight bars in the Gershwin?)

"Think of nothing. God's radiance streams in. God's infinite peace. All will be possible."

(Now, what about those eight bars? God's not streaming into those. They're mine to stream into and a nasty job I've made, too.)

"Quiet, quiet, quiet, quiet —"

(Should I fire Norman? He's playing worse and worse at each rehearsal.)

We stared at one another.

Mrs. Cancellor spoke in the silence. "I don't think you're ready for this."

"Mrs. Cancellor, the theater is falling apart across the street. It's only I can put it together again. Antony Tudor is already so put upon; he can't wait for me."

"Ah, Tudor. He's not spiritually too advanced. Go, my dear. Perhaps next week. Here's a little tract. Read it before you fall asleep."

I begin to understand why Mr. Reed gets so frantic when people suggest Unity.

You know what would help? You know? One permanent dresser, one permanent publicity person, and earned, not begged — one hundred pounds.

Ruth Draper is having the most terrific season. Two weeks in London at £1 a ticket. A week in Golder's Green, a week in Hammersmith, and then the provinces. All the Golder's Green buses carry her name.

Tomorow I have lunch with Rebecca West. She wrote me a letter beginning, "I don't know whether or not you'll remember who I am. I met you when you were a very little girl." I remember her all right. I was goggle-eyed over the teapot in your Blue Garden when you returned triumphantly from the Hollywood Women's club leading your splendid British Captive. I remember you asked me to get her some primroses. There were nine. She got the lot. Apparently she remembered too, which is sort of astonishing, but people do not forget you or your hospitality.

So many, many people ask for you. Keep well, have fun, stay out of the heat. All my love —

Devotedly,
A.

English-Speaking Union
May 25

Dear Mum,

Lunch with Rebecca West was delightful. She's extraordinary company, and welcomed me as a contemporary and old friend. She lives in a beautiful flat in Portman Square.

She has the most beautiful eyes I have even seen, dark, piercingly luminous and lighting with deep laughter as ideas occur. They are heavily fringed with black lashes. Well, several beauties have eyes like this. Hers, however, absolutely burn with intelligence and excitement when she thinks of something, which is quite often.

Her voice is very high, caroling and arabesquing in the English tessitura. Her diction is so British that I don't quite follow the sense from time to time, which is a pity, because there's lots of that. "What an extraordinary thing," she begins and then recounts something so preposterous you can hardly credit your ears. Each human being she meets seems brand-new, a troglodyte, previously unsupposed, unbelieved, a marvel, not always praiseworthy, but real. She has a long and embracing memory — with wicked delight in all human foibles — but not with cruelty. For these reasons she is a wonderful gossip. I don't know her superior. We put our feet up and just gabble. The other day at lunch we consumed two whole onion pies between us while we chattered on. My, the butler was mad, as well as surprised! I think he'd counted on some for himself. We left not a crumb.

Next day: I've been partying on the introduction of your school friend, good old Belle Moskowitz, who wrote her daughter to look out for me. Daughter is married to an extremely wealthy young Jew, and his mother, the Honorable Mrs. Franklin, invited me to one of those extraordinary London lunches that become the main business of the day. This was on a midweek and presumably a business day, but people here don't take business nearly as seriously as lunches. Twenty of them were present, including a dozen refugees from Hitler. Her house was colossal and ugly and full of Sargents, Epsteins, Boutet de Monvels, Kate Greenaways, du Mauriers, and medieval carvings assembled in dark Edwardian Tudor rooms. The waitresses were costumed in green net head veils tied at the back in a *chou*, tiny wreaths of leaves binding the veil to the head in a Burne-Jones Maid Marian style, and underneath there remained the naked faces of elderly English parlor maids. The tablecloth was green and the soup bowls ancient Chinese. In the midst of this romantic splendor, the hostess wore an old silk blouse and skirt cut on no lines at all, a crumbled straw hat trimmed with silk ribbon punctured all over with blackened hatpin holes. The Honorable Mrs. Franklin also hobbled about on a wooden leg, and a stick. And the story of that is that she is such a feminist she took a bad leg to a woman surgeon who didn't quite know her trade, in preference to a man who did; chop, chop and now peg leg — there's feminism with a vengeance!

I spoke to a charming young German girl at the table, asking her by way of conversation if she intended to stay long in this country. "I think so," she said smiling sadly at the young Jew beside her, an impressive, large, black-haired person, Professor Edgar Wind. "I think we'll all be here quite some time," he said.

He is transferring the Warburg Institute (art history) intact from Hamburg to London. Permanently.

Later — May 28: Ramon has taken me to a theater and to a movie. Movies are going to be easy. Sharpe lifts him into his chair and we go down in the lift. I can manage the roll up the King's Road except for the curbs, but there's always a passerby to help. If someone would just invent a collapsible wheelchair of some lighter substance than oak, or a collapsible stretcher seat, we could manage in an ordinary car. Everything is so heavy, so cumbersome. Are there no other paralyzed people in the world? Sharpe lets us go along the embankment past Cheyney Row, where Whistler lived, and the Carlyle House, now a museum (oh, how I long to go in — but Ramon's chair can't manage the steps), and sometimes to the pub Seven Bells, where I've been introduced to my first English ale and watched the clients playing skittles on the back lawn.

Through all these walks Ramon sits slouched with his fedora hat pulled over his eyes. "Why do you hide your face?" I ask. "It's my shame!" he said. "People look at me with curiosity and pity. I can't bear the pity."

I've told you how beautiful he is and how young. He is twenty-two but he looks eighteen and he is classically beautiful. "The most theatric figure in London," says Kirk Askew, of the Durlacker Gallery, as though all this were an act deliberately assumed for attention.

"When strangers ask me what's the matter," says Ramon, "and they never hesitate to, I tell them if I like them. Otherwise I just explain that I'm lazy."

But to get back to the theaters. In spite of Sharpe's grumbling, Ramon arranged to go. Everything in his life takes arranging. This time he had to buy a box and he had to go by ambulance. We ate very early. We both dressed up. The ambulance arrived at 7:30. Sharpe took Ramon in *smoking* and black fedora in his chair downstairs. There were waiting the curious, mainly small boys. With the help of the ambulance attendants, Ramon was hoisted up, chair and all, to the delight of the crowd. They even mounted the steps and flattened their noses on the glass. Then they waited to see what further disaster would materialize and I flowed down the front steps in full evening dress, covered with orchids (Ramon says he will not have me riding in an ambulance unless I wear orchids). I mounted the steps grandly. The uniformed attendants slammed the doors and we drove off (no bells or sirens), waving and blowing kisses to the gaping crowd. At the theater the process was reversed to a bigger audience. The sight of an ambulance at a theater marquee leads everyone to hope that maybe the star has dropped dead or gone mad.

When I alighted there was recognizable bewilderment. I went in first and waited in the powder room because Ramon always has to be transferred from the wheelchair to a cushioned seat and he can't bear to have me see Sharpe lift him.

Ramon and I never refer to his incapacities in any way at all. He told me on my first visit that he couldn't walk. That's all I know. He says he will get well. He says he will walk. I don't want to talk to Sharpe. I don't want to talk to him about anything. Sharpe has indicated he wants to talk, that he would like to be on a real matey footing with me. Thanks ever so — but no.

Oh, how I long for a good gab with Mag — to share some jokes. Familiar jokes, to dish. I have many friends here and everyone is kind and concerned and generous, but there is always the feeling that I am just a little different, because I am American, because I come from Hollywood, because my slang is not their slang, and my impatience snaps at different things. How can I express it? I am deeply attuned to everything here, but, well, it's not my country, my tempo, my lingo. There's a different expectancy. I'd just plain like to be with my folks now and then and let go. I think the word I'm struggling to find is "homesickness."

All — all — all my love,
A.

Henry Arthur Sharpe was a tall, bony, red-faced man with high cheekbones and the expression of guarded energy that every good workman maintains. (Sharpe had been a construction worker in New Zealand.) He was tall. His hands were large, freckled, and covered with rust-colored hair. He was strong. He had a long upper lip and a tightly held mouth. The impression he gave was of a determined, capable man, much the impression a conservative, old-fashioned schoolmaster might make, which in point of fact, had his circumstances been otherwise, he might well have been. He was also stubborn and this showed, too, and he was wary. He had been in some very rough spots — including matrimony, and had come out alive. He aimed to continue that way.

May 29

Dearest Mum,

Last Monday I went with Ramon into Kent. We rode in an open car, Ramon sitting in a sort of wooden stretcher. He had brought the most remarkable lunch — crab and sandwiches and wine and strawberries and coffee, with plates and napkins, most carefully prepared. He delights in doing things fastidiously. We parked the car by the side of a road under a wild rose bush and sent the chauffeur to the nearest inn for lunch. Ramon asked for some flowers. I picked him a large bunch of buttercups and daisies. I wanted to run and tumble in the fields, but when I looked back and saw him watching me from the car and waving as I turned toward him, sitting watching until I returned, my heart broke and I couldn't romp before him.

Arnold Haskell, the critic, not only gave me a press party but asked me to dinner Wednesday at his home, a most extraordinary place so filled with Epstein sculpture that it looks like an indoor graveyard, a parlor Westminster Abbey. You're hard put to find a chair you can sit up in without striking your head on a bronze chin. He has some wonderful pieces. Two or three of Isabella, the model, and one of a sick child that is extraordinarily moving, but large and jutting.

Arnold, by the way, had told me that George Bernard Shaw had mentioned to Orage, the editor, that he had met the granddaughter of "Henry George the Single-Taxer" in New York. I explained that he hadn't, that he'd met you, the daughter, but that if he'd like to meet the granddaughter, she was agreeable. So I think it's going to be arranged; a lunch, I believe, at his London flat on the Thames Embankment.

The second concert is tomorrow, May 30. I'll cable results.

Wednesday, June 1: At last night's concert a packed house, but sticky audience, probably due to intense heat. It seemed to me I danced badly and that the waits were shockingly long. Just before the concert, Ouida Rathbone stopped me at P. G. Wodehouse's tea for a minute to say she must talk to me about my work and intimated that she didn't like it anymore. Thoroughly depressed, I went off to the theater and my performance. I'll tell you more later.

I'm about to look up the Single-Taxers of Petty France even if they don't like dancing. They never buy tickets. I've given many of them free ones, you know.

I gotta rush — devoted love,

A.

CHAPTER 3

MOTHER had permitted my going away unchaperoned partly because of the presence in London of a large group of Single-Taxers. Before all else, Mother was the adoring disciple of her father, Henry George, and Single-Taxers the world over constituted a kind of second family, men and women of unimpeachable character who would, she knew, keep an eye on me.

In Hollywood we had been visited by most astonishing travelers: Count Ilya Tolstoi, the son of Leo Tolstoi, who had been an ardent supporter; Mrs. Edward Aveling, the daughter of Karl Marx, who had not been; Robert Andrews Millikan, the great physicist; and John Dewey, who wrote, "It would require less than the fingers of the two hands to enumerate those who, from Plato down, rank with Henry George among the world's social philosophers."

These visitors of Mother's were quite different from the regular local hangers-on, of which we had a plethora always. The latter asked nothing. They wanted merely to stand up and be counted. Wherever we went thereafter, we were met by men and women who had corresponded for years with my mother and who opened their houses and hearts, even in Paris, which is basically a closed city to strangers.

Across the world there was a scattering of spiritual uncles and aunts expected and expecting to serve not only in emergency but consistently, like real, concerned relatives. Whenever they saw Mother approaching, they knew it would be with a dependent daughter and that much would be asked of them. They loved her nonetheless. They loved her very much. And they did things for my sister and me beyond all reasonable expectation.

This chain of friendship extended back for three generations, was of extraordinary vitality, and I believe, was, with others like it, a phenomenon of the nineteenth century.

Thomas Huxley had been historically the first of what Mother always referred to as "disciples"; just as Sun Yat-sen had probably been the most powerful and hopeful, there were many others of less magnitude. Since, in the nineteenth century, there was no income tax, no mercenary benefit derived from supporting charities, art, or reforms; a gift in those days was a cut out of one's own flesh. It is, therefore, edifying to learn of the type of enlightened industrialist who, having inherited or made fortunes, concerned himself with the welfare of others and acted forcefully with no thought of personal gain. My grandfather attracted many such. He was given a house, several transatlantic trips, and money, which he needed badly, for he took nothing in royalties or lecture fees. Bernard Shaw heard him orating on the London streets from the top of a four-wheeler and was inspired to begin considering economic problems. This led Shaw directly to the Webbs and Fabian socialism. But there was a long line of convinced Georgists who did not deviate but shaped their efforts on the original plan. Lord Philip Snowden; Lord Josiah Wedgwood; H. G. Wells; Andrew Mc-Claren, member of Parliament; Lloyd George; Lord Douglas of Barlock, the governor of Malta. Most of the English contingent were members of the Taxation of Land Values League and most of them were members of the Liberal Party.

I remember my first visit to the great Liberal Club down by the embankment — the wattled stone façade, the empty dining room, the spotted tablecloth, the creaking antique waiters in their high, throttling collars, the flawless manners, the questionable mutton and vegetable, the unspeakable pudding, the *Times* crackling in the hands of the room's only other occupant, a septuagenarian of mottled complexion and dim smile, and the whispering of lofty, selfless sentiments as the dust settled everywhere.

I wish to make one thing very clear: I believe in the Single Tax, and so do a great many recognized economists. George said, "This and this alone I contend: that he who makes should have, that he who saves should enjoy. I ask on behalf of the poor nothing whatever that properly belongs to the rich. . . . The truth that I have tried to make clear will not find easy acceptance. If that could be, it would have been accepted long ago. If that could be, it would never have been obscured. But it will find friends — those who will toil for it; suffer for it; if need be, die for it. This is the power of truth."

He disagreed violently with Marx on the sources of wealth. The wealth that comes from labor, any labor, physical or mental, he felt, should not be touched by taxes: it belonged in full to the laborer; but the wealth that comes from the preemption of natural resources, real estate, common property, should be taxed very nearly to the point of confiscation — for the public needs and reimbursement. It seems as unanswerable as Euclid.

George believed that the income from these national re-

sources and site values would be sufficient for all government needs. He did not, of course, foresee continuous wars,
nor a state where a large percentage of the community would
be kept on perpetual dole. It was involuntary idleness and
poverty he deplored. It was major theft he was battling,
which produces recurring financial panics, injustice and deprivation on all levels. Since his day there have been enormous
complications and diversifications but, whatever the prolifer-
ated refinements, the basics stand. England is now, on the
surface at least, socialistic. Underneath, the great fortunes
remain; the fortunes founded on the ownership of entire
cities by one belted aristocrat or another who earned his
rights with three hours of hard whacking nine hundred years
before. The government has taken away much of the Englishman's property but not his freehold rights, and the nib-
bling at the top of the income is as nothing compared to
the fortunes welling forever and always greater under the
crowded pavement.

Without adequate funds or remuneration, the London
Georgists maintained in 1933 an office on Petty France
Street, a journal, and a constant anger against all the fiscal
enactments of Parliament. They were vocal, crotchety, selfless, dedicated, humorless — and they were all sizes and
shapes, but mostly small. In Mother's time they were headed
by a Scotch dwarf named John Paul (under four feet) with
a tremendous logical mind and a heavy burr. He had miracu-
lously enough found a mate, even smaller, who wore ankle-
length black cloth skirts and a black felt hat which was in
essence the British Gentlewoman's Hat. Sometimes it had
a buckle and sometimes a flower, but it never compromised
in any other way. Her laced boots were formidable, too. The
Pauls' four boots together on their tiny, short legs made a
terrible impression. She had slightly pop-eyes and said little.

In any case, it would have been incomprehensible, being Highland. Whatever it was, one gathered it was in support of her husband. Their poverty and high-mindedness were constant.

At the daily side of John Paul was Arthur Madsen, half Scotch, half Danish, bilingual, ardent and denouncing. It was Arthur Madsen who had negotiated Mother's and my way through the Home Office the preceding winter when we stormed England alone. She had to lay her letter-of-credit on the official's desk and swear she would not take a penny of English money as salary. Madsen swore likewise, vouching for her in strong Scots but muttering loudly as he left, "The Eejuts! You bring labor and therefore wealth. They ought to be grateful to you. They ought to thank you; when will they get any of their economics straight?" Arthur's wife, Lily, was a jolly Glasgow girl with ruddy cheeks and a full bosom who couldn't bear Paul's gloom but was glued to him and to his wife for life. The two couples spent every Sunday together, and their mutton and veg with gravy was shared with relentless economic analysis. Lily thrashed to no avail. There was no question where loyalty lay; it lay with Paul and thence with George. John Paul had known George Jr. personally and that made him special.

The ardor of these crusaders tended to make them seem a little cracked. Any group of people that is content not to get ahead personally, but just to be right, are suspect unless buttressed by a powerful religious institution. The Single-Taxers, however, all of them, even the smallest with bad teeth, were not only spiritually prophylactic but educated and informed; a pity they were not also effective. They squandered their passion in quarreling and refused to reconcile pedantries to get anything practical done. The Danes organized better and put twenty members into Parliament on their own ticket.

The young secretary to the Taxation of Land Values League was a brilliant and handsome lad. I'd spotted him on the first day of the Edinburgh Conference. He was blond, blue-eyed, square of jaw, with a beautiful mouth. His voice was fine, his gaze forthright and brave, and he had the wonderful carriage of head of the finely bred Englishman. He was a brilliant student and excellent speaker. He was twenty. We ran off on the last night of the conference and wandered around the Edinburgh slums under a full moon. He swore as he kissed me in a dark and fairly foul alley that I was probably the most fascinating woman he'd ever met, and next evening I left for New York, not knowing whether or not he was the answer to my fate. I will call him Robin Lennox; but that is not his rightful name. A few months later he stood for Parliament at the age of twenty-one, but was defeated. He cabled when he got a steady job at Odhams, a publishing house, £7 per week. He had left the Taxation of Land Values League. Except for this small salary he was virtually penniless.

It was through Ashley Mitchell, the Yorkshire Single-Taxer, that I learned he'd also got married, an event he had neglected to mention in his letters. When I confronted him with the fact, he replied he didn't think his being married was important since nothing had worked out. Somehow his wife had got misplaced. She was a middle-European and he thought she was presently in the Near East, but he was not sure. He wanted to find her only to terminate the relationship. She did not wish to give up her British passport and so she did not want to be found. His point of view showed a casualness which made me thoughtful.

Edinburgh — Taxation of Land Values Conference, 1929. Counting from
(FIRST ROW SEATED) Arthur Madsen, 5th; Agnes de Mille, 7th; Margaret de ̷
11th; Ashley Mitchell, 12th (SECOND ROW) directly behind Margaret is An̷
Mille; at extreme right Sam Meyer of Belgium and France, destroyed by the ̷

(THIRD ROW) *Lily Madsen, 3rd; Folke Folke and his wife, 16th* (THIRD ROW FROM TOP) *extreme left, Robin Lennox* (TOP ROW) *extreme right, Andrew McClaren, M.P.*

"He won't come to any good," said Ashley Mitchell over Mother's comfortable New York dinner table.

"You're cross with him because he left the Taxation of Land Values League office," I replied.

"It's not that. It takes a man to know men. He won't amount to anything."

I'd rather hoped he would, and I quailed before the firm Yorkshire onslaught. Ashley's stern judgments reminded me that he came from the land of the Brontës.

In any case, when I had returned the previous winter he had been right on hand and constant in his attentions — chocolate at Lyon's Corner House, enthusiastic notes, and flowers he couldn't afford.

So in London at the moment was Robin. Mother knew about Robin, his sound economics and his worrying infatuation for me and his more than worrying poverty. Mother could forgive poverty, even pauperism. Her father and mother had married on fifty cents and theirs was a marriage of legend. But George had been a genius, and how could Mother be sure any of the poor lads I knew were of the same caliber; that is, gifted enough to be worthy of me?

Just before I arrived in London that May, the leader, John Paul, died. I had called up Arthur Madsen immediately on arrival. He had sounded absolutely stricken. Lily was obviously the one who was maintaining sanity.

English-Speaking Union
June 2

Dearest Mum,

Went to the John Paul memorial meeting. Madsen looking shockingly tired, Mrs. Paul like a mummy. (I sent her a huge hydrangea with your letter. She hasn't spoken to me about it yet. Lily Madsen says it's almost impossible to rouse her to anything.

She is just now beginning to cry.) Speeches and speeches —
some good, sincere, and touching — mine hopelessly pompous,
really rather disgusting. Half-empty hall. McClaren, M.P., and
his diabolic wit conspicuously absent, as well as all his young
militants, who take their cue from him. The few present assumed
an expression of resigned disapproval adopted by Georgists on
duty.

Sunday last, Richmond Park with Robin — marvelous flowers.
Late tea — returned to the Union to find frantic messages from
Ashley Dukes and Haskell. Phoned Haskell at the Ballet Club. An
interview I had given a nineteen-year-old reporter had been mis-
quoted as saying that I had come over "to put ginger in the dull
English dancing." Dukes was threatening libel action against the
paper and cancellation of contract and deportation for me. Haskell begged me not to go to the club until I had talked to him,
told me not to worry, and hung up. I ran around frantically trying to find a copy of the paper, then called him again. (This was
all during the Sunday night ballet performance.) I begged him
to see immediately, dressed, and was out at the club in twenty
minutes. Dukes had the article and was pacing the sidewalk. He
led me into a back room, and with frozen courtesy, showed me
the clipping. I burst into tears and denied repeatedly every statement. At the end of ten minutes, Dukes was embracing me,
blushing a little for his display of mistrust, and Haskell, who had
pleaded my case all afternoon, led me, weakened, into the theater
to see the end of the performance. Afterwards, I went home with
Liza Hewitt, the beautiful black-eyed secretary of the club. She
had hysterics all over me in her kitchen. It seems Dukes had
sworn at her in his frenzy. Her nerves, worn thin with fatigue,
promptly snapped. Most of the rest of the night I spent writing
official letters repudiating the article. The matter is not yet settled — Dukes is still suing the paper and my testimony is Exhibit
A. More letters — and very carefully worded, thank you!

I forgot to tell you that at the second concert (the bad one)
Romney brought as his guest Baroness Ravensdale (a very rare

bird, a lady-Baron in her own right), a tall svelte dark beauty with enchanting presence, the unmarried daughter of Lord Curzon (viceroy of India). She gave me, "instead of flowers," she explained, an exquisite piece of carved jade. She asked me to her salon for drinks and there I met her very lovely younger sister, Cynthia, who is married to a queer young man named Oswald Moseley. He apparently admires Hitler ever so and is attempting to set up an English imitation of the Nazi's romps, against real odds.

In a letter some time back you asked me about Ramon. I found out.

He has some form of paralysis; the disease attacked his spine and nervous system. At sixteen he was struck blind and paralyzed, how far, I don't know. Fortunately his lungs escaped.

He says he knows he has a pair of legs, a deep feeling in the bone, though if you were to strike him anywhere below the knees, he would not sense a thing, and he is, accordingly, incapable of any sort of locomotion. But he expects to get well. Apparently with extraordinary vigilant nursing care (which he seems to have), the destroyed nerve fibers in his spine will grow back, although it may take many years. It has taken six years to give him back his eyesight and six inches of life. A complicating factor is a spinal curvature. More than three or four hours of sitting up is too much for him. He spends most of his time in bed, flattened out, and has developed a most astonishing technique for eating and writing and reading in this position. You should see him with tea, bread and butter, jam, sandwiches and cake spread out on his chest; telephone and cigarettes on either side, and Solomon, the huge black cat, lying between his still feet, vibrating endlessly. If there's a short-cut cure to what ails him, he doesn't know of it. He gets simply frantic when people mention Christian Science, osteopathy, or Unity.

Wednesday, May 31: Lunch — Arthur Schwartz at his most charming. He's always been warm and kind but now that there's a hint of West End managers being alert and excited, he's positively attentive! Oh, what a difference professional corroboration makes!

Called on the Hon. Mrs. Lawson-Johnston to discuss the Derby Ball. A newspaper gossip writer at Haskell's tea had been so struck with my press, photos, and Haskell's blurb, that she recommended me to the Hon. Mrs. Lawson-Johnston, daughter-in-law to Bovril, who was hunting for free talent. She knows all the royal princes well and has promised to introduce me to Wales, either at the party or later at her house. She is American, southern, vain, flighty and sweet, with notions about her own singing and terrific social ambitions. I suppose she hopes that as a lion cub I might prove useful. Mrs. Lawson-Johnston's house was very posh, with sprays of orchids in vases around the drawing room in honor of Prince George, who had dined there the night before. She received me in a fancy bed. She promised to give me everything I asked — stage, lights, dressers, quiet and attention.

On to tea with Ramon and Mrs. Elizabeth Bowen Cameron, who is going to arrange a recital for me at Oxford. Elizabeth Bowen is a novelist and short-story writer and is rapidly becoming famous. She is a great friend of the Kirk Askews. She is Irish, tall, rangy, and long-boned, with enormous hands and feet. Her hair is like straw, her skin shiny, her eyes pale and transparent until taking on the color of seawater. She stutters badly. But then she talks, and elegance, wit, zest, liveliness and effectiveness take over the world. She is a creature of grace — don't ask me how. She is. Ramon adores her, plainly and simply. He worships her talent, he takes comfort in her kindness and companionship. He says if he could write one story she approved of, he'd die happy. No, he doesn't say that — he says it would be reward enough. He never mentions his own death. Bowen went to school with Ramon's stepmother, Joan, and Ramon and she share many wry jokes; of course, not in my presence, which would be unseemly, but alone; he tells me all after she's gone.

Saturday, June 1: Out to Cheney's in afternoon with Robin —
an absolutely heavenly old English village with an enormous Tudor manor house owned by the Earl of Bedford, who owns the
town as well and a great part of London. A chapel in the church
contains the tombs (in perfect condition) of all the family —
painted wooden effigies lying stiffly, praying in ruffs and armor
and farthingales. Overhead the family banners hang motionless
and gay. "I wonder," said Robin, looking through the grille,
"what these good folk would say if they knew their line was
going to produce Bertie Russell."

Sunday: Picnic in Epping Forest with Robin. He crammed me
for four hours on the *Intelligent Woman's Guide to Socialism*
against my lunch with Shaw. Dropped Robin rather abruptly
and rushed to tea with Haskell at Jacob Epstein's. Epstein fat,
grizzled, genial and welcoming. (He'd come to the second recital
and particularly liked *Ballet Class*.) Mrs. Epstein, the mother of
the Kings of Israel, a fleshy, pudgy face, a rosebud mouth which
she held pursed up in kiss position and did not move when she
spoke, hair the color of a Florida orange, a body absolutely
spherical, her diameter in one direction being exactly that of her
diameter in another, a black bombazine dress, noticeably soiled,
hanging from the shelf of her breast straight to the floor like a
tent, her pince-nez pinned to the primeval bosom with a huge
safety pin; Peggy-Jean, the daughter and subject of many of his
child studies, sitting in the window, a be-bosomed child of thirteen or so, her yellow hair in a tangle — and not a pretty one —
lying on her shoulders, looking strangely in dishabille because
her figure was that of a grown woman and her hair by rights
should have been up; a bowl of huge scarlet poppies on the floor
beside her, flaming in the afternoon light, their petals all over
the carpet, crouched over them Isabel, the model, the "Tibetan"
beauty (who is a cockney) in purple and scarlet and a tigerish
voluptuous face (she is famous for her strange beauty and becoming known for her watercolors of animals, and she is going

to paint me); behind them a magnificent bronze head of a Negress; the ragtag and bobtail of London's art colony around the rest of the room; a dancer with bright green eyelids beside me in a green evening dress with sphinxes on her forefingers — petals on the carpet, crumbs on the table, and a fat Jewish gentleman with an open shirt who happens to be the greatest living sculptor beaming on his guests.

I was fifteen minutes late for tea, so I didn't get any, but sat staring hungrily at the plates of piled cakes and empty cups. An old ragamuffin got up, went to the piano, and with her sunburned, stubby fingers managed to extract from the keys some pretty expert Mozart. A Yiddish businessman pompously opened his music and sang German lieder superbly. And what do you think they asked me to talk about? Hollywood, Hollywood, Holly—! I left them finally, discussing art in intense small groups, dropping their cigarette ashes all over the carpet.

June 8: Contract signed for a week at the Leicester Square Variety Theater! For money, Mum, Mum — they're paying me this time! One week in June to do a scene based on *Ballet Class* and two solos! £40!!

The Shaw Day. Early for once, I arrived at the Shaw establishment on the Victoria Embankment and waited in the lobby for Mr. & Mrs. Orage, he the editor, and my sponsor. I dared not go in alone. We were ushered, all three, upstairs to the flat and into the empty drawing room, a quiet, large, sunny place fronting the Thames, filled with flowers, books and fine engravings. Mrs. Shaw arrived, gracious, easy, poised, a flawless hostess. Not nearly enough has been said of her. (Rebecca West told me, when I recounted this to her, that she held Charlotte Shaw the direct inspiration for *St. Joan.*) When everyone had gathered we were given sherry and stood in waiting for the Presence, exactly as though we attended royalty. He arrived swiftly, an agile, lean creature, moving with incredible possession and precision from person to person, a demigod, a quickening, a catalyst. All tweedy of suit and downy of waistcoat, all brown, he seemed rustic, sylvan even. His skin was pink and fresh and the white hair of head and beard crisped with energy: Pan himself. I never was in the presence of greater vitality — quite the sexiest man I ever met, if wind, green earth, and the changes of nature have anything to do with sex. He was inevitable, with the economy and concentration of an animal, and the energy of an element.

"How do you do?" he asked; and then suddenly, "What are you, the daughter or granddaughter?"

"The granddaughter," I answered.

"H'm," he said.

"You're looking well," said Orage.

Shaw preened. There was a time, he said, when he could not be certain that every woman he met would fall in love with him, but now that he had passed seventy, he discovered he was utterly irresistible. This was apropos of his admitting that Marion Davies had been taken with him at first meeting, as he with her.

It was Mrs. Shaw, however, who kept the conversation going all through lunch. Shaw only spoke when he saw the opportunity of making a point. The groundwork was laid by his wife, who referred to him always as "G.B.S." and quoted his remarks as though he weren't present. He waited until Charlotte had worked up the material, as a straight man should, preparing and readying it for him. Then he gave the *coup de grace* — and that subject was done for. He spoke always in periods, full complete phrases that came out in measured rhythms, limpid and clear. He never was at a loss, or repeated a word, or left any idea unfinished. No doubt he was thinking out the rhetoric while Mrs. Shaw did the spadework and he munched quietly on his coddled eggs.

Lunch was beautifully served by two butlers. Shaw ate eggs, vegetables and mushrooms. I was offered a plate of chops. I drew back my hand, then concluded he meant me to eat them or he wouldn't have them served at his table, so I helped myself liberally.

Later, after contemplating me for a moment, he asked, again suddenly, "Have you read *Progress and Poverty?*"

"Yes, sir," I replied. "Complete and many times."

"I'm surprised to hear it," he said. "I met the grandson of Bulwer-Lytton and asked him if he read his grandfather's books. 'Did he write books?' the boy enquired."

I spoke of the John Brown play, *Gallows Glorious*, which had moved me so much the night before in spite of the cast's Oxford accents.

"I once intended to write a play about John Brown," Shaw said, "because he always seemed to me an unmitigated rascal on whom the wreath of martyrdom fell exactly like a tile off a roof," — he laughed aloud at the emerging idea — "it killed him, but it rendered him immortal."

After lunch, the ladies went back to the drawing room. The men remained at table with their port and discussed Shakespeare. I wanted badly to listen to them, but found myself cornered with Mrs. Shaw, who showed me pictures of the Hearst ranch, San Simeon. Hearst's rooms looked like Egyptian tombs, packed, replete, crowded against eternity with just everything, including the jellied entrails of his family and retainers. The rooms should have been sealed up just as they were to wait for doom or the robbers. I thought them hideous. "This is not beautiful," I said, thumbing through the large book of full-page photographs of the stuffed rooms, the cement gardens, the penitentiary globular outdoor lamps. "This has been assembled not with care, but with pride and greed."

"Oh, not quite," she said in her little crisp voice and she bit off my objections like a hangnail and spat them away. "Not quite. There is more there." What there was did not photograph. She, however, seemed really to like the place.

What naughty perversity made Shaw and his good lady treat this hoggish jumble with respect? So that they bragged about being there and showed off boasting pictures?

Oh, yes — Shaw had said that he received one of the major

shocks of his life when he read the newspaper reports of the speech at the Metropolitan Opera House last spring. He was well aware that a speaker could hardly avoid grammatical mistakes, unfinished sentences, repetition, etc., but the perfect gibberish he was quoted as saying he could not believe because his audience gave signs of intelligent interest and if he had said what he was credited with saying, they would have booed and whistled or simply left. "Maybe," said Orage, "they were too embarrassed to do anything at all." Well, you did something. You turned off the radio in mid-speech and went to bed. And if Aunt Nan hadn't gone on stubbornly listening and phoned, you might never have known what he said about your father: "One of the two greatest thinkers nineteenth-century America produced." Wow! Remember that when you are blue.

The rest of the afternoon was spent in the Home Office signing pledges not to accept work.

By the way, Ashley's Nameless Theater is reverting to normal habits of advertising. It turns out the audience was also nameless, being absent. The young Auden was done in the eye by the plan. T. S. Eliot will have a fair chance; *Murder* may survive. It would be nice if Ashley could have some success. He might ease up on his ridicule of the dancing classes, which pay all the upkeep of theater and office. He might even let Mim off the hook for a week or two.

I really was appalled by my second concert. I can't get over it. No good. No good.

No sleep that night — hideously depressed. Maybe Ouida Rathbone was right. She keeps saying I'm going off on the wrong tangent. All my dances seemed futile. Longed for someone to talk to.

Three days later: The boys, Tudor and Laing, and I make forays on the Caledonian market, none of us with more than ten bob to spend. Hugh returns happily with an armful of fans and spangled Edwardian scarves for the ballet company he knows

Antony will one day have. I found a Georgian bottle and some flowers that were quite wilted after the hour-and-a-half bus ride home. Tudor, I think, does not have three shillings so he usually buys nothing.

June 9, the day before yesterday, I went up the river to a magnificent rock garden at Ainley with them. We ate lunch on the train, spitting cherry pits out of the window at difficult distances to the great delight of an old gentleman who became almost apoplectic trying not to laugh. On the way back, we were determined to keep the third-class compartment to ourselves, so every time the train halted, Antony picked his nose, Hugh drooled at the mouth, and I rasped out, "Antony, have you the pills? I won't answer for him if you've not brought the sedatives." Quite understandably, no one cared to join us. At the Richmond stop, Hugh hung by his knees from the hat rack while I managed to sob real streaming tears and Antony rent his hair. This was considered a masterstroke and so broke us up that two old ladies with umbrellas were immediately upon us and seated. "Oh, God, I failed you," moaned Antony. "I relaxed. I shouldn't have laughed. I betrayed you." The point of all this was that the acting was extraordinary.

The next day the boys went with me to buy a hat in a fashionable shop on Old Bond Street. After trying on (all of us) every model in the premises, we settled with much arguing on a knitted object for eleven shillings. The exasperated saleslady in the end refused to close the deal. We took it though, threw down the cash, and left. I forget who wore it out.

No one over fifteen should behave publicly like this, but when I was fifteen I was never silly. Remember? I wonder if Antony was. Maybe he has a lot to get out of his system, too.

But the boys aren't silly, you know. They are truly funny. Antony has wit. Anyhow they're my only real cronies.

This letter has become book length but it's a way of keeping close. I'm less homesick when I write. I know my days sound bustling and God knows they're occupied, but I am in a foreign

Antony Tudor

Hugh Laing

land, and the people here, although loving and beloved, are not
mine — not yet. I long for my folks. I long for a good gossip and
laugh with Mag — she'd put me right and toughen me up. I long
for the woods. (The garden sounds great. Did you sow the
whole tennis court in roses? Goodness!) I love your letters. I
think of you constantly. I long for you.

Always devotedly,
A.

Antony's humor was not always so playful. One morning,
he came to us in class with the following news: "I say, where
do you suppose the janitor found Collin this morning? Sitting with his head in the oven, quite dead. It did give him
a turn."

"Antony," I remonstrated, "that's a hell of a way to joke!"

"I'm not joking," he replied blandly. "It's quite true."

Hugh deprecated the tone. I was shocked. Collin was, until
the previous midnight, the Mercury secretary. It is true he
looked like a chrysanthemum with teeth, was unattractive,
complex, secretive, and I think I can say, quite generally disliked, but that the poor young man was aware of his inade-
quacies had become suddenly quite plain. Antony, however,
saw no reason to pretend to grieve for someone he never
cared for. The hopelessness and degradation of spirit which
prompted the frightful step did not apparently touch him
one whit. Antony hated sentimentality and cut through it
with wicked speed. Any show of emotion, however genuine,
always embarrassed him. I slopped and ran over the edges on
every occasion and it always sickened him. And so did Hugh,
sometimes to the point of hysteria. It made Antony more cold,
more withdrawn, seemingly callous.

But if Antony had staged the suicide, then you would have
seen something! Again and again in his work I began to sense

a tenderness, compassion, love, and grief that may have been beyond the power of any other contemporary choreographer or stage director. This is an extraordinary fact. Antony was gradually becoming steel, but Antony always could put passion on the stage.

In life he was candid to the point of astonishment. "Whatever I say against anyone," he remarked, "is said with the intention of doing the most possible harm."

Now I submit this is a remarkable statement, unique in my experience. All of us, from time to time, are driven to brutalities. I'm always sorry later, possibly fearing the results. Antony accepts wickedness as perfectly natural. His attitude is that of a gunman who gives straight notice he is going to shoot to kill; mine is that of Lorelie Lee, who suddenly went blank and on recovery found a gun in her hand and that her gentleman friend had "got himself shot."

Antony was my daily companion and colleague, yet in spite of my frenetic social life I was lonely. Often, I sat in the late dusk weeping for my bewilderment and for my lost love, who would have made me laugh, who would have made me realize dance steps were not the most important things in life, and whom I would never, never see again.

English-Speaking Union
June 12

Dearest Mum,

Monday: Rehearsals all day. I was determined the last concert would be good.

Tuesday (The Day of My Last Concert — the Day of the Derby Ball): In the morning I gave up class to go to the Grosvenor Hotel to inspect the arrangements for the Derby Ball, my stage, etc. Found they had built additions to the musicians' platform that I requested and covered them with linoleum but had left the rest of the stage carpet-covered — was accosted by an overwrought dormouse named Panter who was the go-between for the hospital and Lady Milbank. Conversation for the next two hours roughly as follows, punctuated by trips to the telephone to tell the Ballet Club that I could not get out to the recital light rehearsals.

MRS. PANTER: You cannot have the stage in the center of the wall facing the grand staircase as you asked because Lady Milbank's buffet has to go there.

AGNES: That is the only logical place for the stage and the only place where everyone in the room can see what's going on. Couldn't the buffet be moved?

PANTER: No. Lady Milbank doesn't want it moved.

AGNES: Well then, how about putting it in the center of the floor against these columns with screens behind it?

MANAGER: We have no screens.

AGNES: You can get some.

MANAGER: I don't think we can.

PANTER: Besides, the stage will take up too much of the dancing space.

AGNES: Well then, put it over against the wall. It's a bad place but the only one left.

PANTER: The musicians won't like to play over in the corner.

AGNES: (*Ignoring her*) If it's there, you'll have to cover the wall decoration with a curtain.

MANAGER: We have no curtain.

AGNES: You'll have to rent one. I'm not going to dance Degas against an Italian landscape with columns and grillwork in full relief and artificial palms and box geraniums.

MANAGER: We're not going to ruin the decoration of this room for a dance number.

AGNES: You're going to alter the decoration if it helps the production.

MANAGER: No, we're not. The production only lasts a couple of minutes.

PANTER: How long do your dances last? You're not doing more than two, are you?

AGNES: I had been asked to do three.

PANTER: Oh no — two's enough.

AGNES: And you'll have to cover the stage all over with linoleum.

MANAGER: That will be expensive. We've already spent a good deal on you.

AGNES: How much?

MANAGER: Three pounds.

AGNES: (*Flushing scarlet*) I hate to be rude, but my regular fee is a hundred pounds a performance and I'm giving that to you free. (This was a beaut — you know what I get. No notice taken of this remark.)

AGNES: Well, where are you going to put the stage?

PANTER: We don't know. You see how it is.

AGNES: Why didn't you decide where to put it before you built it?

PANTER: We haven't had a meeting since.

AGNES: I think it would solve everything if I didn't dance.

PANTER: Well, you see how it is.

AGNES: Please phone Lady Milbank and ask her if she'd move the buffet.

PANTER: I don't like to disturb her.

AGNES: Please —

(Fifteen minute interval wherein they go off, leaving me standing, biting my fingernails, and wondering what's going on at the Ballet Club.)

PANTER: (*Returning*) Lady Milbank doesn't want a single thing changed.

AGNES: What does she want done with me?

PANTER: She didn't say.

(The hotel top manager arrives, takes in the situation immediately, and leads me off to look at flooring which could be laid down wherever I pleased and taken up again immediately after

I'd danced. Everything solved — return to ballroom. Lady Milbank arrives, young, dark, beautiful, chic, spoiled — waits for people to cross the room to speak to her. The dormouse in palpitations of subservience. Milbank gives me a lifeless hand.)

MILBANK: You'll have to get through your act quickly, Miss de Mille. We have about ten too many turns as it is.

PANTER: And she's doing two dances.

MILBANK: Oh, she is? What a pity! That will make things complicated. Now how will we order the program?

AGNES: As you please.

MILBANK: I think we'd better end with something bright, don't you? We'll end with the Yacht Club boys. We can begin the cabaret at one-thirty. By one I certainly hope all of us can be in bed. The Prince will have gone long before.

PANTER: He stayed until three last year.

MILBANK: But this year he'll be bored to death.

(At this point I turned my back on her and laughed. Panter saw me and looked apprehensive.)

AGNES: I must go now. Good-bye, Lady Milbank.

MILBANK: (*Barely looking up from her list of table subscribers*) Good-bye. I'm sure everything will be all right for you.

If you ask why I stood it, it's because I knew the publicity would be tremendous and that if I refused to dance, the correct reason would never be given out of deference to the noble ladies running the ball. All the Britishers I have repeated the story to have shut their mouths grimly and said, "I can quite believe it." The love the people bear the royal family extends only to the limits of the family itself. The rest of the aristocracy they loathe and particularly Australian nobility, which Lady Milbank is. This I did not know before. Also I never before knew what it felt like to lust for someone's head on a pike.

Well, I went out to the Ballet Club. My people, Tudor *et al.*, had waited in vain for me and had gone home. I let off steam in a lesson.

Went to Mrs. Cancellor, the bookstore lady, and sputtered. She said with a kind of satisfaction, "There is nothing so rude in all the world as the British aristocracy, except of course, the Australian. They're worse."

I imagine she thinks they're spiritually very low. I went home and went to bed.

Packed house that night at the Ballet Club. An extra row of chairs placed in front of the regular seats. People sitting on the steps of the aisle and standing four deep in back. I danced, I think, as well as I ever have. Myra Hess came back and spoke very warmly to me. Lydia Lopokova (Mrs. Maynard Keynes) had been told by Mim that I resembled her. She accordingly viewed me very closely and with some considerable dislike. One of the Ballet Club boys, Hugh Laing, as a matter of fact, rushed backstage at the close of the performance, threw himself on the ground, and kissed my feet.

At midnight Mrs. Lawson-Johnston's car came for me. I was shunted from room to room in the hotel and finally told to wait an hour, which I did, not daring to take my toe slippers off my exhausted feet for fear they'd swell. At last a surly gentleman ordered me to begin. The ballroom was three-quarters empty, the guests being down at supper. No one was quiet or interested — the lights full up. Norman, the accompanist, began. I signaled him to stop. "Fix the lights," I called through the din.

"Oh get on with it," the rude announcer shouted. I went on and then, thank God, the lights were fixed — *Stagefright*. With the first sweep of my Degas watering can, I realized that no one understood what I was doing, much less cared. The stage was hidden behind the orchestra platform. I used one of the exits to the kitchen as though it were the door leading to the opera stage.

At one point, when I cast an agonized, fearful glance in that direction, the direction of the supposed wings, I grew sick with stage fright, a waiter came out carrying a tray of food and crossed in front of me, causing me to step back.

I collapsed in the dressing room, sobbing. "Nothing," I said,

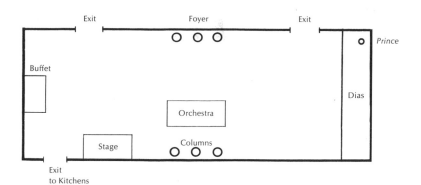

"nothing will make me go out in that room again." "Oh yes," said Norman, hitting me on the back. "You'll go out and dance very nicely. You never know where this will lead you." So I did *Harvest Reel* the best I could down the middle of the ballroom floor. More people were present this time and quiet. At the end I had to turn my back on the prince and run to my kitchen exit. You can't run backwards for three hundred yards. I intended to turn and bow toward them just before disappearing but the applause did not hold out long enough. I got to cover just in time.

Then I dressed in Mag's gold and white gown, white kid gloves to the armpit, and strung a rope of pink and green orchids (that I had bought for myself) down one shoulder and waited. Norman and his page-turner were in white tie and tails. We waited fifty minutes for someone to do something. Mrs. Lawson-Johnston arrived at last. "That second dance was lovely, dear. Prince George loved it. He thought you were a Russian. By the way, can I send anything in for you to eat?"

We'd been promised supper with royalty. I looked at her speechless.

"You certainly may," said Norman with vulgar alacrity. "We've given two performances tonight, the last under unprecedented circumstances, and we're hungry."

Mrs. Lawson-Johnston left murmuring and was replaced by an entire Scotch salmon embalmed in intricate French sauces and spangled with caviar and capers. With it a half-filled bottle of champagne.

"First take your shoes off," said Norman, easing my pulsing extremities out of their white satin bindings. "Put your feet up here, and now tuck in, tuck in. As God's my witness, you've earned this, as well as their blood."

We made quite a good job of it and ordered whatever we could think of from the waiters, who were grumpy and insolent, not liking to be set to serving the not-quite hired help.

Had my glass of milk alone at three A.M. If there'd only been someone to talk to. I get all wound up after these sportings and I can't sleep.

Ah well — well — love,
A.

CHAPTER 4

WHEN I could, I talked to Antony, although he seemed as bewildered and lost as I, but strangely enough, I laid down the law just as though I was sure of myself on all points. Tudor did the listening. I'd had some success, while he was just starting, and in so very diffused a way. "Do you like my stuff?" I asked him once. "I have a big admiration for the amount of solid work you've racked up," he hedged. "I recognize professionalism; also I think you're funny. I myself am fascinated principally by movement."

Was he ever! His plots at the time were badly organized and unclear, his characters dim, but he never once asked a dancer to do a vulgar or a trite gesture, and he never approached music as anyone had before. His talent might be unpruned, but the sap ran strong.

Mim foresaw a big future, and Hugh, his leading protagonist, did, but only these two. Even I, who loved and admired him (I had a kind of crush on him), entertained grave doubts. Who could possibly foresee in this disorganized, patient youth, the volcanic talent that was to make itself known? And although Mim was wonderfully supporting, she was not really sure of his success because she had doubts about his will to achieve. Antony is now a world figure and very bitter.

He occupies himself for the most part with restaging his nine masterpieces, teaching, and uttering sardonic remarks. He was not bitter in 1933. He was bonny, poor and hopeful, diffident and courteous to established artists. And he usually was gentle. "Bone lazy," said Mim.

Hugh was the whip to scourge him on. Hugh was the gadfly, Shakespearean in his undiluted determination that Antony should become famous, and that he, Hugh, should become the great interpreter of Antony's works. He spoke of Antony even then as "Tudor," the way one speaks of "Verdi" or "Michelangelo." Antony was scuffling around in the basement with knock-kneed children, but when Hugh spoke of him, he spoke of the established great "Tudor" — a name in the floor of Westminster Abbey.

So I continued pompously to instruct, while he listened without comment, and I went from him to gnaw at my nerves in absolute self-doubt. It was quite plain to me that if I went on with the acting line, I'd end up in straight pantomime, a form I despised. I had been often called "the Ruth Draper of the Dance." The other alternate was abstraction, i.e., dance.

I was, however, mortally afraid (Tudor obviously was not) of pretty movement per se. One can be trapped with the intoxication of motion and deliver up simple yardage, meaningless decoration, in the way certain contemporary musicians become bewitched by sound. Language, whatever it is, must communicate, and when it is good, no matter how new or unfamiliar, it always does. My taproot was in acting, which is of necessity based on immediate recognition. I was literal, sometimes derivative and repetitious, but always clear and emotionally charged. But I kept trying to find a gesture that was not literal, to become abstract without loss of emotional impact. The difficulty lay in the fact that I felt I was never truly a dancer. My father used to say, "She is more than a dancer because she is also an actress." Nobody can be more than a dancer.

I could make people laugh and cry at will, and sometimes both together. Larry Hart said I was funnier than Fanny Brice. I dare say I was. My timing of comic points, I'm told, was fine. Indeed, I was told I could make every passing thought visible. A choreographer, however, which it never occurred to me I was, must think and feel principally in terms of movement. I did not instinctively so express myself; Antony did.

The abandonment of everything I had made my name on, chiefly comedy, took guts, or foolhardiness. All my professional friends deplored the attempt. The family was distraught. Only Mim was in sympathy, and Antony Tudor, who remained comfortably dubious, not believing for a moment I would ever really succeed in changing. I was not, he decided, to crowd him in his field.

The attempts toward pure dance form that I was making at the moment were dreadful. I had not had the opportunity a young choreographer should have of dancing continually in the works of masters and watching great choreographers in daily rehearsal. America was producing self-taught mavericks who discovered brand-new forms. But it took them a long time, and only Graham and Humphrey came through to greatness.

Whether or not my work influenced Antony in any way is doubtful; our styles were totally divergent. But my industry certainly did. Thoughtful critics have said I was Antony's catalyst, that sheer indignation at my earlier, larger success goaded him to action.

For my part, I was envious of his talent. Naturally I was. It was so obviously more subtle, more rich: wider than mine.

I always knew this and said so heartily. He didn't believe me for a minute; that is, he didn't believe I meant him well. Antony came to feel month by month and later very strongly that lives were ridden by jealousies, and that the person who harnessed the rages and frustrations of rivals learned where power lay.

But I kept talking to him because he was the only one I could talk to. Louis Horst, Graham's musical director and mentor, used to say, "A young artist needs a wall to grow against." I had no one. Antony was my most gifted friend. The only one, in fact, who could possibly talk as a peer.

I couldn't talk to Robin about any of this. For although he was versed in economics, English literature, history and philosophy (he was currently the head of the debating society of the London School of Economics), he knew nothing of dancing, or music, however hard he tried to catch up. We kept seeing each other, however.

We walked the wonderful old streets arm in arm, observing everything, day after day, stopping when tired for tea or hot chocolate at a Lyon's or ABC. I think I paid my way. Robin hadn't a bean. And I'd been paying my way with all boys since the depression. It's a habit one got into. We walked in the long roseate evenings, the ruddy northern light reflected back from Wren's bricks. We walked in the rain, slopping through Hampstead and taking tea and buttered scones as we discussed Keats. We walked through the night city on the embankment, around the palaces, munching saveloys and drinking the incomparable black tea brewed in pails on the sidewalks. We walked and sat in Kew Gardens in a field of silvery bluebells (in reality, tiny hyacinths, I discovered) while cuckoos called in the great blooming horse chestnuts and the bossy rhododendrons lifted up their bouquets. It was an Elizabethan time of beauty and readiness, and I had a lad who was in love with me. He was comely, intelligent, sweet and able, and my heart was a stone.

Robin made love to me as much as I would let him, as far as I would let him. I wanted him; I didn't want him. I wanted him until I remembered. This was different. This wasn't the same. Before, I had not been able to help myself. Robin was lusty, but he was gentle, and he waited. He always kissed me good-night, and he kissed me in the grass, and under the flowering trees, and in the rain, but he was gentle, and he recognized my turbulence. And he was willing to wait. I let him. He was in deep love and I had power.

The trouble was that I was still pining. Something bled away inside me. It was silly because hopeless, but one can die for silly and hopeless reasons. What miserable, whining, crippled thing tied me still to a man who had gone away forever out of pure boredom? I went sick with fright at the thought of another permanent alliance; in my bringing-up, there was no other kind.

I was frightened as I fell asleep. I was ashamed when I woke. I was remorseful while with him.

What did Robin lack that my False Love had? My False Love had laughed with me. He was laughing very hard and so was I the night he said he'd never forget anything I'd ever said and kissed me good-bye forever. "Why do you laugh?" Robin kept asking. I never had the strength to explain.

Robin, with whom I could not talk about these matters, kept walking with me. Ramon, with whom I was beginning to talk, made daily promenades in the Valley of the Shadow. Things like money and headlines and notices were only amusing inconsequentials. Furthermore, he interested himself in a lot besides aesthetics, which the tight little crew of the Ballet Club did not. Like all ballet devotees, they were in large measure pedants.

"Aglet," Ramon would call from his bedroom, "the workers are holding out in Vienna. The army hasn't got them down yet. My God, the courage! Think, in the face of those guns and no food! My dear, we'll drink to them!"

Mother had gone along blindly. Ramon wasn't blind.

"It will come," Ramon said. "All artists go through these wastelands. Look at D. H. Lawrence." I'd never heard of D. H. Lawrence. Ramon began to read him to me. Bits and pieces and at length — even *Kangaroo*, and Aldous Huxley, and James Joyce's *Portrait of the Artist as a Young Man*, and John Donne, the sermons, and also *Variety*, which he subscribed to not so much because of the theatrical news but because of the brand-new language. "Aglet," he'd say, "not since the Elizabethans has there been such invention in language, except, of course, the Irish" — and then he'd smile — "or possibly, the Cornish." Language meant to Ramon what motion meant to me; he was teaching me to listen, I was teaching him to look.

Ramon, of course, had not seen any other dancers. None at all in his whole life, so he was possibly not prepared for perspective in the matter. He, however, had informed taste in all the other arts which he brought to dancing, so that he was demanding, but not confused by scholastic or trade secrets.

So, in the end, my heartening and guidance came from a bedridden cripple who was neither intimidated nor fooled by easy answers. He never tried to impose his tastes, but he backed my best instincts. He refused to indulge my apprehensions.

The changing of basic style, in my case, took longer than Jane Austen lived. Or than Ramon did.

I began going to Ramon's more and more often. There I was safe. There by his bedside I did not feel guilty or frightened. There was comfort and quiet. Ramon, who needed so much and asked so little, was a kind of expiation for using Robin.

"Do you know why I hang around?" I asked once. He shook his head smiling. "Because you can't run away." And I did not add — "Because also you probably won't ask me to marry you."

Although he was my age, there was something of a father in him, the father I'd lost. I nursed a perpetual fear of abandonment, of giving up all and then being abandoned, which was precisely what had happened when Father persuaded me not to dance but to go to college and then having obtained his will, at what dreadful cost to me, walked out on my mother, and therefore me, for good. I was mortally afraid of commitments. I was equally averse to the loneliness of freedom. Since neither of these risks pertained to Ramon, every time I pressed his bell I found sanctuary.

"Come in, Aglet, come in. Look what a great smashing tea I have for you. Ethel's gone to the Fulham Road for special buns — and I've got the brand-new copy of *Variety*."

The rooms were quiet and beautifully furnished. If it was chilly, the fire was lit, and Ramon would be waiting beside the tea table, eager for my news, eager to give his, gleaned from newspapers, books, telephone calls, or his bedroom window. "Aglet," he called as he heard me at the door, "Aglet, come here, my honey, come quickly — just hear what Solomon has been up to." It was home.

Robin took to waiting outside of the houses where I was visiting, Ramon's, for instance, and seeing me back to the

Union. I didn't want this. At all the parties I sat chattering and laughing, knowing he was outside waiting. And yet I couldn't say good-bye and finish it off because I was afraid of loneliness. Under the frantic professional and social effort, deeper and deeper I drowned. My headaches grew frightful and I couldn't keep my breath onstage.

But no one suspected my confusion of spirits. Except, of course, Mother.

She went to call on her friend, the playwright Edward Sheldon, blind and totally paralyzed. "Don't let her see too much of this cripple boy," he said. But there was a salt ocean between Mother and me. And the great trench of desperation.

In London I carried on like an E. M. Delafield heroine. Having been abandoned, I clung to whatever was certain, even if unsuitable, and while never saying exactly yes, I kept up a teasing. I knew this was cruel and I was sorry, but I did it. I think I believed if I myself agonized enough it would excuse the shiftiness. I had bypassed adolescence. I never kissed casually because kissing meant betrothal. I was having my adolescence now, but it was among grown men and this was painful to all, and highly unattractive.

One evening I arrived at Ramon's all in a tremble — and then over the tea murmured some of my personal turmoil. "He's outside now, waiting — staring at these windows — I'm greatly troubled."

"Quite understandable," Ramon said, "but don't on any account go through with it. Break it off clean, now. It's not so hard, you'll see."

Robin was a healthy man. Robin could look ahead. To Ramon it all seemed simple. "Have a bun," said Ramon, picking up a book. "Calm down and listen."

E.S.U.

June 12

Dearest Mum,

I've a new maid now, pleasant and interested; also not quite normal in the head. Anyhow, she has been sweet and astonishingly willing to do favors.

The morning after my horrid snarling maid left, a new one, Valerie, appeared with breakfast sans egg. I thereupon ordered one, which she returned with a few minutes later, but finding me telephoning she withdrew in embarrassment, catching the egg squarely on the doorjamb. Exclamations, apologies, moppings of rug and woodwork. I was telephoning Ramon at the moment. "She dropped the egg," I told him.

"Oh good! I'm glad," he said. Exit, entrance with fresh egg. Blushes. "Oh, miss, how careless of me! I'm dreadfully sorry." "Never mind," I said. "I thought it was funny." "So did I, miss. I thought it was proper funny. I think I shall write it in my diary," with which she dropped the second egg on the bed frame. I called up Ramon again. "She's just dropped the second egg." "That's made my day," he said. "You must forgive me," she said the next morning with tremors of confusion. "I am not used to handling these things. This is not my proper work. I am," she said simply, "by profession, a trained nurse." She is now known as the egg-breaker. She does my laundry — free — refuses pay.

What does Robin do? He works at Odhams, a publishing house, for seven pounds a week. And last Sunday evening he asked me to the London School of Economics, where he is head debater, to have supper with Harold Laski and Bertrand Russell and to attend a mock debate by the two great intellectuals on some ludicrous subject. They were brilliant, I suppose, but it all seemed rather strained in an undergraduate sort of way, flexing their academic muscles in a real showoff for the youngsters. There was a good deal of supportive British laughter, but not by the American present. Robin chaired very well indeed. He has enormous poise and a nice turn of phrase.

Robin is working in his spare time (and free, of course), for a group called the India League. They recently passed around the hat and sent Ellen Wilkinson, a member of Parliament, to India to look matters over. She came back last week and I was present at her report on how matters stand. Matters stink, it seems. One day out of every three in the average Indian's life is a fast day; they starve one-third of the time. In periods of famine the ratio augments and they die off rapidly. They expect this. They take it for granted. This is a sobering fact. She spoke with passion and eloquence. Robin said he'd never heard her so moved or so moving. The remedy she advocates is freedom from England.

The League puts out a paper once a month and it is edited (and I believe written) by Robin and a young Indian lawyer named Krishna Menon, a dark Oxonian with a smile that positively glitters and an accent so British it is mostly incomprehensible. They work in a dustbin on the Strand and the other night when they put the paper to bed, I went down at eleven-thirty and took them up a tray of tea and hot buttered toast. They were sitting in their third-floor walkup cubicle in a clutter of proofs, copy paper and ink bottles. I think there was a typewriter buried somewhere. They were fagged out, and they were surprised and very glad to see me.

I left them at it, scraping away like termites at the British Empire.

What are you scraping away at, darling? I mean besides the biography of your father, and the garden weeds?

Love,
A.

June 16

Dearest Mum,

I'm collecting clippings but first I send this valentine just as it appeared:

Look! Look! Look!
"For Agnes de Mille, the Dancer.
Dermot Spence, New English Weekly, *June 15, 1933*

> *Take, lady, take this sorry, spoiled design*
> *NOt worthy of the moment that it seals:*
> *ReAd it, excuse it: click your scarlet heels*
> *And Give me something that's already mine —*
> *The iNterwoven pattern of the reels,*
> *A giguE to treasure, or the half-divine*
> *Swan. myStery of the Hymn (the faltering line*
> *Halts unDer Beauty's gaze, the Sonnet kneels).*
> *And so givE more than Beauty, since you link*
> *A varied huMan frame round Beauty's own*
> *Penumbras, wIsely witty, gravely great. . . .*
> *Remembering London's homage, smile to think —*
> *How once the wiLdest poet ever blown*
> *Bowed to one AgnEs and fell slave to eight!"*

The concerts are finished and they've been a solid success, but this had been a hard spell, Mum, I haven't written you all — there has been no one, literally no one (now that the concerts are over I can tell you) to help me. Lily and Arthur Madsen offered nothing. Mrs. Denton, the little dressmaker, was too busy to come sew. The maid on my floor was something of a pathological case (they got rid of her a week ago) and absolutely refused to do anything except make my bed and tidy my room. Yes, and prevented the other maid, Valerie, from helping me. Now she does — and free. The girls in the downstairs office (who ask after you all the time) tried to help with secretarial work only to the extent of getting photographs mailed for me and then only after I'd done all the preparatory work, backing, addressing, etc., nor could they recommend anyone. The phoning I had to do alone. There is no one except you who can do that work for me. If I wanted a button sewn on or a stocking

Gigue, *from French Suite No. 5 by Bach*

Ouled Naïl: *café dancer*
(*Photo by Harlan Thompson*)

washed or a press clipping mailed or a ribbon bought, I had to do it. I kept going steadily from the time I got up until bed, and even then I slighted my practice. On Saturdays and Sundays I have tried to go out into the country and sit quietly until I'd calmed down a bit. I've not written a line to Margaret or Father.

I enclose the press:

De Mille is an artist of an exceptional order. She has a vivid personality, is able to concentrate upon whatever mood or feeling she wishes to express with an intensity that immediately conveys its meaning through the medium of an accomplished technique to her audience. She has, too, a touch of comic genius . . . and is an ingenious choreographer with ideas of her own.

— *Times*

A dancer whose sense of characterization is as strong as her artistry is sensitive and her technique is facile . . . Agnes de Mille has an understanding of the creatures she portrays, born of intuition and intelligence — her pity springs from the heart, her satire from the mind. She has a gaiety which leaves you chuckling, and pathos which makes you yearn — and a sense of the ridiculous so stringent as at time to border on — but never absolutely to reach — cruelty.

— *Daily Herald*

She has genius in her feet, gaiety in her head, and a perfect ear and sense of rhythm. The touch on the floor of her feet is as delicate and perfect as the best pianist's touch on the pianoforte.

— The Countess of Oxford and Asquith, *Sunday Dispatch*

Miss de Mille is indeed something of a portent.

— *Punch*

. . . That superb American creative dancer, Agnes de Mille. She is a very great artist, gifted with rare technical equipment and with any amount to express . . . Thank you, America, for de Mille.

— *New English Weekly*

And now, on to Leicester Square, and some MONEY!

Hurrah and love,

A.

E.S.U.

June 17

Dearest Mum,

You ask about Ramon. The story behind his illness is this. He comes of a wealthy family, a town house in London, a biggish estate in Sussex called Netherfield Place, open for charity on Tuesdays. It was designed by a pupil of Sir Edwin Lutyens and immaculately decorated and furnished.

Ramon's chief friends were the staff, cooks, gardeners, and gamekeepers. He was a great tease, Cousin Joan says, adorably funny and a favorite of the lot. He had a normal enough childhood — with morning walks in Kensington Gardens, the Cornish beach in summer with beloved cousins, and even a hunt or two in Sussex. He was present once at the kill and was blooded on the spot. He remembers this as a climactic moment of his childhood, a sort of coming into manhood.

His mother, very lovely from the pictures, died of TB when he was seven. His father, a romantic widower in a cape, a hypochondriac given to melancholia, unadulterated by any larger grasp of contemporary life, a patriotic lover of county tastes and county traditions, married a young lady who had been a saleslady at a superior men's shop in London and who (in the course of her duties) met the widower and quickly grew to admire "Dorian's" cape, exquisite manners, and income.

Ramon was at this point about twelve. He didn't get on with Step-mama at all. She was managing and took over. She was terribly exacting in all things. The turnover of servants was incessant. Papa was given to the vapors and became more and more fragile. Ramon went to Rugby. Ramon said they did not pamper the boys at Rugby. One lad got kicked in the head during rugger. He said his head hurt, but he was told to brace up and carry on. He kept falling asleep. They shook him very hard and told him to pull himself together and pay attention in classes. He fell asleep onstage in a play. That they did find odd. The next week he died.

Ramon's cousin, Joan Reed, says that all public-school boys are undernourished; that is, that they are badly nourished, with ill-balanced diets, no attention paid to vitamins and so forth, and that they get flu and enduring colds repeatedly. Ramon did. One December Ramon played rugger in the mud, stopped at the bun shop before changing, and got a thoroughly bad cold.

He came down to London for his Christmas holidays and began complaining about his eyes. The optician found nothing and suggested a neurologist. The neurologist ordered an ambulance at the end of the examination. Ramon took a bath that first night in the hospital and crawled back from the tub. He never walked again.

Then he went blind. He sat propped up in bed and listened to doctors discussing him as though he could not hear. They said that he would surely die. (He couldn't see at this point, but he could hear.) He lay immobilized and blind and he determined he'd fool them. One specialist said within his hearing, "He'll not get better, you know. But I don't think he'll get worse."

But another specialist was kinder and patted him on the shoulder and said to buck up, there was hope, at least for his eyes. Then they left him alone.

He was just sixteen and he cried.

His father told him that no Englishman cried and to stop it. Then his father left and they took him to a nursing home, where the care was spasmodic.

If he reached for anything, or fell asleep and slipped, he lay as he fell and couldn't get back. Sometimes it might be an hour before the nurses came. His spine is dreadfully crooked.

His sight recovered somewhat, but he still can't discern color. He sees everything in browns and reds — no green — as a dog does. For a time he had some feeling in his legs, but gradually that went.

They brought him home to the Sussex country. He had a motorized chair and tootled about the gardens and watched the hunts pass, but the chair wheels made muddy marks on the rugs, and Stepmother Joan was a tidy housekeeper. It seemed to be simpler not to go out. Cousin Joan, the daughter of his father's twin, told me that he hadn't been taken out of his house into the garden, the display gardens open for charity on Tuesday, for one entire summer. This is hard to believe, but I do believe her. He had a little movie camera and projector and screen but it was so much trouble to set it up and darken all the windows and pull the furniture around that after a bit he let them put his equipment away for good. He was all but slipping from life in sheer boredom and despondency when Sharpe, who had training in the London hospitals, came. Sharpe took in the situation and ran up the pirate flag, declaring open war on the whole family. The hatred is fierce and mutual and lasting. They say Sharpe is after the boy's money; he says he's trying to save Ramon's life and reason, and it's him I believe.

An intelligent and kindly doctor, brought by Cousin Joan's mother to Dorian for his hypochondria, noticed the crippled boy in the chair and asked questions. Thereafter, Ramon was his chief concern. At this point Ramon's grandfather died and left him a small but decent independence. (Paper bags and pulp mills I think.) With this income and the help of the friendly doctor, who fought to get him away from the family to a life of freedom, Ramon straightway moved to Oxford (Step-mother Joan was glad to see him go. He was in the way.) and began to read for a degree while learning to play the flute, which he could do

Ramon Reed before his illness

Ramon Reed at the time I met him, after his illness

flat on his back. But the life proved a little too strenuous and still under the benign approval of his doctor he returned to London to this place with his small household and a regular regime — one-half day up, two days down, and a few outings around the block in his chair. Sharpe has to lift him into the chair and out and doesn't like to do this because, he says, it's tiring. If Ramon goes any distance, he has to take an ambulance, which is costly for him and attracts crowds.

The family has chosen to ignore me totally. I met Stepmother Joan at a tea Ramon gave for her. She phoned later at suppertime to say how much she'd enjoyed meeting his friends and named every single person but me. She couldn't have known that I was sitting on the other side of the phone avidly listening. I had been doing a large gros-point chair seat while Ramon read me Aldous Huxley.

The chair seat is for one of Ramon's Queen Anne chairs — he has beauties, but he says of course he can never sit on it, unless he is ceremoniously lifted onto it and straight off. He has to have rubber air cushions and things.

They think I too am after his money, I suppose. Imagine! After a poor, crippled boy's money in London! But they are County and despise all Americans. Hollywood, however much it may fascinate the intellectuals, repels them. They think I am venal and vulgar. They choose to overlook me, which is easy, as they're seldom around. They're down in the country with their foxes and delphinium — not that they occupy themselves with anything much beyond their digestion, but these are things they approve of. They don't approve of Ramon and Ramon's "Bohemians" (he entertains painters, writers, and theater people) and Ramon's new American friend.

Ramon wants to take me to Netherfield on a Charity Day. The family is always out those days, he says. Naturally, they don't stay home while the rabble roams about. The butler is his good friend and will let us in the back door and will not tell. No, thanks.

Do you realize that, there being as yet no children to the second marriage, he is the heir apparent to a big roaring fortune and a great estate? (Joan says not really wealthy, not enough to cut ice over here, but, my God, they seemed so to me.) — except, I think, they are hoping he will die. They do pay for his medicines, it is true, but he must lie pretty heavily on their consciences. An Aunt Dora, also rich, who gives Cousin Joan handsome presents, buys him fruit at Jacksons, Piccadilly from time to time. They never did. They never sent him anything although they have gardens. The father even questioned one chemist's bill because Sharpe did not send it promptly enough; and cut ten pounds off Ramon's monthly allowance for medicines. Once, after a bad bout of sickness, Sharpe sent a medical report but inadvertently addressed the envelope to "Mr." instead of "Esq." All Sussex rocked. No mention was made of the fact that Sharpe had saved the boy's life.

Stepmother Joan recently asked him if he'd like a Queen Anne cupboard for his papers. His room was so messy, she said. He would like anything Queen Anne, but he didn't like Stepmother's constant cold disapproval of the way he lives. He snapped that he adored having his papers all around and on the bed and on the floor, too. She shrugged and left! One more disagreeable session with a cold and disagreeable and cantankerous boy. If he would only submit to his affliction and be grateful for all favors. Above all, if he would only be humble and accommodating as any cripple should, not continue to rage and snap like a well, virile son, chafing at interference and supervision. If only he would not continue to — well — live!

Later: Sharpe hates the family with black rage but he is becoming, like them, uneasy about me, me and Ramon. He doesn't like our outings. He says they're too expensive. There have been one theater, one picture, one picnic, and my concerts, but of course the ambulance costs three guineas a trip, and there have been flowers — many flowers. And besides, he has to lift Ramon four times each evening and he says he will be ruptured. Ramon can't weigh much (he's agonizingly thin) but it's dead weight. "Wine at dinner," Sharpe says. They never had that before. I gaped. He says all these things in front of Ramon repeatedly, and Ramon copes with humor, with firmness, without bitterness or self-pity or anger. He just insists that it's his own money, and he's going to spend it as he wishes on his own pleasure. "What does he want me to save it for?" demands Ramon, and that is the closest he's ever come to inferring that his future is limited. That is the only reference he's ever made to possible death.

Sharpe accompanies us when he can, especially to the movies. He likes the flicks, but then also, I think he doesn't want to leave us alone too much. He's jealous. The fact that Ramon and I can read together and talk about things in which he cannot join maddens him, although God knows he tries, to the point of utter exasperation. He dislikes conversations in which he cannot insinuate himself as an equal participant. When sufficiently rebuffed, his retaliation is to become brutally and coldly impersonal, to send Ramon to Coventry, sometimes for days. Since Ramon has no one else to talk to and is dependent on him for everything, the treatment is effective. However, as far as I know, he has not resorted to this recently. And I'm there quite often for Ramon to talk to. Sharpe (oh, how he hates me calling him this — he's damned if he'll be treated like a servant) has lost a little of his absolute power. But not much. There's never a substitute nurse. That means Sharpe can have no vacation, not even one whole day. But he doesn't mind. He loves Ramon. Ramon has taken the place of his abandoned wife and son and of any lasting romance, and is, in very truth, his career and, I suppose, his future. There must be a will protecting him.

In the meantime, Ramon continues as blithely as possible. They swear at one another but they knock along, like two old married people. They are both completely interdependent and deeply fond. Because Ramon's family is so outlandishly unfeeling, Sharpe is all the boy has — except for some wattled aunts and his beautiful Cousin Joan whose visitations, like some tropic bird, are brief. Cousin Joan is dark like Ramon with huge black eyes, long lashes, chameleon skin, classic features and tall. (I measured Ramon the other day in bed. He is six feet.)

She has just turned twenty-one and comes into her inheritance, but due to the happy circumstances of an augmenting capital, her portion is somewhat larger than Ramon's was. She has out-fitted herself with some stunning clothes and a little car, and she is living in a small flat here, though she has to check in regularly with Mummy in Sussex. (These independent British debutantes — and believe me, if they have money they are independent — keep a wholesome, not to say terrified respect for Mummy's approval.)

The other day I found her in a marvelous Mayfair hat sipping sherry at Ramon's bedside. She tells Ramon everything, to his great amusement. Apparently, she has no reticences with him. The two of them are pretty ribald about the family: Percy's (Ramon's father) dispirited and feeble attempts to beget another heir since Ramon is so rickety (that's the way they put the matter). Ramon laughs until Solomon gets up in disgust and leaves the bed, stalking out of the room with his tail straight in the air. Joan is merciless about Stepmother Joan. "Have you met my namesake?" she asks, her pansy eyes sliding sideways and her beautiful mouth open over dazzling teeth. "Only once," says Ramon, thumping his pillow. "Nor is she bloody likely to again. Some things I can spare her."

If Joan is a good sample of what the family turns out, think what he might have been! It was extraordinary to watch them facing each other. The same hair, the same eyes, the same gestures and mode of expression, she all physical radiance and he a wraithlike reflection, a sort of abstracted essence of what she is fully and vigorously.

She has become friends with a painter, Anthony Devas, whom she brought to Ramon. Ramon likes him very much. "They click" as Joan says. He is painting Joan and says he will paint

Cousin Joan Reed
(Photo by Angus McBean)

Ramon. He seems to be making quite a name for himself. He also seems to be married, a situation Joan doesn't find inhibiting.

Last time Joan came she brought her 21st birthday present from her two most beloved girl friends. Joan's memento was a £12.10.0 Elizabeth Arden makeup kit which she took all apart on Ramon's bed to his delight. This autumn she plans to go "out" to Canada, where there is a maternal grandmother.

Are Mag and Judy settled in at the farm at Goshen (the largest cow barn in Orange County! What can Bernie be thinking of?) or are they all still living with you? Oh, give them my love.

Devotedly,

A.

CHAPTER 5

THE week at Leicester Square netted me just under $200. It was almost unendurable and it brought no fame. Attempting rather subtle comedy in third-rate vaudeville, with incompetent musicians and careless and overworked stagehands, in sets designed for English knockabout vaudevillians, was a doomed enterprise. I danced four times a day to lethargic audiences, and every tiresome and paltry detail of the experience I relayed to Mother in order to make her suffer also. I was a whiner. I should have taken the money, which I desperately needed, and shut up. Instead, I tried each time as though it were a Theater Guild concert. I never got reconciled. There were a few pleasant circumstances, which I also relayed.

The English-Speaking Union, London
June 26, 1933
Dearest Mum,
I'm glad because it's over. I thought it would never be.
I was sorry to part from my dresser at the end. She was an extremely motherly person, wise in theater ways, and very amusing. The wardrobe woman had originally promised to get me a dresser. By noon of our opening day she admitted she'd failed to

find one. Hours of frantic telephoning and dickering with messenger boys. A poor sick old lady, the one who dressed me at the Arts Theater, showed up, so fragile that I thought she'd faint every time she leaned down to pick up a stocking. She has since collapsed. But in true British form she wrote me a letter and found me a substitute before she allowed herself to be taken to a hospital. The woman I have now is robust and pleasant and worked, if you'll believe it, with Charlie Chaplin in the 'alls. He was the "saucy boy in the box in an Eton collar, and didn't know 'ow funny 'e was at all." He also carried a birdcage in one act — in other words, a stooge. "Wot 'e needs, miss," continued my dresser, "is a good, motherly woman. These women 'e mixes with are no good at all — a kind, motherly woman to look after 'im and keep 'im steady." "Of twelve or thereabouts," I added silently.

After the first show (there are four daily) Mr. Foster came back and said *Ballet Class* was the prettiest act he'd ever had in the house.

I took a class from Mim every morning before I got to the theater, and rested between shows or worked on the Bach ballet, which Mim wants me to start teaching the girls next week. There was a buffet on the floor above, so I could have tea or milk or hot food whenever I liked. My strength seemed to be holding up pretty well.

I didn't get on very fast with Mim's Bach ballet largely because I had so many visitors. Every afternoon at the theater I had a large tea with toasted scones and strawberries and cream. The rich and debonair Single-Taxer, Manny Jacobs, teaed with me and gave me excellent criticism — also took my pay away so that I would not risk having it stolen from my dressing room. Charming, charming man. He advised me to attach myself permanently in some way to the Ballet Club because he feels I should do better work and find greater happiness in an organization of congenial experimenters and students than ever I should in a commercial wrangle like the present one.

I went to the Kirk Askews' — he's here buying pictures — after my last show. Freddie Ashton rather depressed me by telling me that Mim was teaching me to stand incorrectly and urged me to go to another teacher. He has just had a terrible row with her. Constance Askew was very angry with him for talking about Mim that way in public, considered it shamefully disloyal, as indeed it was. But the net result of the attack was to fill me with the greatest foreboding about my work.

The cocktails were eating their way through the party when I left. They played deadly havoc, I learned later. One man got drunk and abused Elizabeth Bowen until she burst into tears and left the house. Kirk Askew sent her flowers the next day, she told Ramon.

On Friday I had a private lesson with Antony and he and I settled in front of a mirror the controversy that has been raging in the school for the past week over my posture. Antony, like Ashton, had contended that Mim was ruining the one good thing I had, my shoulders, and was fast turning me into a hunchback. Mim answered that her aesthetic decisions were far sounder and more advanced than Antony's, and that what she was telling me to do though apparently odd, would work out for the best eventually. Well, I just wept and sobbed at this point. She telephoned two days later, on the eve of her weekend departure for the country, to bid me pay no attention to Antony. Antony countered by leading me to a mirror. We worked for half an hour in front of it on just nothing but standing up and now I know what I'm doing.

The girls at the Union have been angels. My maid, the eggbreaker, came to the theater one night. I gave her tickets. She does all my laundry free. Miss Ireson, of the front office, is marvelous. While I was paying my bill today, one of the other secretaries dashed into the bureau, and kneeling on the floor, stitched up the back hem of my dress. I'd have gone out like that, you know, to get in time for the *pliés*.

Robin and I were having hot chocolate at a Lyon's Corner

House when who should go by but his crony, Krishna Menon, with his latest flame, an extremely beautiful blonde. Krishna looked at us with disinterest and when we suggested they join us, his gaze skidded. She smiled over dazzling teeth. Menon said something impossible to decipher because of its rapidity and Britishness, and they drifted off. It seems they're perfectly miserable. They're both in analysis, but under the same doctor, who is getting their cases all mixed up.

July 4: Early this afternoon I dashed off for an interview in Old Bond Street with Charles B. Cochran about his autumn show, *Nymph Errant*, music by Cole Porter. Cochran was charming. They're different, the managers, I find, when they send for you. For this interview I wore my garden party dress (I was going to an open house party at the embassy later) of white embroidered organdy, and the Watteau hat. I had on the blue satin shoes with bows. I know I wasn't fashionable but I looked picturesque and good for me. Cockie said so.

He stopped and looked at my feet. "Very small," he said. "Very pretty."

I dimpled. He then resumed his talk about how he thought I was probably a great artist but that he didn't really need me — this was regulation to get my price down.

I went on to the ambassador's, where I ran into Arthur Schwartz, who was very excited about Cochran's interest in me and promised to sit right down and write him a letter, which I believe he did from something Cochran said yesterday. I met Walter Lippmann there and your friend Raymond Moley, looking anything but well. His career, it is generally conceded, has been quite thoroughly bitched up. The party was more or less fun, acres of Americans sweating in organdy dresses and frock coats and eating off the ambassador as hard as they could, while a red-coated British band played Dixie in the style of Sir Edward Elgar.

The Massine ballet matinee at the Alhambra, an amazingly fine arrangement of the entire Tchaikovsky Fifth, with extraordinary pattern in the last movement — rotten sets — restored my waning faith in the art. You can't imagine how depressed I get looking at the sugar-icing stuff that's around. This company boasts a new crop of astonishing soloists, Baronova, Riabouchinska, Eglevsky — who jumps, Mim claims, like a lion cub — Lichine, all under twenty, brilliant, virtuoso dancers, and as veteran stars, Massine and Danilova. Haskell in raptures in the lobby. Also Lincoln Kirstein in demi-raptures. Haskell is living in heaven right now. He goes to two performances a day.

July 6: I went to the Alhambra ballet last evening and saw the best ballet of their repertoire, *Cotillon* by Balanchine, a really exquisite piece. It has cheered me enormously. The audience was very gala. The ballet is the thing now, and everyone goes. Andrée was there looking lovely, and well. Mim was there looking frightful in green, but being very pleasant. Diana had been there the night before and had seen young Doug Fairbanks and Gertie Lawrence with the front of her hair dyed blond in a new and unbecoming fashion. Ivor Novello was there, she said: "had grown a new mustache and did look too Madonna."

My faith had been badly shaken up by the Balanchine *Ballets Trente-trois.* They performed *Mozartiana* (very thin), and *Errante* to Shubert, with Tilly Losch in a ten-yard train designed by Tchelitchev which she managed quite well. And such was Balanchine's genius that she seemed to be dancing on beat. But try as he might he couldn't make her emotionally moving.

They premiered a German work called *Anna, Anna* with a spoken text by someone called Bertolt Brecht. I don't understand German but I did get a lot about *Ein kleines haus bei Louisiana.* There were two Annas, a doppelgänger arrangement, one danced by Tilly Losch and the other raucously shouted by Lotte Lenya (German) — music (German) by Kurt Weill. "*Nicht wahr,* Anna?" yelled Lenya. "*Ya,* Anna," rasped Losch. They took bows at the end before a stampeding house. London

and Paris have gone Germanophile — well, Jooss led the way
last November. (I never thought before Paris could like anything
German. They do now, all right. *Wirtlich dernier cri.*) This
man Hitler seems to be losing his country a good many of its
livelier talents.

The other star is a youngster, Tamara Toumanova, twelve
years old and a true ballerina. I sat there and wept. I wept for
two reasons, and the first was genuine wonder at the beauty of
the child's dancing. The second you can figure out — sheer
envy!

The costumes and decor were chic, but the impact of the evening was paltry; I might even say peripheral. I think dancing
should reach the heart; I'm that primitive. But London seems
enraptured by the two companies.

On Saturday I had Mim Rambert and the Haskells to tea.
They could talk of nothing but Balanchine's Toumanova, whom
Mim declares to be a female Yehudi Menuhin. Haskell has given
the child a holograph letter of Maria Taglioni. Mim was naturally very interested in the Balanchine group because four of her
girls (including Diana Gould) are in it. She sent them to Paris a
month ago, although it hurt her season. She is generous in big
matters, and yields her claims unexpectedly, although I must say
she is getting pretty irritated with Arnold Haskell for spending
so much time and print on Ninette de Valois's schemes.

The *New Statesman* is the paper that panned me before. It is
owned by Maynard Keynes, an economist and Lydia Lopokova's husband. The paper is hostile to all other dancers, particularly me, due to Mim's having stated publicly that I resemble
Lopokova. Her husband doesn't think I do. At all.

The other day I had lunch (my treat) with Lily Madsen. It
seems the tiny, widowed, almost silent Jessie Paul is driving her
mad, and always has. She, Lily, is afraid to wear new clothes, or
make jokes, or go out to parties. She is forced to have all her
fun secretly. Husband Arthur, of course, is far too loyal to
John's memory to protect Lily from Jessie. I'm afraid things are

approaching some sort of crisis. I've asked Lily to come to Denmark with me when I go for my August engagement. Arthur is just appalled, first at the possibility of Lily's show of independence and second that a Single-Taxer could squander time and energy on marital emotions. Now, Mum, if you breathe a word of this in any way or drop any tactful hints to Arthur, I'll never tell you another secret. And don't you dare judge the rosy-cheeked girl! You never spent years tied up in a sack with a gloomy pigmy.

I've taken her to the theater a couple of times but, oddly, I've never been asked to their house. It's just as well, I suppose; I have doubts about the menu. Haggis is solid wool, I imagine, and I've a suspicion that I should find, to whet our appetites, Mrs. Paul standing upright underneath the dining-room table.

But there are formal "social gatherrrings" whenever possible at the Taxation of Land Values Office at Petty France. The English Land Values Taxation meetings are sterner than any others because less alcoholic. But Madsen dotes on them. I, as a manifestation of the Royal Line, am seized on as an excuse for an affair, with speeches by devotees from John o'Groates to Padstow. Whenever I speak — and I always have to, as last Wednesday — I make an incredible ass of myself. Oh, for your happy faculty!

As for Arthur Madsen, he hints rather pointedly that I should contribute to Mrs. Paul's fund. Oh, dear — I want to give money to the movement when my debts are paid, but not to Mrs. Paul.

Dinner with Ramon and Elizabeth Bowen Cameron. No high-minded talk about saving the world here — just good robust sense, and very considerable wit.

Mim gave me a private lesson today which nearly ruined me.

I've had my hair cut off. Now, don't shout and scream and yell! I know you've said since birth it was my greatest glory, my only beauty. I know that. It's in the garbage dumps now. I just couldn't stand it. I couldn't find hats that would sit properly. I couldn't keep hairpins in, and every time I got hot, and that's quite often in my way of life, it rose right up Zulu style. Mag had me plucked last year like an airedale in summer by the most expensive coiffeur in Sak's. No use. It's gone. I'm curls to the ears but not to the horizon. Ramon says I look cute as hell and years younger. I don't know how I'll keep my costume pieces in place, but that's a problem I'll face later. Now I can wear those dear little cloche hats that look so absolutely hideous on everyone.

I had some pictures taken in a booth off Leicester Square to prove that life isn't over.

Don't keep fretting, Mum. I will try to dress well and be neat, and I will occasionally buy myself flowers to wear. I can even afford orchids. Orchids are dirt cheap here. You can get a spray (little spotted ones like tropical butterflies) for ten shillings.

Friday, interview with Cockie (Cochran) in which he beat me down from £100 a week and royalties to £40 a week and no royalties. Oh God, I have a feeling the royalties are going to matter! However — there's to be very little dancing, mostly stylized stage business. Easy for me — and a couple of solos for Gertrude Lawrence. The first four weeks will be hard work, the last four not nearly so hard. I think I can do the Bach ballet for Mim at the same time — and take lessons.

Cochran, who has not seen me perform, keeps saying that he thinks I am an artist and that he hopes to give me greater scope in another show soon, but not this one. But no matter how limited, I have this chance. It's nice. It's money. And it's big time. Pray!

Look, can't you ever manage to take a rest and just laze for a bit? Haven't you earned the right yet? You're going to keel over right under the laurel bushes with an insect repellent in one hand and a Single Tax brochure in the other.

Devotedly,
A.

CHAPTER 6

THE Cochran show had been obtained for me by my friend, Romney Brent, who was really not my friend, but like so many young men, my sister's. Romney had fallen in love with Margaret in New York, as who hadn't.

Romney was Latin and he'd grown up in a climate where one accepted obligations with friendship, so he proclaimed his admiration for me by getting me jobs. His real name was Romulo Laralde, and he had been born in Mexico, the son of the founder of the Coaluila Bank and owner of three great ranches near Saltillo. (These were planted mainly in maguey from which pulque was made — but not as a business and not by the family.) Under Porfirio Díaz the father became Mexican ambassador to Paris and Madrid, and had known everyone in the governments. Romney was the youngest of six and the only boy. He grew up petted and adored. His father's properties were "large," he said. "How large?" I asked. "Oh, I don't know, larger than Belgium certainly." His schooling had been in France and Belgium and he spoke French, German, English and Spanish interchangeably. He was the heir, however, to very troubled estates, the Villa revolution having complicated pastoral life, and he left his country as soon as possible to make his way in the New York theater. In no time he was the darling of the Theater Guild and made an instantaneous hit in the *Garrick Gaieties* (Rodgers and Hart's first show) and was probably the only actor in history to get headline notices as Launcelot Gobbo in *The Merchant of Venice*. Noel Coward brought him to London to star in his review *Words and Music* under Charles Cochran's management. And it was Romney in a topi who introduced *Mad Dogs and Englishmen*. His progress through the London salons was even more noteworthy than in New York, and now he was doing his imitations and telling his anecdotes in hammer-beam halls and pleached alleyways, where duchesses and countesses tweaked and twinkled. The theater fawned on him.

Accordingly, when Romney introduced me in one great house, I was introduced to all, because Romney's word was trusted and his friends of the West End came to my concerts just because he said to. Duchesses did not move on the critic's word, they acted on their friend's advice.

The theater in London is cozy, almost eighteenth century in its containment, everyone there is acquainted, friends or enemies, and shows are readied in an atmosphere of intimacy unknown on my native shores. The talk may be sharp in the cocktail lounges and competition active in the office, but the talk is about known colleagues. A show is often cast around one Ivy Restaurant table. Everyone is at everyone's parties. Everyone knows everyone's weekend cottages — and there is a tendency there — avoided here — to work with tried and proved collaborators and not to jettison helpmates in favor of new and less expensive beginners. There's a family feeling about the London theater, almost akin to the medieval guilds. It doesn't limit them. Their output is just as good as ours, often better.

There were, I suppose, gentlemen in the American Thea-

Romney Brent as Launcelot Gobbo in The Merchant of Venice
(*Photo by Florence Vandamm*)

ter, but I'd met none in the musical branch. The London Theater was different, I had been told. And Cochran, who produced every kind of play, was a great impresario and a man of renowned achievement. He knew all that Mr. Lee Shubert did not and he possessed all that Mr. Jake Shubert lacked — notably taste and probity. I might enjoy working for Mr. Cochran — I might find in him an ally — even a friend.

Romney kept saying that working for Cochran would be the most rewarding and pleasant experience of my life. Noel Coward, he said, would work with no one else. He was the best on that side of the water. It would be strenuous, of course, but I was used to that. It would be fun, opulent, considerate, appreciative — Oh good God! Why go on? I was simply now going to move into class. And I would meet under delightful circumstances everyone in London in the theater and in society. All that had gone before would be classified forgotten — B.C. — Before Cochran.

And I would come to him in good style, because I would come not as a beggar or a Notting Hill recitalist, but as a continental soloist from a paying engagement in Copenhagen.

For several reasons I was looking forward to Denmark. It was Danish Single-Taxers with whom I would be living, but they were a whole lot more jolly than the English breed, basically because, I think, the Danes were a whole lot more jolly than the English.

It had been in Copenhagen that we met both sets. Having gone to Single Tax conferences all our lives, my mother, sister and I, we were prepared for the usual, but were surprised to find this one fun.

We got to the fun part, however, only gradually.

The night of arrival my sister and I had our baptism of fire when we attended uncomprehending four hours straight of German dealing with a few points of Boden Reform. Neither my sister nor I spoke a word of German, and Mother only sang it. But stouthearted Lily Madsen passed along notes to cheer us, and Andrew McClaren, M.P., drew the most extraordinary caricatures of the speakers. Mother was numb; she had just left Father and she was in poor shape, but, of course, determined to do her duty because it was her nature to be determined and dutiful.

The meetings took place in what I supposed to be an art museum, but it might have been a government building, even though heroic naked young men and women stood about in classic Thorvaldsen abandon.

In the middle of the first afternoon my sister and I began to realize very soberly that Danish was not our native tongue. But a young man beckoned, a blond young man with a sudden grin and a large black umbrella. He spread it in the atrium between Apollos and offered his arm. He spoke in English, "I am Leif Folke, the son of Folke Folke, the head of the fire department of Denmark, and I have come to save you."

"But it is our duty not to be saved," we whispered.

"Your duty will come later. Now you see Copenhagen with me." It was pouring rain, but we fled happily and splashed through our first excursion in that enchanted city.

In Copenhagen that July patience was long and tempers were sweet. We were all much younger and still hopeful and the Danes had managed things wonderfully, and the fun did happen.

We went with Mother to the Grundtvigs Hus and the crowd rose en masse as she entered, a proceeding which so unnerved her that she could hardly find voice to address them, but remembering the purpose for which they rose and the purpose for which she spoke, she found a voice and talked to them in her light treble with the clear, high, winged words that came to her at such moments.

We all followed afoot behind the open carriage that took her and various senators to the Liberty Memorial (Friheds-stotten), where she placed a wreath in the name of her father. Members of the government, representatives of foreign countries, and writers spoke, and Mother, again almost inaudible with emotion, addressed the mass. Thousands of unassorted citizens filled the entire central square, listening as she spoke in inaudible English (no public address system then), but her audience was composed of the most courteous people in the world and they responded as though she were a native daughter talking a tongue comprehensible.

The next to last night we dined in a private room in Tivoli, in the long opalescent evening. The sons of the northern Georgists toasted us and danced with us, their guests from California. Lieutenant Johannes Wille presented Mother with his sword as he formally dedicated his life to her. Mother had borne up remarkably well under the private woes and public strains, but this time she frankly wept into her champagne and attempted vainly to regain her composure in an outsize Tivoli table napkin. The young men, various Folkes and Bjørners, alarmed lest her two daughters follow suit, whirled them around to the strains of a violent Danish waltz until dawn which was, alas, only an hour later. As we said goodbye, Dan Folke, Leif's younger brother, managed to speak of his own future as a musician and to wish it would touch mine. Dan wrote over the years and visited us in New York — it was Dan who had got me the Danish job, a two-week stint at National Scala, the largest *café-chantant* in the country. Dan and his wife offered me the hospitality of their home as well.

I could hardly wait to go.

The trouble in London intensified.

Robin demanded a showdown, not unnaturally. He sublet a friend's flat — for us — and I went to him.

It didn't work. Although astonishingly enough he professed himself more deeply involved than ever; but for me it was over.

I ran away. I ran to friends in the country in absolute panic.

I said good-bye to Robin. It was only for a few days, I said. God forgive me the duplicity, the sheer cowardice.

"You will be back then?" But he saw my face, and he knew he'd lost me. I couldn't say it, though. I couldn't say it in words. I was going to make the final break later from Denmark in a long letter explaining. Explaining what, for Christ's sake? Why I had toyed and teased for a year? Leading both of us from intimacy to intimacy with every instinct braking. How do you explain cruelty? No wonder I couldn't do *pliés* or jump without gasping. No wonder I was always late. It is a miracle I got out of bed at all in the morning. I awoke spent, to proceed in opposite directions. This used to be called quartering. It takes a lot of strength to tear a human being apart, but it can be done.

Nothing resolved in the country. I walked the lanes drugged with indecision and came back to town as I had left.

But Denmark was directly ahead. The northern months would give me a change and a time to think. I was frightened. I felt as though I was being caught in invisible spider lines.

I said good-bye to Antony, who was going away also. He was taking a freighter that July to Helsinki and planned to walk across Finland to pay his respects to Sibelius, whom he did not know, but whom he trusted would be gratified by the attention. Antony was warm and friendly in his farewell to me. He guessed I was in some kind of mess, but I am sure he thought it trivial.

I said good-bye to Ramon. It was only for a few weeks, I said.

"Sow some wild oats," he ordered. "Have some fun. You need it."

And then I did the simplest thing in the world. I leaned down to his chair in the London dusk and kissed him good-bye. And the world cracked open.

He had not been kissed by a woman since his illness.

There was a long silence. He watched me smiling, then he said softly, "You'll come back to me, Aglet? To me alone?"

"You know what you're asking."

"Yes."

"You really know? Is this possible?"

"Why not? Why ever not?"

"You mean you wish me to come back as your lover?"

"Yes."

"Live in your house?"

"Yes."

"I have not the courage to marry you. I cannot face that yet."

"I understand that. I do not ask that now."

"I may leave you. I may marry someone, someday."

"You must do what you must when the time comes. I live from day to day. Let me have this, however briefly. I'll not hold you in any way. This I can promise you."

This was a woeful, dark courting.

CHAPTER 7

Det Forenede Dampskibs-Selskab
Aktieselskab
July 14, 1933

Dearest Mum,

I just got up from a twelve-hour sleep and I feel considerably different. I ran away last week to the Blisses. I went there played out. I came back rested and like a fighting cock. But somehow I seem to be tired again.

But Copenhagen promises to be marvelous.

Dan Folke and his wife, Lise, flew in from Southampton two weeks ago, did I write you? She is young, pretty, chic, charming and intelligent, very blond with strange slanting eyes. She speaks English in a soft husky Scandinavian voice. He is growing square and mature, very much the successful businessman in expensive clothes, with a complacency that is not at all obnoxious, but rather gleeful.

They were embarked on a Mediterranean cruise but have returned to Denmark and are waiting for me. They're counting on my living with them, you know, while I perform at National Scala, which is the job Dan got me. It's marvelous to have a paying engagement for a month and then to be coming back to a big paying job, and with Cochran! If I make good at National Scala the cafés of Europe are open to me and there's money there. But if I make good with Cochran, the world is my oyster. I am now

about to begin supporting myself. I won't need more from you.
I won't even need to touch Pop's allowance. It can accumulate
in the bank for me all summer. So you're off the hook indefinitely, and Mum, I'm so glad not to have to demand any more.
There are things you must do for yourself. Take a taxi now and
then, for instance, or a lower berth.

This boat is a sweet little white one with pretty blond steward-
esses who speak English only here and there but manage to be
exceedingly helpful. There are few passengers and most of us
eat at a long table in the dining saloon spread with the most
astonishing Danish hor d'oeuvres, pickled vegetables, cold meats,
salads, and odd breads and cheeses. A popeyed Copenhagen
gentleman has taken me under his wing. He is a scene designer
and play director and has worked for years with Max Reinhardt.
He tells me the Scala Restaurant, where I am to dance, is definitely high-class. We arrive at Esbjerg tonight and take the
sleeper for Copenhagen. Dan is meeting me at six-fifty tomorrow morning, a ridiculous time for the regular daily trip from
London to end! Gotta pack!

Devoted love,
A.

Strandveg 20, Copenhagen
July 15

Dearest Mum,

Dan met me at the train and drove me to his new house, very
like a Hollywood bungalow by the sea and in view of Sweden
and surrounded by a small garden. Lise had breakfast on the back
porch in the sun. I slept most of the day. I can't get over my
exhaustion. At sundown we drove out along the sea to an inn in
the country, returning via Lynby to the Scala for dinner and to
get acquainted with my theater. This is a large restaurant for
petite bourgeoisie, like a Danish Alice Foote MacDougall — a
good stage, sinking orchestra, adequate lights. The audience attentive and intelligent; the show very bad, what I saw of it, but

Dan Folke

I imagine that the people will take as good as they're given. I'm going to see that I'm carefully staged. Dan will help me.

Dan sends love. His father, Folke Folke, wants very much to see you.

A.

P.S. I have just seen the *Times* review of *The Philosophy of Henry George* by George Raymond Geiger. I would refer you for comfort to the contemporary reviews of John Keats's poetry when it first appeared. The public criticisms of Galileo and Socrates were even harsher, not to mention Jesus Christ.

Strandveg 20
Monday, July 17, 1933
Morning

Dearest Mum,

At five o'clock today I am to give a special, invitational recital with piano, and for once in my life things have been so well-managed that I have nothing to do this morning. I am sitting by the open door into Lise's little garden waiting for lunch. By and by I'll go shopping for Kleenex and theatrical powder with my somewhat limited Danish and then I'll go to the theater and warm up. I packed my costumes in the restaurant theater last night and they are being brought to Lorry, the garden theater, pressed, mended, and arranged by someone else! They will be taken back to the restaurant by someone else. Oh, God, to have been allowed to live to see this day!

The garden press-recital is a fine idea. Inge Lise Bock, the twenty-seven-year-old manager of National Scala, decided on meeting me that perhaps she could make a real drawing card of me if she handled my publicity correctly. So she and Dan put their heads together and devised this special performance to be given at the small cabaret theater at Lorry (pronounced Loy), Inge Lise's other establishment. The entire press has been invited and the American diplomatic service, who have accepted, as far as I can gather, en masse, together with all the important theater managers and directors of the city. The stage is rough, with a rake, and small, but no smaller than the Ballet Club stage, the lighting equipment primitive but the electrician astonishingly intelligent, so that I think with nothing at all to work with, we'll get some very good effects.

The kindness and interest of the theater staff at the Scala warms my heart. My dresser, Thilde, especially, is like a god-mother — calm, gay and motherly; she does everything for me, even to understanding the outlandish lingo I speak — a mélange of French, German, Danish and English and various expressive sounds of my own invention. But we were able to make the changes last night in less than two minutes.

I have, however, great difficulty with the musicians, the con-ductor understanding nothing, not even the musical Italian I try to explain myself in. Still, he's interested and willing and I've no doubt in three or four days he'll give me the correct tempi.

Last night the orchestra went completely to pieces — wrong time, wrong cues, everything, the drummer not yet under-standing *Ballet Class* although I rehearsed with him for hours. However, I still got my four bows.

I am going to the restaurant theater tonight two hours early and beat hell out of the musicians. If I could only speak directly to the conductor in his own language once! But I don't suppose it would do much good. The pianist told me he'd like to follow me and not the conductor's baton, but that would not be custom-ary. Twice the orchestra got completely out of control. I've had to train the pianist for Lorry in nine dances, the theater orches-tra in five, and a jazz orchestra in the upstairs bar for my Gerhswin piece, besides getting everything orchestrated and copied. I did a bit of orchestrating myself and I wrote out eight bars of trumpets for my entrance. The things one can learn to do! The restaurant was packed opening night but with a very stupid Sunday provincial audience. The *Gigue*, because of its costume, and *Harvest Reel*, because of its movement, went well.

The others were not understood at all. I was frantic, but Mrs. Inge Lise Bock came back and said she was delighted and not to mind the public: (a) It was Sunday and the stupidest house of the week; (b) The people had not been advised by the press yet whether or not to like me. One woman, she said, sitting near her, started to laugh at *Stagefright* and was immediately shushed by her neighbors. If I get good criticisms from the recital, everything will be fine. After the performance I went upstairs to the dance hall and did the *Blues*. No one understood a gesture, of course. As I left, the drummer leaned over and said in perfect New York, "See you in Harlem." "They don't understand me," I said. "Of course not," he answered brightly. "They've never seen anything like this before."

I had rehearsed all yesterday morning at Lorry; I danced *Ballet Class* at the Scala Sunday matinee, five dances in the evening and then the *Blues* at the cabaret. It is a comment on my health that I am not tired this morning.

I had the feeling after the matinee that Dan and Lise were disappointed and my heart broke for them; he had boasted so much of me. That night I danced at Scala very much better than in the afternoon — very much. And I did get four bows after *Harvest Reel*. That's not bad for a restaurant.

Wednesday: Well, the recital came off. All of artistic Copenhagen present and cold as the first Paris audience. The pianist played wretchedly, all of the tempi wrong — hell, I can't go on. My braids fell out of my new bobbed hair; I haven't learned the trick of anchoring them to short hair. I counted on *Harvest Reel* to pull the house up. The pianist played it like a polka, and the waiters turned the house lights on so that every bit of atmosphere was destroyed, and in the middle of the dance walked down the aisle with refreshments. Somehow I ended. Then I had hysterics to the point of vomiting. It seemed just too bad with such extremely important people out front. It was enough that the stage was so ragged and bumpy I daren't go barefooted

Agnes de Mille: Beethoven — Scherzo, *1934*
(Photo by Henry Waxman)

and that I could hardly keep my balance on points without these other stupid, stupid, amateurish mistakes. However, kind, darling Inge Lise came back and said the audience liked it and so I started again. The second half was very much better. Perhaps because of the cocktails in the intermission, perhaps they had talked me over and formed some idea as to what I was trying to do — anyhow, I got a hand on the *Gigue*.

Why do I write all these rotten things to you? Well, partly because there's no one else I can say them to, and I must put my head down and weep, and there's your shoulder — there's always your shoulder. But, of course, it's cruel to you, so far away and so helpless, and caring so much. You're right — I do make you a whipping boy. Why do I? Why do I avenge myself on you? The last spanking you gave me was for being a crybaby — remember? Or was it because I very rudely said you were one too? I was five, I recall.

The press was part good and part bad. All the papers said I was original and clever but all were equally unanimous in saying that I had neither grace nor charm.

But Ramon has sent a cable — "Mine Eyes Dazzle."

I went in to see William Jennings Bryan's daughter, U.S. Minister to Denmark Mrs. Ruth Bryan Owen, a day later. She had sent me a great bunch of pink roses and attended the performance. She was charming, introduced me to her friends as your daughter, no "niece" business at the embassy, asked after you, whom she remembers very warmly from a meeting at Fanny Hurst's. She wished her greetings sent to you. I went to a party given at her house the next night for the officers of two destroyers in port. Mme. Minister looked extremely handsome in black satin and pearls with an artificial water lily on her bosom. She is very much in the press over here. But the Danes do say it shows the U.S. doesn't hold a great opinion of their importance if they are willing to risk a woman.

Toward midevening a girl in pigtails and freckles and an ill-fitting printed chiffon, looking like hell, was seen lurking forlornly about the floor. "Poor child," I said to my partner, "who can she be? And what a criminal her mother is letting her go out like that! She'll be miserably lonely all evening." Just then all the white-bearded, beribboned, bemedaled noblemen did nip-ups and rushed over to pay homage. She was swept from one dignitary to another and carefully and tactfully kept from vulgar contacts. The wrong person never got a chance to ask for a dance. The little frump was a princess of the Royal House and her presence was a real honor to our embassy.

Mme. Owen spoke of you again as I said good-night, very, very warmly.

Cochran has written for my name and nationality in order to obtain working visas. You plan to come over in September. Maybe Mag could come, too.

How is the garden? And the livestock, Judith et al? Ah me, I must get back for October!

All, all my love to Mag and Bernie.

Devotedly always,
A.

My performances might be going well or poorly, but I didn't care too acutely. At the other end of the present stint was safe harbor, for a time anyway, a quiet, kind, sophisticated, purposeful and loving man waited for me. He couldn't walk and his activities were limited, but not his ranging mind. And his devotion seemed boundless. He was steady and steadfast, with a gentle way of living. I knew he wished to marry me. At the moment I hadn't the courage for this, but maybe with time, who knew? In the meanwhile, there was shelter and rest and a hope I hardly dared to recognize. With him, I sensed reassurance and quiet. All my youth I had been running, whipped on by furies until I seemed destined to heart failure. No peace, no peace, no place to lay one's head. Come in, Aglet, tea waits and just hear what happened today!

So, all through the professional strains of the summer months, I knew the mysterious, troubling, and exquisite anticipation of discovery in love. For him it would be the first time. I would not prove disappointing to this youth — nor boring — nor unbeautiful.

"My undiscovered continent, my America."

I began to read *A Farewell to Arms*. I dared now contemplate what passionate, fulfilled love meant.

His letters came three, four a week, bidding me to make a clean break and be free, bidding me to be of good cheer, bidding me to look forward to happy, great adventures, to be quiet and sure, to come home, when I was ready, to come home freely and with high hope. He waited with joy and no fear. He waited. "Mine eyes dazzle."

In Lise's garden among the bee-busy zinnias and snapdragons, I wrote the dreaded letter to Robin, my bonny, brave Englishman who filled me with such trouble. It was as truthful as I could make it, as totally candid. And it was final. That door was shut. I shook as I signed my name at the end. But, at last, I'd been honest.

Strandveg 20
July 20

Dearest Mum,

Dan and Lise are golden-haired angels, frantically in love and so delighted with their own happiness and so generous-hearted and interested in other people that it is good to be with them. Their home is sweet, somewhat Scandinavian in taste but spotlessly clean and simple. I have a tiny room with a bed, a closet, a revolving table of shelves. My trunk stands in the kitchen next door, and most of my other belongings on the floor of my room. I thought after a few days I'd move in town to a hotel. But it's too much fun here. Besides, I like the food: fishes and meats that I'm not acquainted with, and marvelous Danish breads and cheeses and butter — oh my, the sweet good butter! And beer and marvelous wines. Dan is very proud of his cellar. And of his Chevrolet, a mouse-gray roadster, and of his platinum-blond wife. Dan, it seems, is one of the most important young men in this city. He is the second most popular composer in Denmark. Writes lyrics and music for revues (I saw one revue for which he'd written lyrics and sketches — pretty bad, but naturally I could pass no outspoken judgment). He writes for talkies (yesterday I saw the preview of an unfinished one, *Tango,* with Else Skarbo — very good! — and Dan's music better than I dared hope). He furnishes ideas for comic cartoons in one of the leading papers — an idea a day. He does publicity for three professional friends. He is head of the department at Wilhelm Hansen that buys and publishes foreign music and sells copyrights of their music to other countries. He also buys books — Wilhelm Hansen, for instance, publishes Aldous Huxley in Danish. He also manages concerts — Gigli and Yehudi Menuhin, who he said failed here, but who came into his office the next morning to return part of his fee because he did not wish the concert management to lose so much money. I think Dan may someday be a great impresario.

Our street, Strandveg, is on the straits between Sweden, plainly in view, and the Danish mainland. It is well out in rural suburbia.

I go by trolley into and out from the city — past two miles of truck gardens owned by office workers — each only a few yards wide, but quite deep and containing a small pavilion and enough vegetables for the family meals. In the evenings as I go to work in the late sun, the owners are all out either mowing or raking or reading the evening papers while the Danish red and white pennant flies gaily overhead, making carnival the long narrow strips of green. As we approach the business districts, crowds of silver-haired bicyclists, girls and boys holding hands, skim past at an even *presto,* like flights of gulls. It is all so happy! At one-thirty A.M. I return alone, but quite safe. There is no crime in this blessed country. My steps echo down the pavement, and the hedged gardens give off pungent smells in the wet dew. I have never met a single questionable character. Dan and Lise would not let me do this alone if there were any problem; there is none.

Devoted love,

A.

Lise's garden

July 29, 1933

Dear Maa (a good sample of the manner in which I speak Danish),

The Scala season is finished. I got through alive! The reason for my not having written has been simply straight physical exhaustion — an hour and a half to two hours class every morning with Sven Aage Larsen — as hard work as I've ever done. An hour and a half in the theater before performance, an hour between performances — never out of the place before half-past twelve. I kept moving like this to keep my nerves screwed up. I had to spend the afternoons in bed. I've written some letters long overdue. But most of the time, I've been unfit for anything and really lay about the house working up what vitality I could. The program I gave every night was extremely exacting and because there was no cooperation from the audience, it did me in regularly. It took me about forty minutes to come to afterwards — mentally, I mean. Dresser Thilde was a help. Bless her. But only as a sponge for my woe. Although the reception got gradually better, I'm glad to say. At first the people turned their backs and ate, then they began looking. Then they began standing up to look, and the last four days I noticed the appearance and increase of opera glasses. The last night I had a brilliant reception. I don't know how many people knew it was the last night.

You probably think I was a fool to attempt lessons at the same time, but I wasn't. First, I had to feel I was making good use of these weeks or my morale would have snapped. The nightly performance tore me to pieces. And second, this is the first

The Parvenues, *1933* (*Photo by Henry Waxman*)

opportunity I've had for regular uninterrupted work with a good teacher. And I've made genuine progress. I could do little or nothing with Rambert — business kept interfering with the classes. I always arrived late and I was always being interrupted by phone calls — no way at all to study. I've never in my life studied the way I should, the way a piano student does, for instance — four hours a day every day. I'm beginning to realize that if I did that, there's almost nothing I couldn't accomplish.

I'll write a note tomorrow and tell you the social news.

It's after one o'clock in the morning — I must to bed.

Later: I nearly forgot. Mrs. Haskell, Arnold's mother, as a hobby is making miniature rooms, exact replicas of period houses. She knows the shops in England where the miniature museum pieces come from. If she does not charge too much, I shall ask her to make an early American farm kitchen for Mag for her Goshen manse. She makes the rooms (and entirely by herself) like stage sets, complete with lighting. Rambert has a charming early Victorian living room, flowers under glass on the mantel, eyeglasses lying open on a book! Mrs. Haskell has never sold one so I don't know what she'd charge — we'll see — But I know how you dote on these things. And I think the workmanship is finer than the Queen Mary doll house at Windsor.

Mag's silk stockings have started to arrive — marvelous!

Dan has records of a young American singer, a Negro named Marian Anderson. He was astonished I never heard of her. Well, who has? All of Europe has, that's who, but not one of her own countrymen. Scandinavia has gone mad about her, and when I listen to the range and quality of that voice, I easily understand why. I've never heard better. When do you suppose she'll be able to go home? Do you remember Graham Reid's pupil, the Negro soprano that you went to hear in a church? and how he explained she'd never be able to sing anywhere else? Well, Miss Anderson's broken through — over here at any rate.

This kind of gift makes me uneasy — first there's my wonder

at it — and then the fact that it's directly from God. Glory is in her throat — also, she does not have to write her own music. Well, such talk is silly, but it seems to me I try to do too much and miss out all around. Anyhow, she will be crowned with stars. I must be grateful; I have a restaurant stage under my feet tonight. At least you're not paying for it.

God, I'm nearly dead. I just can't seem to unwind.

Devoted love,
A.

Strandveg 20
August 5

Dearest Mum,

I promised the social gossip.

Well, to begin with, words fail me in attempting to give due credit to Dan and Lise. There never were two kinder, gayer, and more sweet-minded children. Living with them has been perpetual picnic. Dan is successful, which gives him the money and the opportunity to do what he wants. He lives to his fullest bent with gusto and art; alternating hard work, frequent and enthusiastic play, and an awareness of all that's happening in his city, or, for that matter, in his world. He misses nothing. And he knows just where he's going. He's on the top of things in Denmark. He gives himself another two years to ensure his position and save some money and then head for the open spaces. Lise is a swell playmate. With one woman to help her in the mornings, she keeps the house going as though it was automatic — cooks, launders, gardens herself, and without the slightest bother or sign of fatigue, always looks fresh and tidy, and if not chic in the New York sense, certainly very attractive. She has waited on me hand and foot. I have been too tired to do anything about helping with meals and you know how useful I am at my spryest. She has even left parties to come home and get my dinner when she and Dan have been out together. Neither of them eats breakfast, but every morning she has got up early and cooked me an enormous one — meat and eggs and rolls and tea, and milk and cakes set out waiting for me when I came home at night, unless they were up romping around the house with a bottle of wine waiting for me. Dan has busied himself refusing invitations for me. "This afternoon and the next two days you will do nothing," Dan would say, pushing me back on the bed. I then would find that I'd sleep three hours without moving. So perhaps he was right. "If I had you in hand for a year," he said, "I'd make a fine girl of you."

Bouë Bjørner, the son of the Single Tax leader, Signe Bjørner, has been to see me five times — my most faithful admirer. Your knight, Johannes Wille, showed up one evening with his brother and two friends. It was one of Bouë's nights so we had a party afterwards. Wille took me out into the country the day after my engagement ended in an army limousine with a soldier at the wheel. He is a captain-lieutenant now and does engineering work for the air corps. He had to visit a farm way off in the country which is going to be made into an airport. The farmer's wife was giving a birthday party in the garden for neighboring wives and children and she invited Wille and me to join them, bringing up a child's chair to the al fresco table. I could not talk to any of them, of course, but they were extremely gracious and I had a delightful time. Wille announced that I was the granddaughter of Henry George and the ten-year-old son, if you please, was impressed. He also understood English, but was too shy to speak. We had a second tea afterwards at Mr. Folke Folke's — he had asked me at an hour he knew Dan could not come. They all ask repeatedly after you.

My teacher, Sven Aage Larsen, has been charming, and so has Else Højgaard, one of the best-known dancers here. She had been at the recital and was rhapsodic about my work. They came to my midnight cabaret performance last Sunday night and oh, what a difference it made having someone in the hall that knew what I was doing! I got a salvo of applause on my entrance and they had infected the entire audience by the time the dance was over.

The last performance was touching. The pianist handed me a

*National Scala, Copenhagen, July 1933. Agnes standing in the coat
and hat Mag helped her buy*

Burgomaster's Branle: *Agnes de Mille*
(*Photo by Doris Ulman*)

bunch of his own pink garden dahlias tied into silver leaves. The stagehands came to my dressing room to say good-bye and not to get tips, and as I was leaving, one of the musicians, I don't even know what instrument he played, rushed down the hall, kissed my hands, and then gently and slowly leaned down and kissed me on the mouth. I was staggered. I thought he was drunk. But Lise says no, that was a respectful tribute to my work.

The night after my last show Dan had the official opening of his new film, *Tango.* The company sold every bit of sheet music in two days and two thousand records in the same length of time. His office has been filled with flowers and every company in the city, movie, music and theater, has been offering him jobs. Actors have been telephoning their congratulations all day. The day has been gala. Dan's songs are not really good; that is, they are European jazz, and I, who have grown up on Gershwin, Berlin, Arlen and Rodgers, cannot rate him very high. (And by the way, when we stopped at a beach en route to Helsingør, a whole crowd of girls and boys were singing, in English, "Stormy Weather." Now, that's a song!) However, Dan names any price he likes and the managers jump for him. A real hit means these things and nothing less. But it is not all joy. There has been not one word from his father of praise, encouragement, or congratulation, now nor ever before. He's behaved shockingly to Dan about his work, about Lise, about everything. Dan says his father is the big disappointment of his life. And then I think of you and what you've done for me, and with what kind of success do I reward you?

All — darling — my love,
A.

Boat
August 10

Dearest Mum,

I hated to leave, I can tell you. I'm in love with the city. We must spend a summer there sometime.

The train left at six in the morning. Fran Schwabe came with chocolates, and Thilde, my dresser — imagine getting up so early after the hours she keeps — with carnations, and Dan and Lise, of course, running beside the cars and holding my hand, just as Dan did seven years ago in New York. Ah me!

I tried to get Mag a Greenland suit to wear in the snow — you know, pants and jacket of beautiful leather, big beaded collar — but couldn't find one. I got her something pretty cute, however.

And I sent a silver bowl from Jensen's to Dan and Lise — little enough. I've lived off them for a month. Besides, I didn't give them a wedding present. So this went "to the house that sheltered me."

I also bought an exquisite unglazed Jensen figurine (all white) of a Javanese girl, for Lily Bess Campbell of U.C.L.A. When teaching me to write she kept repeating ad desperandum, "You'll never dance. You haven't the body. Look in the mirror. It's your duty to write. I may be sentimental but I think it's your duty." It used to make me pretty mad. She did add once, "You'll never dance but you may" — this was after seeing me in a Chopin mazurka — "just possibly be a great actress." Well, I vowed I'd earn enough money dancing to shut her up. And I have. Hence the figurine.

I sent Inge Lise Bock a lovely basket of flowers. She's been grand.

My best love to the folks.

Always devotedly,

A.

P.s. I'm known in Copenhagen. My hairdresser saw me, and the boy in the shipping office where I went to book passage back nearly fainted with delight when he saw my name on the ticket.

CHAPTER 8

I n London Ramon was waiting for me. But as the boat train slid into the station, it was Robin who stood on the ramp. I had not told him the date of my return.

I must have changed color.

"I didn't mean to impose — I couldn't let you come in alone, unmet." I could barely speak.

"I'm going straight to the Union and then to Ramon. He's waiting for me. He's waiting dinner."

"I'll take you to the Union." As he kissed me good-bye there he said, "Are you really going to Ramon? That's your decision? I hope you know what you're doing. God willing you're not making a mistake." And he left white-faced, and I was free to go to Ramon.

Ramon met me like a bridegroom. His house was filled with flowers. He had presents for me. And I had brought some for him and a lovely new negligee.

That night Ramon told me that he was totally paralyzed from the waist down.

I also learned that he had no idea of the situation he'd placed me in. He didn't beg or whimper. He didn't threaten. He did not even excuse himself. We held hands in terrified silence for ten minutes. Then he spoke.

"I thought you knew."

"I didn't. How could I? After what you asked? How could I?" He said nothing. He was going to die and sooner or later depended on me. That was as plain a fact as that there could be nothing physical between us.

I was trapped.

Sharpe had given me his room for the night and himself had taken the parlor sofa. I remember sitting, as the night thinned, by his bedroom window. He had covered his table with a rich brocade and Ramon had had placed on this a bowl of heavy-scented summer lilies. I was aware of their searching perfume in the unmoving air and the gleam of white as the street lamps paled. After a while the morning drays started down the King's Road and a bus ground up.

I could have left before morning. I didn't. I stayed to begin a life cored, gutted, concerned with trivia, where daily household happenings are events and the main reasons and dynamics of living are not, and the main goal is to be alive tomorrow morning. This is the life of the invalid. This is the life of the condemned exile. Mine was voluntary. Ramon had no choice. I held his hand, but I knew I could go someday. There's a difference.

Sharpe came back to his room with the understanding that if there was any sleeping on the sofa to be done, I would do it. (I quickly found that a nice little bed could be made on the floor with the sofa cushions.) Ramon learned that I was staying and he now faced the days ahead with radiant anticipation. For the first time since the tragic onslaught of his disease, for the first time since his sixteenth birthday, he was happy. He felt loved. He had someone to care for.

I kept my room at the Union and operated entirely from there. The life in the Paulton's Square flat was absolutely secret and known only to the occupants.

Vacation was finished. Charles Cochran of London waited with his fine new show. This was Big Time, not provincial restaurants, and success was to be now or never. I was quite clear about that. The initial encounter with the great man was to be at his house in the country and I dressed very carefully and prettily, a red-checked gingham and little high-heeled red sandals (size three) that set off my feet.

The English-Speaking Union
August 14, 1933

Dearest Mum,

A Rolls-Royce met me at the Windsor station, a great Rolls-Royce with a silver cockerel on the bonnet — Cockie's trademark. Cockie was most gracious. He is a delightful, urbane and kind gentleman. Oh, how different from our breed! And Mrs. outdid herself. Gertrude Lawrence was there. She's nice and we'll get along. Dorothy Dickson, the musical-comedy star, completed the party, a sprightly spirit with a beautiful face. Unfortunately, she had a cold and couldn't talk. Romney was there too. He's staying there for a fortnight, working on the script which he personally is preparing from the novel. Isn't that fine? I hope it's good and successful! Gertie drove me back to the station and insisted on coming in with me to see that I got my ticket successfully, thereby forcing me out of shame to buy a first-class fare which I couldn't afford; but it was a pretty gesture.

E.S.U., August 17: Well, I'm hard at it now. Today was to be the official beginning but they rushed me into rehearsal four days ahead of time, and while I was a bit frantic at the lack of preparation, it has turned out for the best. I have already outlined with the chorus one of the major numbers. That's a load off my mind, for one thing, and for another, we have learned how to work together. The girls, I think, have confidence in me. At any rate, they are behaving beautifully. Attentive, diligent,

and respectful, they go at the dance if not with talent, at least
with determination and enthusiasm, and I'm sure when their
initial shyness wears off, they'll perform with more gusto than
they are now aware they possess. There are eight of them, English, pretty, chosen by Cockie and his assistant, Frank Collins.
Only four of them are trained. It would not have occurred to
Cochran to let the dance director pick, or even sit in on auditions. However, their drill sergeant, a passé vaudevillian of sweet
nature and vast experience, thinks I'm just wonderful and she
calls them an hour before my rehearsals and polishes off what
I have set the day before. Soft for me! At that, I can hardly
whisper tonight. Two hours of counting and calling and I'm
done.

The woman in charge of the music is fascinating, white-
haired, with a witch's profile and horizontal teeth. She is, however, one of the most expert musicians in the business, the liaison
officer between Cochran and every musician who works for him,
from tympanist to composer. Noel Coward will not do a show
without her. She does all the actual music dictation. She is
known the world over, calls herself unaccountably, Elsie April,
and is mistress of enough theater gossip to keep anyone open-
mouthed.

There are to be ten dances including bits and pieces ("Hardly
anything for you to do at all," said Cochran as he jacked down
my fee), one of them a real chance — a Greek Dionysian ritual.
Romney told me to shoot the works. I asked Cole Porter to do
me a Greek dance in 6/4 and thought I might get some routine
tin-pan alley excuse; not at all. His eyes twinkled and he came
back the next day with a charming piece with astonishing
rhythms and harmony. And he'd written it out himself — he
hadn't dictated it as Irving Berlin, Arthur Schwartz, Noel
Coward and so many others do. Porter has studied seriously
with Satie and Milhaud, I'm told. He's also done a darling Turkish number, which our extraordinary little Scotch contortionist
will perform on a silk pillow. This one is a proper treat, very

exotic looking, the spine of a boa constrictor and the diction of a Glasgow schoolgirl. She goes by the name of Eve. When she warms up, one hour uninterrupted, she sits on a mat on the floor anywhere and gradually loosens every joint in its socket until she can pull her legs straight up and tie them in a knot over her head; but she dances with phrasing and expression. And, I believe, Balanchine, who was her last choreographer in a Cochran-Offenbach extravaganza, thought she was a fine artist.

The Keeper of the Harem, the Eunuch, is played by a remarkably fat old "femascumale" (Ramon's term), Bruce Winston, who is amusing, able, and very pleasant to work with. His chief claim to fame is, however, that he makes hats for Queen Mary. He tells how he sits her in front of a mirror and places the basic toque on the Head, and then tentatively adds, one by one, buckles, lace, feathers, roses and veils, watching for the barely discernible inclination of approval. Not a word is said. At length a finger is raised and Royalty speaks, "Enough!" Winston bows. Another Imperial Hat has been achieved.

I was touched by your suggestion that I get a secretary to keep track of my social connections. Don't you realize that London is absolutely empty? No one here who doesn't have to be? Mim Rambert in the country. Antony Tudor, her lieutenant, in Finland calling on Sibelius, and all of my classy acquaintances far, far off. Besides, I've got to be quiet, not necessarily working all the time, but quiet. When rehearsals are finished I can't afford to go places where I have to make an effort. For one thing, I simply can't talk — voice gone.

I have seen almost no one, lived like an ascetic, and worked.

The Massine ballet is still running (over a month, a colossal financial success) so I've gone twice there. Had dinner with Robin, and some odd meals and teas with Ramon, who lets me come late if I like and reads to me while I do gros point — exceedingly restful. I practice every morning before rehearsals — while Cissy is cleaning up my girls — at the Ballet Club with one of the pupils who trains me marvelously and won't accept a penny — says she is glad of the opportunity of learning to teach. Ramon wrote the enclosed the other day while waiting for me.

August 14, 1933

(Written by Ramon Reed on learning A. de Mille had been born a month late.)

> *En retard, Agnès! Ça fait presque cent fois*
> *Mais ce n'est pas drôle. Comme ça c'etait, ma foi!*
> *A ta naissance. Mais dis, pourquoi celà?*
> *Pensais tu qu'une vie penible arrivat?*
> *Rien ne va mieux parce que l'on le prévois.*
> *Mais les attentes! Eh bien — vraiment pour moi*
> *Elles ne sont pas mauvaises. Tu triomphes, vois*
> *L'avoue que c'est donc, oui, de te due: Ah!*
> > *En retard, Agnès!*
> *Mais viendra la mort, ma chère, à toi,*
> *Mauvaise affaire ou l'on n'a aucune choix*
> *Il n'est pas possible d'être en retard là.*
> *N'y pensons plus! C'est trop serieux ça.*
> *Il vaut mieux vivre et être souvent chez moi,*
> > *En retard, Agnès!* *

E.S.U.
September 5, 1933

Dearest Mum,

There literally hasn't been a moment even for a note, and I thought this would be easier than recitals! I have worked from early morning until midnight and frequently taken my music to

---

* "Late again, Agnes! This makes nearly a hundred times but it's not strange, because this is how it was at your birth. But, tell me, what made you think a hard life awaited you? Nothing is better for the foresight. But the waits! Never mind. They're really not so bad for me! You conquer, here's my pledge: you deserve to be waited for. Late again Agnes! But here comes death for you, my dear. A nasty affair, where one has no choice. It's not possible to be late here. Let's not think of it. That's too serious. It's much better to live and come often to me. Even late, Agnes."

bed with me and studied it there for a couple of hours, dreaming all night of the dances and waking to go on with them over the first cup of tea. I have seen no one since I last wrote — a couple of lunches next door to the theater with Robin — a couple of milks after rehearsal at Ramon's bedside — one dinner with Mim Rambert — and nothing else outside of the festivities of the company, which are gay enough. But more of that later. The work is all outlined now. Polishing to do, of course, but that's not too wearing. "Not since Diaghilev," said Cole Porter, "have I seen girls move like that," and this of a troupe which included only four trained dancers.

Cole Porter is a small, finely boned and fastidious little man with a round doll head like a marionette's (Charlie McCarthy), large staring eyes, and a fixed and pleased expression that I rather think has nothing to do with his emotions. He is supremely well-groomed and sports a carnation in his buttonhole. He walks mincingly and very gingerly with tiny steps, and he leans on a cane. He seems unattached to the situation and barely concerned. His voice is soft and husky and rather light. He purrs. His presence is quiet and deferential, as unassuming as a visitor's; he sits surprised and intrigued at all rehearsals like a good boy with hands clasped on the top of his cane. He barely speaks, but, make no mistake about it, he is the most powerful person in the theater, not excepting Charles Cochran.

His rhymes are fabulous, male, female, middle word which I suppose could be called neuter. "How do you do this?" I asked marveling. "It's easy," he replied. "It's just fun. Anyone can. Get a rhyming dictionary." That's the answer, of course.

His wife came with him the other day, the legendary Linda Lee, all silver and exquisite, with pale, luminous skin and a veil over her pale hair and face. She looks the way duchesses should and so seldom do. Our soubrette, our special little sow's ear, XY, a common little chit with the taste and manner of a carhop, said loudly after she left, "That's the way I want to look when

I grow older." This remark drew a general and audible giggle; everyone knows what she's going to look like.

Our author, James Laver, is a bookish young man in a bowler, with a muted, slightly eighteenth-century air, the curator of prints at the Victoria and Albert Museum. It seems he has his raffish moments, this play being one of them. I think it's silly, a mere excuse for good songs and Gertie's dresses, which, by the way, are marvels and together with the sets are designed by Doris Zinkeisen, a ravishingly beautiful brunette. Her costumes are not only pretty, but, thank God, practical. Evidently Laver agrees with me about Zinkeisen because they sit side by side and hold hands, but then, I guess he's nervous. She may be also, although a pro and a beauty. She's almost as beautiful as Gladys Calthrop, Coward's designer, and much, much more gifted. Calthrop looks like Nefertiti — same neck and carriage of head. She is almost conditioned to showing profile without any formal request.

The other morning, in bounded Tilly Losch, looking adorable in a little striped silk Phrygian cap. Rehearsal came to a dead halt while she twinkled and shimmered with Porter and Brent and with Cochran, whose star she has been. Finally she tripped away, and we got on with it.

"Isn't she pretty?" cooed Romney, who might have been expected to be annoyed at the interruption.

All these people wander continually around rehearsals, although not connected with the enterprise.

I believe, I pray, I'm sitting pretty. I know I've done my best work under helpful conditions. Romney is heaven to work with — asks how I prefer to rehearse; asks my permission, if you'll believe this, every time he walks in on one of my rehearsals. If I've felt unready to take a scene, I tell him and he gives me as much time as I like, setting the date for the first showing and leaving me alone until then. He did make one mistake — insisted on my showing the Greek dance in front of the entire company

before it was ready — when it was just lousy. Eve, the lead
dancer, nearly went to pieces with nerves, and I was shattered.
Cochran came to my rescue and promised the dance would be
good if I was given a chance to finish it. I went home shaking
and lay awake all night.

   Actually, it was to Ramon's bedside I rushed shaking. I fell
asleep, hat still on, and woke up crying.
   "Steady," he said. "Steady."
   "I can't do it."
   "You can."
   "I'm going to fail."
   "You're not."
   "The best thing I did today was by accident. A girl did
something by herself."
   "But you recognized it. That's the whole point. What does
it matter how it happens? Now have some Bovril and quiet
down. Try taking your hat off."
   Sharpe listened to my reports of daily work quite coldly.
"How do those men like taking orders from a woman? I
don't understand that," was his one comment.
   Sharpe really disliked women very intensely. He used girls
but he did not trust them. He had walked out on a wife and
son in New Zealand and he was not going to be hoodwinked
here.
   Sharpe had a girl, invisible and not always the same one,
every Saturday night in the next room. Ramon read unper-
turbably throughout. Sharpe considered himself a womanizer
and gave himself top marks for performance. When sufficiently daunted by Ramon's superiority in argument, he
would flounce out of the room with the remark that Ramon
might be right, but that it didn't matter, because he, Sharpe,

was a very great lover. To which, of course, Ramon had no rejoinder, except to laugh in kindly amusement.

Throughout the rehearsal period Ramon continued to participate in all my problems and victories. He began to talk about following me to Manchester for the tryout period. This proposal struck me as profoundly impractical, not to say undesirable. Yet, he stubbornly set his heart on the plan and began to write to real estate agents in Chester. I was to spend all spare time with him. Sharpe was appalled. Ramon had never been out of his flat for a night, and the proposed trip seemed dangerous.

September 6: The day after the Greek fiasco Romney apologized and said he'd learned a lesson and would never demand to see an unfinished piece of work again. He has, however, made few such mistakes and is achieving brilliant success with the job. Cochran pronounces him the best director he ever had. All the staff members talk all the time in superlatives. It's heartening but it makes one wary. Romney is being teased for further musical shows already and can probably have his pick of jobs on both sides of the water. I'm glad because he has ability and is by all odds the pleasantest person to work with I have yet encountered, as well as the most intelligent.

Gertie, on the other hand, although warm and charming, has been something rather special to deal with. In fact, I've left every rehearsal cursing with frustration. I finally asked Cochran if she really liked what I was giving her. He says she adores it. It dawned on me then that she actually thinks she is doing exactly what I ask. She never does eight consecutive bars twice the same way. She's more particular about her hats, I can tell you.

Gertie's art is built on instinct and improvisation. She disciplines her performance, I'm told, no more than her rehearsals, changing with whim and temperature and without warning. You expect Gertie downstage; she comes in center back — even with curtain up and a paying audience. You expect her to play *grazioso* and gently; she is *allegro vivace* and sharp. You expect her in a dark-green silk; she is in transparent gauze.

But she's always fun, on and off stage, always.

As for me: Cochran said to Romney, "Agnes is a great virtuoso." Cole Porter to Romney, simply, "She's great," and to me, "I'm crazy about everything you do." Romney is pleased, I know, since he was my sole sponsor. He is getting the company all hopped up about me as a performer, too. They keep asking when I'm going to dance myself.

I feel that Cochran is on the point of doing something really important for me. I have an idea of working out a pantomime on some Hogarth pictures. Romney is enthusiastic and thinks Cochran might produce the show. Romney even went as far as to suggest his being in it. I spoke to your friend, Arthur Bliss, about this. He professes real interest and might do the score. This would be a tremendous coup.

I remember so well the afternoon in Hollywood when he played the "Agincourt Song." "There's iron in that," he said. And a new sound came into my life.

He is making a big name for himself here and in Europe and has been commissioned by Ninette de Valois to do a long ballet for the Sadler's Wells. He composes symphonies and cantatas and all sorts of things, which get played by the leading orchestras. I wish his music wasn't quite so loud, but it is vigorous and he is a master. And of course he is as delightful as anyone I know. He and his Santa Barbara wife, Trudy, have been adorable to me.

Oh, everybody here is full of plans and hopes. The tea talk is all *scherzo!*

The people in the company are friendly — including me in their lunches and beer bouts. I feel, for the first time, part of the group, Romney and Cole Porter are particularly sweet, and

Gertie and Doug Fairbanks (her steady at present) have taken me twice for food across the back street to Rule's, the two-hundred-year-old theatrical restaurant in Maiden Lane, Gertie in her gorgeous streamlined Molyneux, and me in — well, what I wear — but I do try to be neat.

> All love — and very, very happy,
> A.

> September 7

Dearest Mum,

Cockie's done it! Cockie's done it! Last night at Rule's he said, "Aggie, I'll give you a recital. I'll put you on in our theater one Sunday after the show's opened. The only other solo dancer I've ever successfully produced and believed in is Argentina!" This was after we'd run the Greek dance on the stage and the whole cast cheered. The whole cast yelled and cheered and Romney raced down the aisle and kissed me. The tide's turned, Mum. This is it!

The other day Marc Connelly came in to rehearsal and asked me to stage the dances for a revue which he may produce in October or November — all very tentative — but he stressed the fact that I could have anything or anyone I wished, and that I would consult no one but myself on the dances.

The more I think of the Molière play (translated and adapted by Lawrence and Armina Langner), *School for Husbands,* for the Theater Guild, the less I like the idea:

1. The pay is bad — $50 per week including solo performances. No pay for rehearsing or choreography, no royalty, all of which I am told is their custom.

2. The people arrogant.

3. The opportunity small. Doris Humphrey and Charles Weidman are to be in it also and Doris has sneaked the big mime from me. I would have two dances, it's true, but no production number. So, I think, no!

I'm pretty well. I expect to get out into the country when we go for the tryout in Manchester. Antony Tudor gave me a lesson today and is giving me another tomorrow here at the theater. Rambert is clamoring for my projected Bach ballet.

I had dinner the other night with Judge and Mrs. Samuel Seabury. He seems exactly as calm, no more, no less, as when he had Mayor Walker in the witness stand committing perjury, but surely he must be — what I mean is — that he is absolutely calm. He spoke glowingly about your biography of your father — real, genuine enthusiasm.

Lily Madsen has been saying also how fine she thought your biography was. Arthur, it seems, had wept outright at the close and declared that you wrote with tremendous and poignant feeling. She longed to have you come over and lecture, she said. You could pull the whole movement together here, and it wants some pulling. Her eyes glistened with enthusiasm as she spoke. Think about it. You have a real reputation as a speaker here. Everyone, Englishman and Dane, comments on it.

The rich and debonair Manny Jacobs says he never will forget how you made strong Danish farmers weep. And Adrienne Meyer constantly writes that she thinks you are the most amusing conversationalist she knows although, due to language blocks, she can't understand a word you say. Hey! Maybe your success is due to incomprehension! But no, hoary Scotsmen wept and Yorkshiremen and creeps from New Jersey.

Devotedly,
A.

p.s. Aunt Marie wrote me sweetly. Obviously you omitted to relay the painful passages in my chronicles. My relations' idea of my trip is a rose-strewn path to fame and social prominence.

I must make up a waltz number for Lawrence now — dear, dear — pure piffle and so difficult to do! This game isn't worth any candle at all I can think of, except interesting Cockie. That way lies glory.

COLE PORTER
who wrote the music

AGNES de MILLE
who arranged all the
dances, and ensembles
with the exception of
"Georgia Sand"

JAMES
LAVER
who wrote
the original
novel

"NYMPH ERRANT"

CHARLES B. COCHRAN
WHO PRODUCED

ROMNEY
BRENT
who adapted
the novel and
directed the
rehearsals

DORIS ZINKEISEN
who designed the decor
and costumes

All my love. Your letters are wonderful. But not a word yet from Father since I left in May.

> Midland Hotel, Manchester
> September 14, 1933

Dearest Mum,

This is as tough a lapse as I've subjected you to yet, and I'm heartily sorry. The work has been terrific and increasing. I thought I'd have leisure once we opened, but I swear, the strain on me has been almost as severe as before, except, of course, that I'm no longer as frightened as I was.

I received your cable this morning and I was sad to hear that you were not at the moment boarding a boat. You must be here at the end of October when the recital comes off. Cochran is still too *distrait* to be pressed into naming a date, but he stipulated the other day a time that would permit three or four weeks of publicity. (Evidently he intends to put on my show properly under his own personal supervision.) It will perhaps be better to have you then. My heaviest work will be done, everyone will be back in town, and we can really play about. I expect to put in two or three weeks of grueling practice immediately after I return to London — classes every day and rehearsals, *no* parties, and regular bed. I feel I don't need to do any social advertising with Cochran taking charge of that end. The point is to get some new dances ready and technique in impeccable condition so that when the big day comes, I can really take a step forward.

I have the four hundred dollars you lent me last spring safely lodged in the English-Speaking Union strongbox, so that helps toward the money end of your visit. And if you need further conscience salve for the trip, there's a possible lecture tour around London and a smaller subsequent one under the auspices of the Manchester folk. I addressed them on the subject last night.

I went out to dinner with Dr. MacDougal, a local Single-Taxer, and his daughter — very pleasant. And then we went to a small early gathering of the Single Tax clan. Dear me, what a crew! So sweet and so inevitably marked as failures! If anything could make me believe the cause is moribund (and nothing can), it's the people who gather together in the name of Henry George to pay tribute to his flesh and blood. The fustiness, the emptiness, the frustration of them all! I was introduced to one pillar of the Movement in dark glasses, two canes, and an arrangement of teeth ingenious and effective as design but good for no practical purpose whatever, I should think.

The men all had high collars and watch chains and elaborate figures of speech. The ladies of simple means wear mustaches and friendly, timid smiles. And the hats! The evening started with one of the women remarking (she was pointed out to me as a firebrand, a Boadicea who went around the north rural districts rousing people to fury and action) that she'd seen me at the Leicester Square. "Oh dear," I said. "I wasn't so good there." "Yes," she said, "we were sorry we'd gone. It was a wasted evening!"

Then there were a few words from the honored guest, salutes in lemonade to the flesh and blood, an announcement made of a religious service to be held in honor of George, and a question put to the Guest as to how she stood in regard to orthodox observance of creed.

Dr. MacDougal, an otherwise sensible man, was charmed with the way the evening came off, but did not hesitate to rush me away to the theater and sneak in with me to see rehearsal.

What they need is you to rouse them up — so plan to come; I shall plan to have you — even if it's only for a short time. It will do you good and won't cost much. The only thing you'll miss will be the opening, and that's really just a circus — fun, of course, but not too impressive. The play doesn't permit of any spectacular demonstration. It's all about nothing at all, and some of it's very thin and some of it's very dull, but parts of it are bright, impertinent, and amusing. The parties connected with the opening will probably include me only in a minor capacity. Cochran has made several charming gestures, partly because he left me out of one big affair very noticeably and was distressed afterwards. No — you come over when I'm the whole show and the fireworks salute nobody else. I'll absolutely plan for your coming, see?

Well, now what's happened? We rehearsed feverishly until leaving London, then came up en masse. Cochran had chartered nearly all of one entire train. This was good fun although everybody was tired and a bit nervous. C.B. had a large box of pink and yellow carnations waiting for me in my seat (first class). We are rehearsing endlessly without stop until opening — you can imagine — and I really think I have spent more time in the theater than anyone else.

The dancers and idiot singers, my charges, a godforsaken group who are breaking my heart and wearing out my patience (my anguish over them has become a company joke), are left always until everyone else has finished. And so last night — for the third straight night — rehearsal was turned over to me at two in the morning, as everyone left. I am also given them at ten A.M., before anyone else is up, and I'm told to polish off this bit of solo business or simplify that messy mob scene, and in the meantime, during the other rehearsals, I remain constantly on call. I no sooner stretch out on the floor for a snooze than Cockie summons me. "Aggie, Aggie," he calls, "sit by me." And he asks my advice about music, cuts, costumes, characterizations, etc., things that are none of my responsibility, but on which he apparently feels my opinion is of some value, and I naturally am flattered enough to be as much on hand as I can manage and a bit more than I can stand. I keep by Romney's elbow all through the staging of the big spectacle scenes. I coach the soloists in movements. I inspect costumes and makeups and always, during every company rehearsal, I sit from beginning to end out front — Romney's orders. Not that he needs me, but he wants all the directors present in case anything should have to be changed.

Things look very good for me. I'm on top. Keep your fingers crossed. I'll cable any good news.

In the meantime Ramon had arrived in Manchester against my most solemn entreaties. I naturally could not have him in the same hotel, although I knew he'd be lonely in another. Sharpe hadn't wanted him to come. Sharpe threatened and warned. No use.

Ramon ordered Sharpe to bring him to a mean little third-rate hotel across the city. They could not find a cab that would take the chair, so Sharpe had to push him through the streets half a mile over rough cobbles. I was able to sneak away only once and have tea with him in his hotel lobby, a paltry tea with smashed buns and old deaf people and north country traveling salesmen hanging about. My heart broke to leave him in this drab boredom with absolutely nothing to do and knowing not a soul, but I was overdue at the theater. After resting quite alone two days, he went to a rented house on the moors in the country. And there he waited for me alone — and all through rehearsals I know he was waiting.

September 16: At dress rehearsal yesterday Gertie suddenly decided onstage she hated her first act final costume although, naturally, she'd been at all the fittings. Suddenly at that moment she couldn't abide it. She pouted and fretted and Cockie, instead of saying it was too late and to get on with her job, patted her on the cheek and said, there, there, she'd have a new one next night.

My heart turned over for Zinkeisen. If anyone had carried on in dress rehearsal about a dance this way! Zinkeisen was already making a pencil sketch of a new red velvet. The specifications were phoned to London, and a messenger dispatched on the next train with the drawing. Gertie will have it in time for opening. Throughout all this, our author, James Laver, sat by admiring. Well, by God, so did I.

Before openings, I'm told, Gertie goes to the theater with three or four outfits of her own for every scene and spends the day choosing. It distracts her from nervous horrors. It also gives the costume designer — who is never consulted — fits.

More soon.

Devotedly,
A.

Midland Hotel
September 20

Dear Mum,

The show's a hit, as I cabled, but I'll give it to you blow by blow.

The day of the premiere I left the theater at five in the afternoon, after grubby, useless rehearsals with the goddam singers and ran around the city looking for a beauty parlor that would take me on. Every place was full up. All the actresses were being done, of course, and whole trainloads of people had arrived for the opening. Well, I finally got my hair washed and curled, but not my nails, flew back to the hotel, threw myself into my flame-colored chiffon evening dress, and with a spray of lilies-of-the-valley two feet long that Ramon had sent me hanging like a great feather from shoulder to waist, I swept down to dinner, looking on the whole extremely well. Romney was having cocktails with Noel Coward, Gladys Calthrop (set designer), and Lord Geoffrey Amherst. I was introduced to Lady something — important, started to shake hands, and gasped, "My God, my ticket!" then blushed and said, "Excuse me!" Noel said, "It's all right, dear, we like it." I rushed upstairs, took the ticket out of a drawer with shaking hands, dropped it, leaned down to pick it up, broke the shoulder strap of my dress, threaded a needle, lost the needle, found it, rethreaded, mended the dress, ran back to Romney — Romney all the time suave, cool and gracious. We had dinner alone. We drank each other's health. "The first of many collaborations," said Romney. "Agnes, you look lovely — very stylish and lovely. Can't you do this more often?" He had a new dress suit for the occasion. Coward and Doug Jr. leaned over grinning from their table. "Oddly enough," called Romney, "we're talking shop." "Have you heard anything lately of Laurette Taylor?" asked Coward.

We all went to the theater together, wedged in one taxi. I sat on Coward's lap, my arms around his neck. When we got out, the crowd, held back by cordons of police, eyed us excitedly, then recognized Doug. Romney and I were pushed across the lobby, buffeted, elbowed, kicked, shoved. I was somewhat spared, being a female, but Romney was trampled on and entered the theater unnoticed, his new suit definitely abused. He began to show signs of tension. I sat in the front-row balcony with Cissy, my assistant, Elsie April, the accompanist, and Frank Collins, next in office to C.B. Ovation when Doug Jr. entered and sat beside Gertie's young secretary, bigger ovation for Coward — prolonged applause for Cochran when he took his place in a box with Mrs. Cochran, white-haired and extremely handsome, and Romney, oyster-color.

The show began, and it was, as I'd suspected, piffling. The Cole Porter songs are enchanting. The dances stopped the show, however; that's the God's truth. The Greek dance absolutely. For whole minutes — not seconds, whole minutes — Gertie couldn't go on with her lines.

And Gertie. Ah, Gertie! As Frank Collins said, "She is like a racehorse. When the curtain goes up, her best foot is always forward. You can count on her as on the Queen. There will be no public error. She delivers. She leads the field. She breaks the tape" — and also my heart a little because it is never by any chance my exact work she is performing. Who cares? She sells tickets. She proceeds as I have told you by improvisation. This may be rough on the play and on the other actors but it means that her great nights are incandescent, and on this night she was pure magic. I've never witnessed the like — indeed I haven't. She was, as predicted, nothing like what she's been in rehearsals; the stage was nevertheless jumping with excitement. Acting shimmered. Gertie moves like a fish through shadows, the creation of her unexpected invention. She is funny, bright, touching, irresistible. When she walks she streams; when she kicks she flashes. Her speaking voice is a kind of song, quite unrealistic but lovely, and her pathos cuts under all, direct and sudden. Her eyes fill, her throat grows husky, she trembles with wonder. The audience weeps. She can't sing, but who cares?

At the end Cochran made a short speech to great reaction. All this clapping had little or nothing to do with the show — they adore C.B. in Manchester.

There were supper parties afterwards. Cole Porter entertaining Lady Sibyl Colefax, Cochran entertaining members of the company, including me. I sat between Doug and a most charming man named Bates who is the European representative of NBC and who is getting up a transatlantic coast-to-coast broadcast of a rehearsal of the show. He sat out all the rehearsals and I became well acquainted with him. He and his pretty young wife are good friends, I believe, of the Prince of Wales. We had caviar, and pâté de fois-gras, and grouse, and ices, and cham-

Gertrude Lawrence in Nymph Errant (*Courtesy of John F. Wharton, Trustee, Cole Porter Musical and Literary Property Trusts*)

pagne, and nausea. Too, too, too tired. Also, conversation lagged or grew hysterical. I fell into bed at last and mortified.

The next morning the inquest was held and we were all set to work again. One of us was fired — a tragic warning to others of us. The firing was without any notice and involved a leading man that everyone (except Gertie, who claimed he wouldn't look at her) had raved about and petted and entertained. "That voice!" said Romney. "Imperial, like the czarina vomiting!" "A new Chaliapin," said Cochran — and even Cole Porter sighed with rapture. He was fired without one word of explanation or a good-bye and taken to the station ignominiously and alone by Danny, the stage manager. The rest of us shook in our boots.

Changes were ordered in Eve's Turkish solo (which I like very well as it is) and a new dance for XY, who isn't doing well. She says the dance is no good. She can only tap, nothing else. And I know only three and a half tap steps. Cochran knew this when I signed on. I've tried to use what she has, but I hoped to give her some style and irony besides. After all, that is what the lyrics have, and the chorus girls achieve the effect very well all around her, but she wants to do precisely what she made a hit doing two years ago on Broadway, and she finds she is not making a hit in Manchester and she's getting panicky. There's trouble ahead.

I changed and spoiled the number and now Cochran's sorry and has ordered me to put it back again.

6:00 P.M.: Romney just phoned to tell me that Cockie in the middle of a soccer game this afternoon declared himself delighted with my work, though he wants changes. I am reassured somewhat.

Now, as to where I was over the weekend and why I didn't answer your cable — Ramon got himself and Sharpe invited up to friends at Winsfield (near Chester) so he could get me invited out for my birthday because he thought it would be fun if we could have a party together. And fun it was. The hosts, a Captain and Mrs. Hastings, were nice people but I saw little of them, sleeping most of the time, or reading with Ramon in a lovely walled garden, or walking alone through the high quiet fields and being chased over stiles by three village yokels who had a fairly lusty idea of gallantry. I called the theater Saturday afternoon to ask for mail. I left my telephone number and I phoned back on Monday to see whether or not I'd be needed before Tuesday, but I didn't ask to have someone go to the theater and get my cables and read them to me because I expected them to be birthday messages. It was extremely careless of me. This is why you heard nothing to your questions about coming.

I had left Manchester with a good deal of apprehension. And I left a very nervous theater staff. I knew I should not be going. I was well aware of how vulnerable to panicky advice a worried producer can become. The sovereign cure for any trouble, whatever it may be, was the hiring of someone new, and it was usually the dance director because the dance director usually had the weakest contract. It didn't matter that my dances were now stopping the show. In each show previously, one or more dances I had contrived had been show-stopping smash hits. It didn't help. Sometimes they were retained under someone else's name. I did not know what decision would be made over the weekend behind my back. But I had to go because Ramon was waiting alone after an expensive and exhausting, even dangerous, trip.

Just before I had returned to Manchester, Sharpe got me into a corner of the kitchen. "Did you know," he asked, "that the boy had endangered his life by making the trip?"

I could only shake my head.

Had he told me the truth about himself before I returned from Denmark? Had I walked into this situation not knowing what I was getting into?

"Yes," I murmured.

Had he told me how sick he really was?

I shook my head. "He promised he had told you everything. I made him promise. It's not fair to anyone — to you,
to me, to anyone. I'm responsible for his life — I alone."

"He didn't," I said.

"I couldn't believe he had. No woman in her right mind
would accept this — well, he won't live," continued Sharpe.
"Not long — and you're not helping."

I felt for a chair and sat down.

Sharpe was absolutely baleful. All right, so now he'd tell
me. Did I know Ramon almost collapsed after every unusual
effort? Did I realize all the things that were the matter with
him? The trip over the Manchester cobbles had torn open
his thigh and there were running sores; he hoped no gangrene, but that was a possibility.

"Any damp or cold brings on gangrene," Sharpe said —
"spots of wet gangrene. There are open sores on his thighs
and buttocks that infect easily, and worsen until the bone is
visible." — I wondered if he was exaggerating — "A bump
or a push tears the flesh. That is why he always has to be on
pneumatic pillows and mattresses. And because this paralysis
extends above the kidneys, he is in perpetual danger of kidney infection and blood poisoning. And this," Sharpe added
emphatically, "is what eventually will get him."

Sharpe went on and on. The boy lived from day to day
only because of Sharpe's nursing. Once someone had put a
water bottle on his legs too hot; in the morning the flesh came
away. You could stick a knife into him anywhere up to the
waist and he wouldn't know. He would never, never get
well. And I would probably be the means of hastening his
death. Before I came he had settled peaceably to his life and
now he was all upset and trying to do things he shouldn't.

Also he was hoping again — something Sharpe had beaten down in him. In short I would kill him. "Don't let the boy know I've talked to you," he concluded. "Run upstairs and don't let on you know anything at all. He'd never forgive me — never. He's waiting. I'll make you a cup of hot tea and bring it up."

As I passed toward the stairs Sharpe pinched me firmly on the behind, a real intentional hearty goose. "What you need is a man, a real man."

So I took a deep breath and went up, and Ramon was as cheery and gay as always. This scene went unreported and it took place on my birthday.

September 20 — later: The vacation did me real good. I was getting too tired, no fresh air, no daylight, and constant nerve strain. My head was tightening on me, my throat getting sore, and my face beginning to look like decomposed meat. The rest did miracles for me — country food, country air, and sleep. I hope the trip wasn't too much for Ramon. He is much sicker than I'd any idea — kidney and bladder complications among other things. Sharpe told me that nothing keeps him alive but astonishing courage and a heroic will to exist and accomplish. Naturally he values rather simple pleasures, such as a trip to the country, as of momentous importance. Anything I can give him in the way of fun is little enough, all things considered.

I returned to find two small coffins of flowers, one from you — white chrysanthemums and pink carnations (there wasn't, so Romney says, an orchid in the town) and four dozen roses from Frank Collins, Cockie's assistant, whose birthday it also was. Romney gave me as a somewhat pointed hint, a charming and accurate clock. Ramon gave me three Lytton Stracheys.

Gertie didn't like Eve stopping the show so we moved the position of the dance, which hurt it somewhat until I changed the lighting, and wonder of wonders, Eve still stops the show cold — absolutely cold, but not now to Gertie's disadvantage. Gertie continues unpredictable. The other night she wore two dresses no one had ever seen. Also, she took off all her underpinnings for the Turkish scene, and the actor who was playing opposite her, on being confronted by his star virtually naked, was so surprised he had to leave stage to recover himself. Gertie and Young Doug thought this very funny.

There is a fog here, not thick and obscuring and frightening as I'm told it is in London — you can see all right — but it eats you. It goes through brick, glass, wood and cloth, and while you haven't particularly noticed it, you suddenly find your throat flayed, the lining of your nose raw, and your eyes smarting. Rehearsals are painful because my throat hurts all the time. There's grit in the air, soot and coal dust. Perhaps this partially explains the Brontës who lived nearby, but no, they had wind and drinking water from a well in the burying ground. The w.c.'s here are as cold as in London but much sootier, and the toilet paper is both slippery and gritty. The natives don't mind. All this goes to build up the fierce pride of the North. I find it exhausting and mightily depressing, but the natives take comfort in buns and wool. There's marvelous wool here and everyone knits and embroiders. I'm stitching you a gros pillow of Victorian dahlias, or rather I will as soon as I can find someone to read to me.

My complete and devoted love. I'll be seeing you soon. Kisses and hugs to Bernie and Mag. Is everything all right at the farm? I sometimes wonder — Mag sounds strained.

Devotedly,
A.

Midland Hotel, Manchester
September 28

Dearest Mum,

Hell's popping! Cochran has a bad fit of nerves! Rehearsals night and day. But sit tight — I'm coming out on top. Nothing must hurt my chances for the recital. There's been an awful lot of underground dirt. It's all coming to light now. I've been working and working. I'll explain fully in two days. I haven't had a chance to write this week.

But the news about the show is heartening. There are queues down at the Strand for the advance bookings in London. The box office here has been shut for three days, standing room only. Unprecedented. In spite of that, I must confess the show is pretty thin. Hence C.B.C.'s nerves. Romney is slowing up in all his capacities — exhaustion, I suppose. I'm o.k. professionally and physically.

Devoted love,
A.

At this moment Mother cabled she was on her way to join me. The thought of her arrival under my present circumstances threw me into panic. I wired my sister to keep her home and used the unfortunate phrase "too busy for unnecessary social whirl." Not having received any direct word, Mother demanded to see the cable and was more hurt than at any time since her separation from my father. She did not reply. It was my sister who relayed her anguish.

The Adelphi Theater, London
October 4, 1933
Rehearsal

Mother, Mother,

I'm so distressed I hardly know what to write. I wouldn't have hurt you for anything on God's earth. It was my desire to save you from worry that led to this hideous development. You must believe that I didn't mean what the wire to Margaret sounded like. I tried to explain something to Mag in short cable form about not wanting to be dragged into a social whirl, which I thought she could explain to you. I thought she would sense trouble without my having to wire details and throw you all into a panic. I've only succeeded in wounding you as no amount of anxiety or worry could do. I'm so profoundly sorry. Oh, Mother, you must believe me. I'm simply frantic over what's happened.

This is my story from the beginning.

I've written and wired all the pleasant things that have happened to me — all the kindnesses and attentions of the company, and they were all true. But there have been other aspects of the case not so simple and not at all pleasant.

The show is far from first-rate. The loss of morale in the cast has been profound and subtle. Cole Porter has disappeared, as I believe he always does under similar circumstances. Cochran has been in Paris, whence he cables Romney orders for new dances. I was scared to death, but armed with the music, I went off as I wrote you to spend my birthday with Ramon in the country.

I found him considerably weakened by the trip, but delighted with the change from London. I reworked my dances and spent quiet hours in the fresh air. It was restful and happy. I telephoned regularly to Manchester to see if there were any messages for me. My assistant Cissy said, "None" and rang off before I could ask her about cables at the theater. I let the matter rest there. Don't think I've not regretted this lapse bitterly.

Now, I must tell you what I've just learned. Ramon is much, much iller than he's ever let on. He has gone to heroic lengths to keep me from knowing. Once, in my presence, Sharpe had to lift him up in his arms. This was in the theater when the commissionaire had not been brisk about bringing up the wheelchair. Ramon ran a temperature for two days with the anguish of his embarrassment. Sharpe cannot leave him for more than five hours. If anything happened to Sharpe — but Ramon says Sharpe won't hear of a substitute.

Anyway, Sharpe told me he expected that Mr. Ramon would have a severe crisis in a day or two. He'd pleaded with him not to come, told him that he was deliberately risking his life. But the boy said that was his responsibility and that he was going.

You see, Ramon loves me. You've guessed that long since, I

suppose. When I discovered this, I told him I was never going to see him again. He said that would be a mistake. He had very little in his life. He asked nothing of me but my company, such affection as I could give him, and the right to love me in return, but in an absolutely unpossessing way — no strings of any sort — no promises — no demands — perfect freedom. Knowing there could never be anything legal or permanent between us he saw no reason why his life should be robbed of the intellectual and emotional comfort I brought him. I was frightened. I told him that I would be going back to America and asked him how he would face that loneliness. He said he'd face it when it came, that he had faced other losses in his life; he knew all about loneliness. I told him that I'd sometime unquestionably fall in love and marry, and what then? He said I must do what I needed to do. That he understood all this perfectly, had thought it out, and made his choice. This was all before I went to Denmark. I wrote him from there that I thought I was doing wrong to see him again, and he replied that he thought otherwise and that on this point he must be allowed to decide. So I've seen him constantly since my return and I haven't known such peace in years. I've had little peace — Mum — very little. This may seem strange, but when he hears me at the door and calls, "Did you give them hell today? Tell me how the new cross-step worked out," I enter my own house.

And so when I returned to Manchester from the country I found that XY's number was going worse and worse, and I started rehearsing a new dance but with dreadful premonitions. Dreadful — I've been fired before. I wanted terribly to have you come but not until I saw what was going to happen. I cabled Mag something I thought would show that all was not in order, that it would be better if you came later, that I was working like hell and probably would have to continue to do so. I chose a most unfortunate expression. But more of that later.

Ramon's temperature rose all week, the bad week, following my birthday. I phoned every day.

Cockie returned from Paris Thursday, where he's been having a rest. He promptly threw a fit. Long conferences about what to do with XY. The day after I got back from Winsfield, I learned what that little hussy had been up to. I learned what she really is! The naughtiest girl I have ever had any dealings with — lazy, spoiled, neurasthenic, selfish, featherbrained, and oversexed, who proved in her first rehearsal incapable either of working on count with the girls or of learning anything new. I pulled the number to pieces twice under the instruction of Cochran and I ruined the dance doing so, but Cockie, Cole, and Romney professed themselves delighted with the results. I, however, wasn't pleased. I tried to discipline her; she absolutely demoralized my rehearsals. I went repeatedly to Romney; to whom else? He promised to scold her but his admonitions were somewhat weakened by the fact that he was temporarily in love with her. The encouragement this familiarity gave her led her on from one excess to another — in effect, a prolonged temper tantrum to gain sympathy and attention, particularly during Gertie's numbers: phony faints, phony hysterics, sprained ankles, stitches in the side, dizzy spells, and as a climax, tearing her clothes, so that her bodice fell down twice in public, leaving her stripped to the waist. As Gertie was singing her star piece, the "Experiment" song, during one of these demonstrations, there were some forceful instructions given to the wardrobe woman. But XY was resourceful. She had scissors and she cut her way free by slicing the shoulder straps. Cockie is flabbergasted. I think you might call him liberated in his own life, but public exhibitions he won't have. His chorus girls and mistresses are "Mr. Cochran's young ladies" and they behave themselves when on view.

God knows what all went on in my rehearsals. Yet I would not be worn down. Rehearsals that should have lasted ten minutes went on for three or four hours while principals sat around biting their lips and swearing. I held her to her practice. I made her learn to drop a curtsy, three hours work. I made her learn to kick on a turn, three hours, hysterics in the dressing room afterwards and a faked faint on the stage that night *in full view of the audience*, and on Gertie's entrance in the new red velvet dress. I explained to Romney that she was merely manufacturing an alibi for her behavior during the afternoon rehearsal. His answer was to rush up to her bedroom and hold her head. Loathed by the entire company, she was abetted in her insubordination by the very man who should have been first to call her to order. So she said amid sobs and wailing that she could only work with a male dance director. I rushed to Cochran and pleaded to be spared the interference of someone outside the company. Cochran promised me that no one outside would be called in.

At this point, Sharpe phoned again from the country. Ramon, it seemed, was good and sick and would be very grateful if I could go to him. This was a crucial moment to leave because my position was in real jeopardy. But so was Ramon's life. I asked Cochran to excuse me over Sunday. He said, "Delighted. Nobody is going to work before Monday. We all need a rest."

I found Ramon with a fever of between 103 and 105 degrees (it varied according to the time of day) but gay and jaunty as ever. I sat beside him that night and held his hand. He kept apologizing for his behavior and adding that I had no idea what it meant to have someone to hang on to, that he'd gone through so many hours of this sort of thing alone, except, of course, for Sharpe. That night the crisis passed. The fever broke — the sleeve of my dress was drenched with his sweat. The next day he was bright yellow and so weak he was groggy, but he definitely had turned the corner. I went back to Manchester to find. . . .

Cochran, contrary to his promise, had called in Carl Randall, a tap dancer, to restage my work. I had been the darling of the troupe, the white-haired girl. Yesterday they had all been asking my advice. What had happened?

The night I got back, after the performance, Cochran confronted me on an empty stage alone. And this was a man I'd never met before. He was frightened and belligerent because,

I suppose, he felt a little guilty. I accused him of breaking his promise and hiring the new guy behind my back while I was away. He blasted.

You'd have thought I'd cut dialogue, changed costumes, re-orchestrated music the way he went on. He denounced all the things he'd hitherto liked. What I'd done was no good. No wonder XY failed. I couldn't do a new tap dance for her. (Well, he'd always known I couldn't. We had tried to make do with what she had, since she couldn't learn new things, since she wouldn't learn.)

I stared at him white-faced and shaking. I think if I'd cried it would have been better. He must be used to tears although I don't suppose he likes them much. He's not used to accusing silence. He hates scenes and avoids them when he can. Silence can be a scene.

Cochran was obviously frantic with worry — so was I. I handled him badly. Cochran was a small, compact man, bull-chested, with pugnacious shoulders, a pink and white skin, exquisitely manicured and scented hands, Saville-tailored and corseted torso, and manners impeccable, until something frightened him. Then, without a minute's warning, Bill Sykes stood there. The roll of flesh at the nape of the neck swelled, the eyes grew small and hard, the face clotted, the mouth became a fist, the voice high, drained of tone. It was the suddenness of the change that was so startling, the sheet-lightning revelation that Mr. Cochran's love for the theater, and Mr. Cochran's veneration for artists and artists' feelings, simply disappeared at the threat of failure. This was not the kindly gentleman who had understood so well Gertie's need for a new costume the day of dress rehearsal. This was a desperate man trying to shore up a show in trouble, a man who had run off to Paris at a time he should have been minding shop. This was an employer facing a deficient hireling. This was a bully.

Later: I asked not to return to London with the company. I think they were glad not to have me. I'm a drag on their high spirits and certainly on their consciences. There have been a great many parties I have been left out of, in some cases almost pointedly. I'm an outsider, a youngster, an alien. More and more I've been left to my own devices, and as nerves tightened and continue to tighten with the approach of the London opening, people have been colder and colder. I have literally been left by a group of the company standing alone in the lobby while they went in to a supper party given by Cole Porter or Gertie. I don't expect even to be asked out by Cochran after the London opening. I'm making my plans privately for ham and eggs with Mim Rambert and Arnold Haskell. One of the results of this strange freezing has been that I've been separated from Romney and Cockie at crucial times.

Now I'm in London, but haven't been allowed to rehearse yet. The new Randall dance is charming but is largely dependent on tricky, difficult props and for this reason may very well be a fiasco on Friday. I hate to wish him bad bad luck but . . .

In Randall's rehearsals XY is behaving like an angel. Oh well! And that brings me up to date.

Now, Mum, as to us — you must understand. You must. It's absolutely vital to our happiness. What I meant by "social whirl" was just this: that I might have to spend hours by Ramon's bedside (I don't think I shall but I didn't know that then) and that I've got to work as I've never worked before. In all your letters you keep repeating how you believe I should keep up the social end here, how important you think it is. Well, I've come to the conclusion that that's the one end I can well afford to drop. It's my work I must concentrate on. When that excels, everything else will follow naturally and easily. I've failed right along in the important things because I've scattered my energies, dissipated my interests, lost sight of my direction. This is the important fact I've learned this summer. I'm cutting free of everything except those people and pleasures which are vital to me. Everything else is canceled. I think I shall probably go to the other extreme. But that's all right to begin with. You must help me in this — it's fundamental to my future. You see what a bleak prospect I have immediately before me? That's why I cabled Mag. You've helped me more than anyone else on earth, and what you did for me last fall was nothing short of miraculous. Whatever has happened this summer is only the result of your earlier efforts. But now I must work, quietly, steadfastly, tirelessly, and then the way will open. Do you understand this, Mum? Do you see why I mustn't party in the next three weeks and why I can't play with you? I know you've had a lousy summer and you deserve some fun and I sympathize.

Come for the recital. With all my heart I want you, and if you don't believe me, then I know that you've lost all faith in what I say to you. Come then — the work will be done and we can really see one another. Cochran has set no date, and I can't approach him on the subject until after the opening Friday, but I have every reason to believe that he expects to go through with the project.

When I read Mag's letter today at rehearsal, I put my head in my hands and sobbed. Such is the peculiar self-centeredness of any theater company that though I was sitting in a group, no one paid the slightest attention.

Write me, Mum. Answer this. I'm really distracted.

Devoted love,
A.

P.S. Ramon was brought home today. I don't yet know how he is.

P.P.S. Later — I've just phoned. He had another attack last night. I have been calling every half-hour. He's still with us, but barely. I sit weeping through costume fittings. Zinkeisen thinks it's because I don't like the new dress she's done for Eve. Naturally, no one knows anything of my personal concerns and they just think I'm disagreeable, stubborn, self-centered, and definitely unamusing.

I've just phoned again. Ramon's temperature has dropped half a point. It looks as though he'll make it this time.

> English-Speaking Union
> Day after opening, October 7

Dearest Mum,

Well, it's a hit, a real one, and the dances got raves, all except the Carl Randall number for XY, which was signalized in the press as vulgar and out of style. Well! Well! Whee!

And don't fret about how I looked. I looked gorgeous in Mag's white and gold, and Ramon's orchids, which he had somehow found the energy to order in his terrible duress. I took as my guests (circle seats, but center good ones) Arnold Haskell, Mim, and Antony Tudor. The dances stopped the show, really, truly — you'd have been repaid for much. The dances got cheers, hearty ones — but Antony, who sat next to me, didn't say one word — not a word — nor for that matter did Arnold and Mim, except just to indicate that for this medium, which neither of them took seriously, the dances weren't too bad. They're snobs, you know. How dare they scorn Cole Porter's music, unmatched lyrics, the beautiful scenery, and my dances, for God's sake? Mim, with her eighteen-square-foot stage and fat-legged little girls? How dare she? It's not just that our show is expensive, which of course enrages her; our show is good in certain ways. You can't just brush Cole Porter aside — nor Gertie. Well, as to Gertie, they both agreed she was extraordinary, and, my dear, last night she blazed like a beacon. I think the glow might have been seen in South Kent.

Come to think of it, I don't believe Mim thanked me for her ticket. She was too busy trying to get a word in with Cochran, whom she professes to despise.

The downstairs had been completely bought out by Young

Doug and Gertie's other friends, all of Mayfair. There was enough nobility there for a Royal Garden Party. It was pretty dazzling. (I had tried vainly to find a beauty parlor in the afternoon — all driers between Knightsbridge and Piccadilly Circus having been preempted by the female half of the audience.) Whoever wasn't going to the Adelphi last night might as well have retired from public life in London. Last night there was one occupation and one theater in London — that theater. I'm not sure Parliament did not recess!

I went into Gertie's dressing room to wish her luck. (She'd been closeted in there since ten in the morning trying on dresses without, by the way, either the permission or the assistance of the designer — not even her secretary dared speak to her.) She was making up in a state of manic euphoria. Beside her were Young Doug's flowers, £50 worth. Two men had to lift the basket down from the stage door. The top roses brushed the ceiling.

"Good God!" I said.

"What a mercy they're white!" she replied without taking her eyes off her technical business in the mirror.

She did add, "How sweet you look, dear!" and "Thank you for coming in!"

Then she handed me a present — a big box. I asked her secretary what it was. Her secretary shook her head. "She does these absolutely by herself."

"Truly?"

"Oh yes — always — herself, personally. I've no idea what's in there."

What was in there was a milk-white vase from Asprey with a spray of absolutely exquisite pastel-colored flowers made of feathers. It sounds tacky. It was enchanting — leave it to Gertie.

There were tremendous parties afterwards at the Savoy and elsewhere, but somehow I was not included. The new dance director, Carl Randall, was, all right, all right. I had supper with Arnold and Mim, who talked about Massine throughout. I phoned my good news by relay through Sharpe to Ramon when he should awake.

Ramon had, of course, sent flowers besides the orchids — more than he could afford — and there was a simply gorgeous Moisses-Stevens basket from the Fieldings — a miracle basket — more than they could afford. (You remember Mag's extremely attractive beau, Paul Fielding? Who went around with the fat boy, James Beard, interested in cooking? Well, Paul is here with his entire family from Nice. And they've all been attentive.)

From Romney there were roses. Mr. Cochran's office did the routine, but he was personally cool; not chilling, however, especially not after Eve's absolute triumph. I know you're sorry I didn't go to the big party, but I don't think under the circumstances I could have endured it. (I'd been on the phone to Sharpe every three hours.) The shutting out and ignoring that has been going on is a process I've seen so often in Hollywood. People survive it; they really do. Last night I honestly didn't care! There's my heavenly press this morning and when I go back to the theater there'll be a lot more courtesy.*

This afternoon I'm to be allowed to see Ramon.

---

* For an alternate view of the proceedings here is James Laver's account in his memoir, *Museum Piece*, Houghton Mifflin, Boston, 1964:

". . . The combination of Cochran and Gertrude Lawrence was, indeed, irresistible.

"I suppose I shall never be involved, in any capacity, in a more 'glamorous' affair. Manchester had suffered an invasion of fur coats and orchids and white ties. The Fairbanks [only one — not at the time married and now known as 'the'] had taken a whole row of stalls for themselves and their friends. The London critics attended in force, and when we got back to the Midland Hotel the stairs leading up to the dining room were lined, five deep, with people clapping and cheering Gertrude Lawrence. One of the pressmen asked me what I had to do with the show, and I replied: 'Not much. I merely wrote the book.'

"The first night in London was dazzling, and the inadequate foyer of the Adelphi was full of well-known faces, from Somerset Maugham to Elsa Maxwell, from Lady Lavery to Cecil Beaton. And at the Savoy afterwards the scenes at Manchester were repeated. I suppose it was natural that I should have been made a little dizzy by all this, especially as my share of the royalties was rather more than ten times the amount of my official emoluments."

Tomorrow I talk to Cochran about the recitals. Oh, thank God, thank God for those notices!

Herbert Farjeon wrote, "If the Greek and Turkish dances were in the Alhambra Ballet Russe repertoire what serious attention they would get! And they deserve attention! They are splendid and they are subtle." Farjeon is a well-known playwright and critic. His sister, Eleanor, writes charming children's books.

Now for the concerts: class every day — class on time — all of class — and five hours of rehearsing a day. This can be managed — Cochran's taken over — and I can keep my mind on my proper concerns — four new numbers.

Antony Tudor and William Chappell will partner me.

Wire your sailing date!

A bientôt,
A.

October 19

Dearest Mum,

Wednesday night, as soon as he was able, Ramon came to see the show. That was a gala evening. He knew every step of every dance, but had not seen one except as demonstrated by me in the space between his wardrobe and his bed.

Last night my costumes came. I went to Paddington Station and in the cold sooty gloom of the six-thirty dusk the boat train came in and there were Henry Andrews and Rebecca West standing at the lighted window. He was avuncular and beaming; she just a touch brusque after having taken all my costumes through customs. How do you persuade people to do these onerous, appalling chores? Well, you do — and they go right on loving you without irritation or resentment. It's extraordinary! She said she'd ask me to lunch when they got settled, and then she marched wearily off. Mr. Andrews kissed me.

I'm trying hard to save money; the galling aspect of all this is that every night my dances play to sold-out houses and get ovations — and I do not get one penny royalty. Three guineas a week would ease matters, but I daren't offend Cochran by asking.

I dropped by the theater the other night — mobs at the box office. I saw Gertie; Gertie's dressing room is always a mass of flowers, and there is always a bucket of iced champagne in the corner.

"Come in, darling. Come in," she carols. "Have some champagne," her eyes moving beyond me to see if there were possibly a man in attendance. She never looks at me directly. I imagine she looks men in the eyes. But how can I be sure? She has never looked into mine or any woman's I've noticed. She fixes on men wholly, and although sweet and pleasant to women, is in the end oblivious to them. She is a coquette *par excellence* and unfailingly successful. Many women, however, adore her.

In her house in London every night at midnight is spread, I am told, a rich supper, pheasant, caviar, crêpes, roast beef, and, of course, champagne. She gathers up whomever she wishes and takes them home. The staff is always ready. She lives on the scale of a duchess.

She collects jewels as people collect gramophone records, and after every admirer's visit there is a fine new piece. The white ties and black tails flash in and out of her dressing room like blackbirds and there have been near encounters and narrow misses. Gertie bubbles through it all, vastly amused, and the new pins and bracelets keep on appearing and being replaced. There was the tale of how on the opening night in a short-lived comedy drama, she found to her astonishment that all the stones in her stage jewelry had been replaced by real ones.

There are rumors of Young Doug saying at breakfast to Gertie the other morning (Joan Reed brought this tidbit), "Look out the window, Gertie," and there, tied up in the Thames, was her new yacht right before her house in Cheyney Row.

None of this is to imply that she is anything less than a great big stunning star and deserving of all. The greatest actress I have ever seen, the most deeply moving, the most searching and spellbinding, the most evocative and versatile is the French *diseuse*, Yvette Guilbert. The most magical, hypnotic stage personality was Anna Pavlova. The most enchanting and bewitching, Geraldine Farrar, but right behind her on a totally different plane is Gertrude Lawrence. Farrar had elegance, beauty, dazzle and manner, with a heart-reaching common sense and practical wisdom and a directness of approach that made fast friends of little girls, cowboys, scene-shifters and great conductors, as well, of course, as royalty. Lawrence has bewitching, quicksilver grace, wit, prettiness, chic and outrageous fun. Her energy is legendary. Her chic and fun have set the style in whatever city or place she graces.

Paul Fielding cites Gertie as an example to me. He keeps saying that if only he could arrange my concerts as they should be done, costumes made by the great houses, enough assistance, dressers, stage managers, conductors, advertisements on all the hoardings, at all the theatrical agencies; he wants to get me dressed properly; Elizabeth Arden-ed. The other day at lunch he drove his points home brutally. It seems that Cochran, Lawrence, *et al.* lost interest in me because I looked messy at rehearsals. I wonder if I shall ever learn? Every atom of my attention was going into my work. I really believe I should have got on better if I'd looked smart at two in the morning during those twenty-four-hour bouts in the cold and empty theater and relaxed on the directing. The fact that the audience cheered at the opening meant nothing, nor the fact that that night I looked ravishing. It's a point of view I can't get used to.

"You shouldn't live at the English-Speaking Union," Paul continued. "It sounds like a woman's hostel. It depresses people and puts them off."

"It's inexpensive and charming," I said.

"It gives a gloomy impression. People don't want to ask you out. They think you're poky."

"I don't believe you," I snapped.

"It's true. You've got to surround yourself with glamour.

You've got to cut a figure. You don't know what glamour is. For instance, how dare you go out to lunch with me in that sweater?"

"I'm cold. My coat is thin."

"You have no right to look like that when you go out to lunch with a man, even an old friend like me. You have no right. Your hair is wisps" (I've been rehearsing three hours). "Your stockings wrinkled" (Would you enjoy lunch more if I took the sweater off, or my stockings?). "You've got to get glamorous" (I haven't the time). "You've got to make the time. This is why everything is so hard." (I don't believe you.) "Well, one day when my affairs resolve, I'm going to take you in hand and do you up properly." (Will that make the dancing better?) "We'll turn you out so that everyone will gape at you. You'll be the talk of the cocktail parties."

Now, Mum, don't say it — "Haven't Margaret and I always, always insisted that . . . ?"

You have, you have, you have. I try to clean up, but I would like a good arabesque as well — more. That's the trouble — I'd like it more.

I was, however, shattered by the talk and didn't sleep for nights.

And, by the way, the other afternoon Sylvia Ross, the millionairess from Bangor, Maine, also took me apart. She is over here to buy a bulldog. The bulldog is to chase the children off her lawn, I suppose. When the animal is ready, it will return to Bangor, Maine, with her chauffeur. She goes back next week to prepare lodgings for it. She spends a good part of her time in the London Zoo from which she derives, she says, great companionship. I encountered her at the Fieldings', and over tea she began with Judy. It seems she gave you some money as a present and you bought something for Judy, and you, not knowing Sylvia as well as you should, told her, so she was extremely put out. When she gave you a present, she said, it was to be for you and you were not to modify it or share it or take pleasure in it in any

way except as she designated: and that was to be selfishly and
with total and undeflected gratitude to herself, the donor. If she
wanted to give Judy something (which she didn't, not liking
children), she'd give it to her directly and then Judy could be
directly grateful, not indirectly through you. All this was delivered in the voice that only her lawyer could love, and then,
finding herself warmed up, she turned on me. How long was I
going to bleed you white? Take all you had and throw it away
on dances that obviously were never going to pay back. I was
depriving you of comforts, luxuries, all the delights you were
entitled to. You were getting old (I thought you would like that
bit) and I was continuing indefinitely as a self-indulgent parasite.
Margaret didn't do that. She had married very well, to a rich and
successful man who was even able to help you, and she dared
say that if Margaret had continued with the theater, she'd
have . . .

I must have gone chalk white, for she halted. Paul said, "Sylvia,
don't," and led me to the bathroom, where cold cloths were
applied and whisperings. "You're a great artist. We all know
this. Your mother knows this. She's proud and happy to do what
she can. It gives her her greatest joy," and more of the same,
sotto voce. Well, I didn't say good-bye — I just left.

I didn't sleep that night. There are many nights I don't, but
that night I got up and read my press. Oh, Mummy, I know so
well what I'm depriving you of, and it seems so long. I just can't
do otherwise — but, well, I don't sleep.

Oh darling! —
A.

There was much in what Sylvia said. Whatever I wrote to
Mother, or withheld, she continued to send me all the money
she could spare, even to her own pitiful deprivation.

I lived indentured to her, a state she did not altogether
mind, for as long as I was dependent on her for the continu-
ance of concerts, I was physically her toy, even if realistically

I was draining her and she was forced to do without all luxuries. Mother never under any circumstances took a lower berth and even began going long distances by coach so that she might keep me in ballet slippers. I permitted this because I didn't know how not to. We had nailed our flags to the mast. The foundering of the career would have been a second marriage failure. She wouldn't have it; and neither would I. I lived as inexpensively as possible on a ridiculous budget. I ate in tea shops, bought no clothes, wore only my sister's hand-me-downs, did not smoke and did without drinking. Every extra penny went into production and training.

But theatrical production costs money and I was earning so little. The apprenticeship of a performing artist of necessity is very expensive. None of these financial outlays were tax deductible, nor were my classes, and when years later I began to pay back the ten-year debt with what I earned from *Oklahoma!*, *Bloomer Girl*, *Carousel*, and *Brigadoon*, these repayments were not tax deductible to either of us.

In the meantime, I couldn't get a job, nor a stage I didn't myself buy. Everyone official said, by way of explanation, that I lacked sex appeal.

What in God's name is sex appeal in an artist? What Chaplin had? or W. C. Fields? or Gracie Fields? I think what is meant is magic, a kind of hypnotism based on the knowledge of power. It is as true as fire and just as unanswerable. I had it only in flashes. I could make people laugh or cry, but I couldn't make them believe I knew I could do it.

"Don't worry," said Ramon. "It will come. Why can't you believe in yourself? Your power is so obvious to the rest of us."

I didn't know how to believe him. I became extremely nervous at this point, wept easily, and was always cold. Once Diana shouted to me unexpectedly in a crowd and I burst into tears. The same thing happened with Antony. But while Diana was apologetic, Antony was sardonic and remarked that although late for lunch with him, I was sauntering along window-shopping, which was true. I brought him to the ground with me as he attempted to prevent a faint — and I recall the instant, wonderful clearing of the sidewalk as the Londoners observed a man and woman writhing on the pavement. Antony thought the whole thing a fake and revolting and said so. Perhaps it was. What I was doing was screaming for help. And that was not fake.

CHAPTER 9

RAMON had guaranteed me freedom — but how could he know?

One night I went out to dinner with Robin. Relations had not resumed, but he still loved me enough to want to keep an eye on my well-being and to share a meal and a conversation now and then. Ramon wished me a fine evening. That night he didn't sleep. The next evening I was reading by the fire and Sharpe suddenly bolted down the hall to the bathroom. "We're in for it," he called. There followed much running, opening and shutting of drawers, scraping of basins, rushing of water, while I sat white-faced and staring.

Then Sharpe came back. "He's in rigor," he said. "You can see him. But you mustn't show any alarm. He's not a pretty sight. Have you ever seen it?"

I hadn't. Where would I? But I went in.

Ramon lay smiling wanly and holding out his hand. His whole body jumped and convulsed with nerve spasms. His legs, which I had never seen move, were shaken with such tremblings and twitchings that the bed rolled on its casters and the covers jumped.

"It will pass," said Ramon. "Don't be frightened. It only goes on an hour or so. The only disagreeable thing is the temperature, but Sharpe has that under control. It's bound to drop in the morning."

"You know why this happened?" said Sharpe as he let me out. "Temperature 104 degrees and the rest? Because you went out to dinner last night with a young man. You see what you're doing to him? He was at peace before you came."

Then, as I put my face in my hands, Sharpe said, "I've some flowers for you in the bathtub. Take them with you, but don't mention this to the boy." I was touched. I was frightened. I was not a little shocked.

Mother once said to me, "There are times when one is clothed in the armor of the Lord. Nothing can reach you." I grew to know what she meant. Ramon put my hand to his cheek and said, "I've brought you to this." I couldn't answer. "All I can say is," he went on after a while, "I'm no longer afraid to die. You've given me that much."

English-Speaking Union
November 1, 1933

Dearest Mum,

Now listen — you mustn't worry about me and my depressions; I go blind every so often, when everything I touch, both in my personal and professional life, seems to wither. There's nothing to do but leave me alone and let me fight my way through. I don't think I'll ever be as bad again as I was last winter. I took most of it out on you, unavoidably because you were closest. It was as though you were part of me and involved too intimately for explanation. However, it won't happen again. It certainly wasn't decent and I'm ashamed. Only don't fret when I go silent. I have to. I'm drawing on the deepest reservoirs of my strength. I'm better alone at such times. Everyone, I think, goes through similar periods. Only most people don't behave so badly.

Ramon's reply to all this has been to give me a new beautiful

Gardenia hat and a pair of walking shoes, which I needed. Sharpe naturally does not approve, looking askance at undue expenditures. I think he wants me to pay my share of exactly everything, but, of course, I simply can't now; I'm buying costumes. So he sulks.

Ramon pays not the slightest mind. "I'll manage him," he says to me. "Go home. I'll straighten him out. Don't think about it."

There he is, helpless, dependent, bereft, and he conducts his daily affairs with a zest and equanimity that is way beyond the rest of us. We fret. We fuss. We lose our tempers. We gloom. Not he. Perhaps living in the vestibule of death has given him a certain coolness of view, a certain evaluation, but it's every day, all day. He never loses perspective. He never just loses his temper or cries out. He never does, and Sharpe's nerves are like a nettled horse's. He has much to put up with also, of course. But he refuses outside professional help. Absolutely refuses. It's scary.

I've pleaded and pleaded for an alternate nurse to be trained and ready, for a doctor to supervise. Sharpe won't hear of it. He wants to be indispensable and wholly responsible and wholly unsupervised. The family doctor is far away. In any case, Sharpe doesn't trust doctors — certainly no one the family recommends. He doesn't trust the family. Ramon is his entire life. He is mother, father, brother, husband. He is Sharpe's and that's why I've become a maddening interloper. I don't belong to this pattern. Ramon clings to both of us, to Sharpe for his life, and this is not a figure of speech — it's only good daily nursing, the mechanical cleaning of his body that keeps him alive — and me for his comfort. Because Sharpe, while supplying much, does not supply all. He is ignorant, opinionated and vulgar. Also, he is not a woman. Don't forget, Ramon lost his mother when he was seven and grew up an orphan without love, cruelly neglected, even despised.

But if Sharpe should break a leg, or sprain his back, or just get ordinary London flu, and a stranger had to be called in — then what?

Ramon knows the hazards, but apparently there's nothing he can do against this brute stubbornness, and he risks all without flinching. And the extraordinary thing is he believes in no after-life. You ask how he dares not believe?

He dares.

I'm working like a maniac and I love it. There will be four new dances for the Cochran concert.

I take two lessons nearly every day and am really getting along. I wear sheet rubber wrapped around my hips. That ought to do something for my figure. My progress in technique has heartened me beyond anything. I know I can be a great dancer if I remain calm and persistent. Madame applauded me the other day in class. Do you know what that means? It's unheard of.

However, life at the club doesn't vary much from month to month. The other day Mim had hysterics on the sidewalk about Andrée Howard, but Andrée had been having them all day about Mim — Andrée weeping in one room and Mim in another, with me waiting to go to lunch with Andrée and Ashley waiting similarly for Mim. Ashley suddenly winked at me and we walked out on them to have a tête-à-tête lunch ourselves, leaving Liza Hewitt, the beautiful club secretary, behind, hollow-eyed and weary, with the weepers.

Hugh continues the same, driving Mim nuts. He has discovered how to rule by blackmail. He makes his demands Saturday morning, the day before performance, and then declares that if they are not met he will not go on the next night. This is a breach of every theater ethic in existence. Of course, she could withhold his salary, but as this is something in the nature of 5/6 (not quite one dollar) he feels he can risk the loss. Last week he followed his pattern but with the added fillip of a message stating that he had taken his mother to *Peter Pan* and would be out of reach for four hours.

For a long time the boys had no phone, and one was forced to send for them to their flat in Campden Hill. They liked this.

But it was hard on other friends and so secretly they got themselves "on the telephone."

Hugh whispered the number to Liza. "On no conceivable account give this to Mim."

A strong hand gripped his shoulder and wheeled him around. There she was. Boiling. Quite understandably. "How can you?"

He cut her off. "If you ever call that number, I will lay hands on you. More, I will change it and you'll never, never know. No one will know."

"How am I to run a theater?" rapped Mim. A fair question, I think.

Outside of the insane crew which inhabits the Ballet Club, the inhabitants of Notting Hill maintain the harmless but busy grotesquerie common to the British lower class. There's no question about it; the stolid Briton is more often tetched than not. Last Sunday in the quiet crescent of Ladbroke Road, quite empty and lined with two-story, late-Georgian houses, all shut in Sunday silence, a plump little gentleman was chasing a pigeon down the middle of the street, trying to catch it with his outstretched bowler. I stood transfixed. He regarded me for a minute, then smiled sweetly and said most reasonably, "But, you see, they'll get hurt if I don't catch them!" Of course, I saw. It was obvious.

There's a fine old lady goes dashing about on a bicycle with a cabbage in a string bag and her mink coat flying behind her.

There's another, not so respectable, who makes a round of the garbage bins every morning. Antony went over to see what she was up to. He went over gently and politely. She looked up and spat straight in his face. It did take him aback.

After the curiosities in the streets pall, we go inside the Mercury to pure Mardi Gras.

Do you suppose I'll ever hang out with a bunch that makes quiet sense?

Devoted love,
A.

When all the plans for the recital had been made and
Mother was in midocean, en route to London, Cochran announced that he could not go ahead because he could not obtain the free use of the theater at which *Nymph Errant* was
playing. He certainly had no intention of investing money in
the rental of another theater. It was characteristic of him that
he got his wife, Evelyn, to break the news to me. Cochran
hated scenes. I made one. Mrs. Cochran was sufficiently disturbed to persuade him to continue, but under altered conditions. I was to share the expenses fifty-fifty, also the profits.
"There won't be any," I said. "No," he chuckled. "I never
grossed more than fifty pounds on any dancer except Argentina." The risk was real, but I thought the kudos of his name
and the grand help his organization would furnish would be
worth the loss of money to me.

But there was to be no organizational help. Cochran turned
my performance over to a couple of contemptuous under-
lings and forgot about me, his concerns at the moment being
the new production of *Escape Me Never*, starring Germany's greatest actress, Elisabeth Bergner, and the return of
Constance Collier to the London stage. No one did anything
for A. de Mille, and Cochran's name and prestige were used
as sparingly as possible.

Mother arrived to catastrophe. The day after she joined
me at the Union, word came that Cochran had stopped every
penny of advertising because the box-office advance justified
no further expenditure. A third-string publicity person came
to discuss this with us. I was so depressed I refused to speak to
her, but Mother did and won her heart. She turned out to
be a charming gentlewoman, extremely able and militantly
concerned. The tongue-lashing she gave the Cochran staff
when she got back to the office about the shameful ex-
ploiting of two helpless American women pulled them some-

what together. But she could not reach the boss. Her professional name was Philip Laing — her personal name was Peggy. She lived across the square from Ramon and she became our lifelong friend.

We went ahead — we always did. Mother was dogged. It was desperately dangerous because we had no money and Mother was selling her last savings bonds.

The first matinee was well attended and the press fine. Mother had enlisted the help of Young Doug, who in turn dragooned Gertie. It never occurred to me to go to her directly, nor to anyone else. I did not know how to beg for help — Mother did, for those she loved. Gertie filled half a house and sent me an incredible basket of flowers and was the first backstage. I was in my *Harvest Reel* black wool dress, sweating, smelly and exhausted, with makeup running and hair dampened, and sitting in a corner of the stage with my head against the wall. (I'd just completed thirteen solos.) "Look at her!" said Gertie. "Look at the girl!" Well, it was a far cry from Gertie's dressing room. Gertie that afternoon was in gray and lavender chiffon — I remember she had on a wide hat and a muff of tiny gray ostrich plumes — very strange for the period and absolutely lovely. Doug smiled at me in affectionate distaste. Charles Cochran did not come. Mrs. Cochran did but had to leave at the interval, sending a note backstage of frankly surprised admiration.

At the repeat concert, which was sold out, Cochran sent a wire, a miracle of inscrutability. "Sorry I could not be with you again." It cost a shilling. He sent no flowers. Someday, I told myself, under suitable circumstances, I'll return that shilling.

The expenses were padded. I lost everything I had saved on the whole summer's work, about $1100. I went to a lawyer. There was no redress short of suing Charles Cochran of

ST. MARTIN'S THEATRE

UNDER THE MANAGEMENT OF REANDCO

WEDNESDAY, NOVEMBER 22nd
THURSDAY, NOVEMBER 30th
at 2.45 p.m.

CHARLES B. COCHRAN

presents

AGNES DE MILLE

Assisted by

ANTONY TUDOR and WILLIAM CHAPPELL

in Two Matinee Recitals of her

Dances in Character

At the Pianos:

NORMAN FRANKLIN and CHARLES LYNCH

London, and under my present financial situation, he advised seriously against that.

I had been presented as a soloist by Cochran — I and Argentina — and this fact must content me.

Twelve years later, after six Broadway smashes, after the London success of *Oklahoma!* and *Brigadoon,* I received a letter from Cochran stating that he had just learned what had happened in '33 and that he was appalled. The fact is, as we both well knew, he had known about everything all the time. When *Carousel* opened at the Drury Lane in 1950, he apologized personally. I thought of pushing a shilling across the Savoy tablecloth. I didn't, however. He was now Sir Charles, and I, having delivered three enormous hits to London, was in a very fortunate position. I smiled benignly. Success makes one forgiving.

Just after the London Cochran concerts my father sent word in relay through Mag that he was unable to continue any financial assistance. When I left he had promised me fifty dollars a week and since none came I had hoped that perhaps this money might be accumulating for me in America. It seems not. He had not been able to give me a cent since the day I sailed. I was accordingly left penniless and in debt. Mother sailed for home to spend Christmas holidays with my sister and her family. She left me with misgivings and what money she could spare.

English-Speaking Union, London
December 20, 1933

Dearest Mum,

I'm waiting fairly impatiently for the arrival cable. Probably it will come tomorrow. You had such a short and backbreaking time here — you left exhausted. I'm afraid the crossing has been pretty rough; the weather here for the first few days after you left was appalling — sleet and bitter, strong winds. Unlike anything she'd ever known, Gardenia, the milliner, said. It was no worse than New York every February, but apparently it was rare for London and must have been brutal out where you were. I'm dreadfully sorry because otherwise the trip with the Ballet Russe aboard promised all sorts of fun.

I'm trying to get a tremendous lot of sleep and quiet, steady work. When I get the mess cleared up with Cochran, I'll breathe better. No word from him yet. I wrote him finally, asking for an appointment. He'll see me Friday, I think. In the meantime I've paid all my debts I personally incurred except the pianos and had an interview with Dan, the stage manager, who was flabbergasted at the state of things and urged me to see the boss. Elisabeth Bergner, he said, had raised hell in Manchester and that was why, Dan thought, he had given me so little attention. It seems to be generally recognized that Cochran is in love with Bergner. Frank Collins has said repeatedly that Cochran, within his memory (twelve years or so) has never behaved like this. The staff is ashamed. Well, on Friday I'll pull the chain on the whole business.

There are no classes now, so Antony is giving me three private lessons a week for thirty shillings. The other days I practice by myself.

I'm all packed up and ready to jump out of the Union, which is too expensive. I've looked all around the Mayfair neighborhood here hoping to find a place I can continue on in but they're all too dear and all slightly sordid — a general feeling of hard beds and old hair-combings in the grate. I'm laughed to scorn when I inquire about central heating.

An eeeenormous package has just this minute arrived from Denmark!

I gave £1 to Valerie, my voluntary laundress, and £4 to the hall porter, who accompanies me to the door now with waving of palms and blare of trumpets. I have ordered flowers for Inge Lise Bock and Dan Folke. I'm giving a perfectly beautiful British Museum reproduction of a Hindu painting to Norman Franklin

(5/) and a Chinese one to each of the little Bateses. They're really beautiful and quite large and full of amusing figures. £1 to Ramon's Ethel, a pair of gloves to Sharpe, and a sweater to Ramon, and that's that. You'll be glad to know I got the brown velvet hat — £2-10. Ramon lent me the money for this.

Ramon sends love. (I'm writing at his bedside.) Except for one lapse, he is better, I think, than I have ever seen him.

Large juicy kisses to Mag and Bernie.

Devotedly,
A.

The English-Speaking Union
December 31, 1933

Dearest Mum,

Well, day after tomorrow I move in officially to my new abode, 16 Glebe Place, S.W. 3 — a large front room pleasantly furnished on the street that goes by Lady Colefax's house. There is no central heat, a shilling gas meter, and baths cost sixpence, but I tried a small room over Christmas and found I could survive so I signed up for the large one and am taking my trunks down directly. There is good cupboard space, the street is quiet but leads onto the King's Road and a direct bus route. The place is clean, and my landlady, Mrs. Daviel, businesslike and efficient. I have bought a tea kettle and will get a reading lamp and then I'm all set. The room costs twenty-two and six a week and breakfast ten bob. So there you are. A pay telephone on the landing outside my door and a maid always on duty to take messages. Don't worry about me. I shall be fine. I'll use the Union, of course, for all entertaining. I discovered the place through an estate agent to whom I went finally, having despaired at the addresses given me by the Union — all expensive, all sordid, their only virtue their location and now that I'm no longer appearing professionally, that's not so important.

Christmas was grand. Rebecca West had asked if I had anywhere to go for Christmas. "Come to us. You're a child of the house. There's always a place at our table." How about that? I could only kiss her and explain I believed I was taken care of. "If anything goes wrong," she said, "just ring the bell." Even so I longed to pop in at Mag's farm at Goshen. I'm crazy for news.

Sunday — Christmas Eve — tied up gifts with Ramon in the evening.

Monday — Christmas — rushed over to Ramon's in the morning and trimmed his tree (the first since his fourteenth birthday), white candles only — all I could get after the Christmas mob had cleaned out Woolworth's — but a great many of them. Piled the presents around the tree, lit the tree and the fire, put one of the Messiah choruses on the gramophone, threw open the door, and Ramon rolled in. I wish you could have seen his face! We had champagne and Ethel drank with us and the charwoman who helps clean and when Ethel touched glasses with me, she was so happy she had to turn away her eyes and she covered her mouth with a knotted red paw. But she got gloriously drunk on one glass and fairly flew around as she waited on table. And we all got drunk and felt perfectly heavenly. And Ramon said it was the best day of his life. And that was nice.

We opened the presents. He had lots. People do give him things, I'll say that for his friends. Books aplenty and gramophone records. I had things too. Your slips, which were badly needed, and what a beauty the fine one is! So many thanks! I swear I don't know when you had the time to get all the presents you did before you left. The package from Denmark contained not Copenhagen porcelain as I'd hoped, but two of Dan's records, one sung by Inge Lise Bock simply horrifyingly, and a box of chocolates made by Lise *elle-même*. Was I mad! The Adelphi present turned out to be from Eve — a bird, carved inexcusably from a horn. A menace. But the thought, of course, touched me deeply. It really did. It was she alone of the entire company who remembered to send me even so much as a card.

Ramon gave me books, bath essence, and crystal earrings, and a large box of glacé fruits. He does all this shopping very painstakingly from catalogues.

At three I went to the Bateses', feeling simply grand and laden with my museum prints for the kids. And who did I walk in on toasting their toes by the fire? Right. The Cochrans! And the missus said with that smile which is like we know what, "Aggie, darling, we'd thought you'd gone home!"

Inasmuch as I'd been trying to get in touch with the boss (unsuccessfully) every day for the past week, I thought her remark just fine. "Oh, did you?" I said. "Why?"

"Well, you didn't phone me," she whimpered.

"No," I replied tartly. "I've been extremely ill. I had a nervous collapse."

"You're looking well now," said the boss. "I like your hat." And that, so help me, was the only reference he made to me all afternoon.

C.B.C. left to rush home for Elisabeth Bergner. The Bateses were going to dine with them that night. Indeed, all London was going to the party. After talking about it throughout the afternoon right up until they left, Mrs. Cochran returned from the door and said that if I had nothing better to do to drop in around ten. I declined.

There can be no question of further recitals either here or in New York for some time. If I could only get a job! If the Home Office would only let me teach! If there's a job at home, of course I'll come. In the meantime I can live here on almost nothing, and I can rest a little. I need to do that. Also, it's going to be hard on Ramon when I leave him. I want him to be a little stronger before I try. Don't worry about me, Mum. Your worrying is the one extra thing I believe I cannot bear.

There will be an American job one day and I will take it. If Uncle Ce would only offer me something! I mean, besides roadshowing me with my own company, for which I was in no way ready. Now I'm nearly ready. Do you suppose he has retained any interest at all?

I think I may after all ask him for a loan of a thousand or two. Surely by this time he must believe I'm worth helping.

Pop has sent me a surprise fifty pounds, which will last me out the month. So I'm feeling better. But I can't seem to come to the end of the recital bills. They keep cropping up and cropping up for items and services I knew nothing about. I don't believe Cochran himself paid anything at all.

Romney says Anna May Wong wants to study pantomime with me. So there's some money in view.

I'm pining for news of you.

Ramon said to send love.

Devotedly,

Agnes

P.S. I'll be thinking of you at twelve tonight. I wonder what the New Year will bring? It's bound to be different.

If there had been anything in America to take me home! But every channel was closed. Every plan withered. The Theater Guild offer (at $50 per week) had been the last good one. No concerts were possible. My only alternative would have been to open a studio and teach as every other American dancer did. But teach what? I did not feel capable. Comedy? No one has ever done this — nor projection. The two gifts I most surely had. If I could have taught that I could have made thousands.

The next month was spent in just keeping going and doing any jobs that would bring in shillings, any shillings. Ramon was my nearest source of strength. He floated along day by day concerned in everyone else's doings. He wrote, flat on his chest, stories and poems he never thought to see printed. He read to me by the hour. He advised me about work and the next steps to take. I was very truly appalled at my predicament — I had been compared to Charlie Chaplin. Who cared? I had hit dances in a London success — who cared?

We had a pleasant social life in Paulton's Square. To his

delightful parlor I brought Rebecca West and her husband, Henry Andrews, all the actors of my show, except Gertie, Romney, of course, Trudy and Arthur Bliss, Mim and Ashley Dukes, the dancers, the Clifford Curzons and the bearable Single-Taxers; everyone I could. And he had a fire in his grate and a marvelous tea for them, or sherry, if they wished, and his princely manner and grand laughter, and everyone left enchanted.

> 16 Glebe Place
> January 10, 1934

Dearest Mum,

The marvelous Blisses come to visit Ramon on occasion. Arthur is really one of the sexiest men I know. I think it's his laugh. He throws back his head, rather like a stallion's, his ginger mustache fairly jerks in excitement, his strong teeth flash, and he's off in a roar.

The other day he was talking about H. G. Wells. He's composing the music for the movie of *The Shape of Things to Come*. And he wanted, he said, a great six-part fugue to illustrate the machinery of the future. "But," said Wells, "the machinery of the future will be silent."

"You see?" shouted Bliss. "You see? The perfect nonartist!"

Once Arthur brought no less a person than Julian Huxley. He had dirty fingernails and struck me as being a bit awkward in handling a joke. I've heard that he was the Will Beebe of England (though that may be black malignment). I asked him about the Will Beebe of Sixty-seventh Street, and he said that once he'd had occasion to write him and had received a reply addressed to "Miss Julia Huxley." I discussed economics with him after dinner: Cock-eyed, of course, doesn't even believe in free trade. He struck me as a charming but not really profound mind. His wife, a blond delicate French Swiss, slightly faded, got me into a discussion of dancing and at the climax of the argument asked, "But can dancing ever be profound?" At which I stared at her in such genuine amazement that she apologized. Trudy was sweet, and Arthur his best, which is terrific. He says he'll compose the concerto and mail it to me, which is not at all the way I wanted to work. Still, I'll have to follow his lead in the matter. Trudy says not to count too hard on his promises as to date of composition.

Elizabeth Bowen lives in an extremely handsome Regency mansion at Clarence Terrace, Regent's Park, with her husband, Alan Cameron, who is the head of the grammar school at Oxford. They give dinner parties for Oxford exquisites, Alfred Knopf, and all the young, budding writers in London, like Cyril Connolly. Ramon and I were asked the other night. Ramon wears *le smoking* and sits at the eighteenth-century polished mahogany table with the men over their port and cigars . . . enjoying the most delicious conversation, which he repeats to me later. Last week's was the latest dirt about J. W. Turner's disreputable private life and scatological paintings. The girls up in Elizabeth's pretty parlor have not nearly such juicy things to talk about. I wish Elizabeth were not always surrounded by young daffodils from Oxford. She says they're very bright.

Mim came to Ramon's for tea Thursday (oh, how she admired his Venetian mirrors!), but she came late, when we had finished tea, so Ramon gave her some of his Welsh gin, and after an eighth of a glass she had to telephone Ashley to fetch her home immediately, she was so dizzy. I tenderly escorted her out into the fresh air, where she somewhat regained her clarity of speech and vision. My attention was so occupied with her that I did not notice what Ramon was up to. He quietly in his corner drank three straight glasses and was put to bed roaring. When I came upstairs again he was yelling in sheer drunken glee and very funny too, but Sharpe was so mad at me for letting it happen, holding me responsible for the boy's physical condition when he is off guard, that he has hardly brought himself to speak to me yet. My God, if a man of twenty-two can't tie one on now and then, it's too damn bad!

I went the other night to a lovely party at the Raymond Massey's (Adrian Allen). Late in the evening Gertie and Noel Coward arrived, Gertie looking unsurpassed in a white satin sheath (oh! that body!) and a scarlet-red velvet coat with great stiffened double cape shoulders and a pussy-cat bow at her throat. She plumped herself down on the floor in a pool of ruby and ivory while every man gaped and was rapturously attentive to the entertainer. One was a guest, an elderly, pretty dowager, Lady something-or-other, who had been Gertie Millar, the greatest operetta star in prewar England. She sang one of her favorites in a small, silky, wavery voice and Noel Coward burst into tears. "I can't bear it," he said. "I used to stand in the gallery when I got in for sixpence. She was the goddess, she was my dream." He sobbed audibly in a pocket handkerchief. Everybody looked at him sobbing but everybody was touched, too. Gertie patted his hand. Gertie Millar, I'm happy to inform you, is covered with diamonds, an encouraging example for our Gertie.

Don't fret about me and C.B.C. If he wants me for a job he can send for me and pay handsomely for my services, and if he doesn't want me, I don't give a bloody damn. I wrote once and telephoned eight times asking for an interview and he has consistently ignored my requests without an answer of any kind. I'm not stooping to truckle to him; I'm passing right over his head.

Opening night of the Jooss Ballet I went with Ramon and saw what Cochran can do when he tries. Leadley, the publicity man, officiated in a dress suit with tails. C.B.C. likewise, with a lady covered in chinchillas; the house packed (paper). I looked awfully well in my new brocade dress (white satin and Parma violets — material c. 1870 from Kate Kiniaar Irwin), price made up: £4.4, and a large bunch of camellias and valley from Ramon. But none of them recognized me, and I didn't dare go backstage for fear of a direct insult. Twenty-six tickets had been given the Ballet Club. Not one was offered me. We paid, Ramon and I.

I think the way to treat Cochran of London is either to have him fall in love with you, as Elisabeth Bergner has done (Mrs. Cochran's heart is accordingly broken; she has not been seen sober since before Christmas) or insult him, as Noel Coward does, ordering him rudely during rehearsals to keep quiet, so that he goes away and is chary about coming back. Of course, if an only somewhat successful girl ordered him out rudely, the end effect might be different. Gertie handles him through personal dazzle and pecuniary glory.

Love to the folks. I get absolutely strained with homesickness at times.

Devotedly,
A.

p.s. Thank you so much for the little chemical hot-water bag. Where did you find it? Ramon never gets tired of playing with it. It's wonderfully comfortable. I keep it in my lap while I'm embroidering. I can warm my hands on it. You do find the most extraordinary things!

CHAPTER 10

THE weeks slipped by. I'm sure Mother was apprehensive. She must have been scared to death. Other girls got married and had children. Some earned their own living. Some even were recognized as successful artists.

I seemed to be having a busy and bustling time, but it was not a real life. She knew it, and I knew it. She wrote two or three times a week and sent money whenever she could. One of her friends, the daughter of a great Georgist, lent me £50 — just saying she'd be my bank for the moment. I had not asked, of course; she sensed desperation.

But all the friends were staunch. Box-office success was not the criterion to these people. Yet in a sense I was having it. Now and then I'd pass the crowds in the lobby of the Adelphi. There never was an empty seat. I used to go from time to time to the theater and warm my heart as at a grate at the applause for the dancing. One night Danny, who had stage-managed my recitals, drew me aside and said that whenever and wherever I appeared again he would give me his services free.

I was cold in my new room. I'd never lived without steam heat, and I remember going to sleep in my coat and putting the floor rugs on top of the thin quilt. But I was never hungry. Ramon saw to that.

16 Glebe Place
January 20, 1934

Dearest Mum,
My room is fine and I'm really very comfortable, a bit chilly at night but cozy by morning, and feeling really snug when the maid comes at nine-thirty, lights my gas, and spreads a little mahogany gate-legged table by my bedside. I have good breakfasts, eggs and kippers (which I loathe), kidneys and sausages, not all at once, of course, on different mornings. I do all my entertaining at the Union, and Valerie still takes charge of my laundry, being most emphatic about continuing and about not being paid, not one shilling.

On Monday I experienced my first fog. It took me an hour to get from the Ballet Club to Ramon's and I crossed the King's Road in a state of terror. I couldn't see ten feet away and the buses were upon me before their lamps showed even a glow. The fog curled visibly like sea mist and stuck raw in one's throat. All sense of distance was distorted. A faraway light glimmering down the street turned out to be a street lamp five feet in front and people dissolved into nothing at a few paces. The buses ran in chains, the leader feeling its way at some peril and the following ones creeping behind in its wake of light. In many parts of the city all traffic stopped.

Interpolation by Ramon: We had the other day what we've not had properly for two or three years — a London fog. Thick, heavy, throat-wrecking fog which lasted twenty-four hours, slowed the traffic, brought about a few accidents, and was generally most unwelcome. Agnes, who had not encountered one before, was quite amazed. When really bad, it has, as you may know, a habit of penetrating through closely shut doors and

The view of the King's Road from Ramon's window
(Photo by Ramon Reed)

windows, so it is not very much more enjoyable indoors than out. Thank God it is now not so cold! You, I suppose, back in the city of central heating, are a good deal happier.

In this country one is resigned now that Christmas is over to a dreary kind of festering gloom until about April when spring begins very tentatively to creep in.

I constantly swear nothing shall stop me getting to your country. England is lovely; but most of the English land invites one to contemplation, while I suspect that in America one can be hit hard in the solar plexus and feel oneself overwhelmed, a little dwarfed and much awed; all of which I should like. In England we too often feel owners and manipulators of the land. In America, I imagine, one is put in one's place: a relief.

I must end up this letter to entertain a highly loquacious friend to tea. Outside, while I write, it pours with rain; the houses across the road are dingy brown and the sky above dingy gray; one could be intensely gloomy. But I feel fine — and hope you do too.

Agnes resuming: Ramon has been fairly well. He went to the dentist, our American dentist you recommended, and had one of his front teeth out. His English dentist had left a dressing in it for three months. The gap in his mouth gives him a peculiarly funny impish expression, and he lisps, but he'll have a lovely new tooth tomorrow.

He mixes me vitamins all the time which Ethel, the nitwit maid, continually throws out, but in spite of her I've got a good bit down me in the last few weeks.

We read together every day, Elizabeth Bowen's *To the North,* which moved us both. Elizabeth is quite a remarkable novelist, and while her prose is involuted and sometimes self-conscious, she can on occasion express the absolutely unexpressible. She seems to have found a new medium, as though she were dealing in tone or color or touch, not words. She gives you direct sen-

sation. We read *Women in Love, The Rainbow* and *The Golden Bowl.* We talk over our tea for hours . . .
    About the trouble at Goshen . . .

                            Love,
                            A.

The one subject on which he would not talk was Single Tax, and the one book he would not read was *Progress and Poverty,* and when I got on a soapbox, he would roar, "For God's sake, shut up, darling, and come kiss me." Which, of course, was a pure male illogicality. To all Mother's attempts at conversion, he remained gracefully evasive, but never in any way derisive or unsympathetic except possibly the time she, on her return to New York, relayed her outrage at finding that the resident farmer in my sister's place at Goshen had been making use of Henry George's bed. This was a four-poster mahogany and stored in the barn against its installation in a museum. Mother's indignation at the man's lack of reverence reached across the Atlantic; Ramon was plainly enchanted.

                                 January 28
Dear Mum,
    Don't fret about my being cold. The gas is lit before I get out of bed. I spend all day at the Ballet Club either dancing or working in the basement sitting room by an open grate, have tea with Ramon, and then write at his big table in front of the living-room fire, with electric heaters focused on my toes when it's very cold. The maid at my digs wraps my night things over a hot-water bottle and puts them inside the sheets. People don't get chilblains in London anymore — you're remembering your childhood. I've used only two shillingsworth of gas in three weeks. I live on £3 a week, not counting lessons. I take no taxis.

About once a week I go in evening dress on the buses — other people do. It's all right here; no theaters, no movies. I do very little entertaining.

I wish I did not have to beg the Home Office for permission to do everything and anything here, even lose money. Very occasionally I can bootleg a small job, but it has to be absolutely secret. The other day, Lucille Wallace, harpsichordist, the wife of the pianist, Clifford Curzon, asked me to reconstruct pre-classic dances — so that she will know something of the tempo and lilt of Dowland and Bach. She will pay six guineas. This is found money and only means a week in the British Museum and Mim's library, which is very good indeed. But there are not many such bonanzas — this one bought me two dresses. I may get two rich pupils next week, Anna May Wong, through Romney, and a social charity performer, very rich and anxious to have me coach her.

By the way, Romney has continued most loving and helpful. He gives me his flat to write in during the daytime while he is away at the Noel Coward rehearsals. His valet serves me a tray lunch in front of a roaring fire. He asks me out to dinner and to the theater. The others may have fallen off because of Cockie's displeasure; not Romney.

Thursday: On Tuesday afternoon I tried out my rich society pupil. She's dreadful to look at, but sincere and stubbornly anxious to improve, so I agree to take her on for one dance at twenty-five guineas. She was delighted. I got some music, worked out a dance, and today she phones me that there's something wrong with her insides, that she must have special treatment and can't dance. And I needed the money good and plenty!

On Wednesday I lunched with la Wong at the Claridge. She does herself nicely with three rooms and a piano and sable coats cut like old mandarin costumes. I said fifty pounds for the dance she wants. She blinked and said all right. It's going to be a tussle. She has no taste, no background, no good instincts, but she has a high opinion of her merits gleaned from a truly enormous social success. If she starts getting in my hair, I'll have to throw up the whole job. She can't dance and she can't sing. But she has the world's most beautiful figure and a face like a Ming princess, and when she opens her lovely mouth out comes Los Angeles Chinatown sing-sing girl and every syllable is a fresh shock.

The school was highly excited one morning last week because Doug Jr. phoned to ask me out that night to a theater and I had to refuse, having a previous engagement with old Mrs. Evershed, which I kept. But Doug called again on Saturday and asked me out last night. Called for me, took me to the Berkeley for dinner, to *Mala the Magnificent*, and then to his house for ginger ale, then home, kissing my hand as he left me. He was absolutely charming all evening and I had a grand time. He'd had a fight earlier in the day with Gertie. I don't know how serious. I'm sure she doesn't love him, and I think he's beginning to find it out. But don't worry about him. He's got a well-seasoned hide. He's no ingénue.

Joan came in the other day from a triumph. She and her buddy, Diana Rose, had gone into Claridge's (I thought only Wong could afford this), ordered lunch, demanding an extra chair for their dog. There was no dog. A plate was placed and chopped meat. At the end of the meal they tipped the waiter, thanked him for his help, and whistling to the invisible animal exited grandly. The entire staff stood open-mouthed.

Ramon is well and sends love. His new tooth is exceedingly lovely. Which reminds me that on Saturday I at last pulled myself together and reported at the Bow Street Station about my status as an alien, only to receive a severe reprimand from the police. In the middle of the admonition the officer suddenly began to giggle, hid his face in his hand, and said, "Forgive my lisping, miss — I can't scold you good — I've had teeth out." Anyhow, I've got to go back again with pictures.

To my astonishment, Robin was waiting for me at the police station, having discovered my whereabouts from the Ballet Club.

He was swept and beautiful in a new suit and overcoat and very happy, anticipating an editing post on the *Herald*. He took me off to lunch. No explanation given or asked concerning his recent prolonged disappearance.

I've heard from the Folkes. His success continues and this is a good thing because, do you know, Mum, he was on the point of bankruptcy last summer while I was with them? He was on the point of losing all. The little house, and the mouse-gray roadster, the servant, all. His manifold occupations should have hinted something of this to me. It was his pride to keep me from knowing anything was wrong. What courage! What style! I lived right in the house with them for a month, and I never guessed a thing. He treated me with generous, with opulent hospitality. I think he must have spent a great deal more on entertaining than he should have.

I've seen Haskell for tea at his house and am going there for dinner on Thursday. He raves about you; says you made the transatlantic trip an entirely different sort of affair than what it would have been without you. He was definitely struck by Mag's beauty and won by Bernie's charm. Ah me, what a family! Also, he says Mag's a good mother. On the subject of John Martin, he is hysterical.

He says Martin should be fired from the *New York Times* because of his notices on the Ballet Russe season — and in point of fact, the impresario Hurok is going to see that this is done. Some chance!

Sunday afternoon I had tea with Andrée Howard in her house. She is designing the costumes and scenery for a season of intimate opera and ballet at the B. Club. She is, I think, a prospective Schiaparelli. She has genius for clothes. And sometimes she does the most lovely choreography.

On Friday last, Young Doug came to tea. The Union was all agog naturally, and bellboys and waitresses found an awful lot of unusual things to do in the room where we sat. He was very pleasant but, my heavens, he is young! You should hear him on

economics! And he still takes such joy in dirty jokes. He's going
to do a new Clemence Dane play with Gertie next summer, so
there's small chance of her coming to New York with *Nymph
Errant*. Cochran wants to close the deal, but she won't see him,
not wishing to commit herself on that yet.

Last night the Clifford Curzons drove Norman Franklin and
me down to Haslemere in Surrey to the Dolmetsch festival. The
Dolmetsches are a family of Belgians — father, mother, four
children, children-in-law, and grands. Their contribution to civilization has been the discovery and preservation of medieval and
Renaissance music, dances, and musical instruments which they
and their pupils manufacture as well as play. Last evening they
gave a program of de Medici music and dances, in homemade
costumes of portière brocade with British trousers and walking
shoes below, and above glasses, clipped hair and rustic English
expressions. The dancing was unbelievable, performed uncer-
tainly through failing memory and without an atom of understanding about moving in cadence, or walking, or for that matter
just plain standing still. The old instruments sounded, as always,
dreadful. The voices were poor and untrained. Music stands
crashed, lights flickered, performers called out instructions
(there having been no predetermined agreement on how often
the choruses were to be taken). Nonperformers strolled on and
off the stage eating light snacks, and yet withal it was, and you
must believe me, a most wonderful performance and I would
not have missed it for anything. A very first-class job of research, stimulating and instructive. Wait until you see me dancing the canaries!

The drive down was simply grand, through Guildford, Godal-
ming, and Esher. The Curzons drove back after the performance
but I stayed — putting up at the George Hotel — and went to
the Dolmetsches' the next morning for a lesson on sixteenth- and
eighteenth-century dances. A nice, upright, girl-scoutish creature and a flowerlike young man all twirls and arabesques
performed for me authentically and ineffectively the eighteenth-

century dances in a cluttered parlor. Her mother accompanied them on a harpsichord made locally. I wrote down the steps and asked questions and I learned plenty. All the toe-pointing, bowing, and peeping under arms belongs to the cotton-batting-wig school of dancing, it seems. The real thing was restrained and quiet and flowing in a most lovely and expressive style. I learned everything I could, court bows, street bows, manner of holding hats and swords — everything. They had read all the contemporary works on the etiquette and dancing of five centuries in as many languages. It is wonderful always how much more effective the authentic gesture is than the vulgarized theatrical adaptation. I'm going to do an eighteenth-century suite using all these graces and conventions exactly as they were performed. You wait and see. Well, I spent all my money on extra time and music! And hadn't enough to tip the hotel porter, not daring to attempt the London bus without a couple of extra shillings in my pocket. I sneaked away furtively —

I asked to borrow Diana's downstairs Bechstein so that Clifford Curzon could come play to Ramon, but Diana has been quarreling with her mother and doesn't dare ask favors. Imagine living together under a tension like that! Diana doesn't dare invite anyone to play on a piano in her house — not even such a distinguished pianist and someone she wants personally to know. I'm trying to urge her to leave home for a bit. I've suggested that she come to New York and study with Martha, who would do her a world of good psychologically, as well as aesthetically.

Devoted love,
A.

February 5

Dearest Mum,
Rebecca West has asked me to some grand lunches, sometimes with distinguished literary figures, sometimes alone.
She is very age-conscious and always asks me how old I am.

(On your instructions, I don't reply.) In this she is terribly feminine, but she is that totally. She tends to think she is put upon by all (some people think she's a genuine paranoid), but then, so do I and so am I, and we vie in naming the undeserved blows we have taken. It's quite bracing. I don't know where she gets her reputation for being waspish, to me she has been golden-hearted.

I've been down for the weekend to Anthony West's (Rebecca's son by Wells). He looks very like his father, but is much more gracious — he could hardly be less. He is also friendly. He has a pretty pastel wife and myriads of cats. I think he wants to be a writer — but oh boy! That's a heritage to compete with! She paints, and Henry Andrews says she paints very well.

I went to Lifar's special matinee. This was a most astonishing performance, a collection of great male solos from all the big repertories, strung together one after another without relation or reason, simply to show that Lifar could do all. They were danced by our hero and two female assistants, each a ballerina in her own right — Alicia Nikitina and Felia Doubrovska. After every turn it was Lifar, not the girl, who was presented with a bouquet and he varied a hundred-and-fifty-year tradition by favoring the lady with a single bloom instead of receiving one. This singular ritual was reenacted after every dance with the exception of *The Afternoon of a Fawn* (which Lifar did quite alone without nymphs to show, I suppose, his independent all-inclusive sexuality). At the finish he was handed a large bowl of fruit. Toward the close of the program, Doubrovska was finally granted a solo either because she had the power to demand it or because the master needed rest. At all events, she performed so exquisitely, so enchantingly, with her long flexible legs, her long svelte torso, her long liquid arms, her long noble neck, her long sad face, and her great burning huge eyes, that she damn well stopped the show. The audience was no doubt delighted to see someone of straightforward, recognizable sex and honest craft do something pleasing that they all but rose to their feet. Thereupon Lifar refused to reappear and the afternoon was brought to an abrupt end by three ballet boys who were there simply as filler and wound up the business to no applause at all.

"Well," said Anton Dolin in the foyer, rather smacking his lips. "That was a pretty spectacle, I must say!"

Tuesday night I went as Mim's guest (complimentary seats) to the Sadler's Wells Ballet to see Alicia Markova dance *Giselle*, the hundred-year-old ballet which has been the vehicle for all the great ones from Grisi, for whom it was created, to Pavlova.

Alicia had been invited to join the Ballet Russe de Monte Carlo as a first soloist (an unprecedented opportunity for an English girl). All her friends cheered. But Ninette and perhaps Freddy too, or even patriotism, persuaded her to cast in her lot with the budding native Sadler's Wells Company and she has stayed here on the promise that Ninette will mount all the great classics for her; at least it was to be on a normal-sized stage. This decision plunged into acute consternation her advisers, including Arnold Haskell, who is a sort of foster-father. They implored her not to bury herself in a group of students in the suburbs. But she followed her instinct and last week, the first English full-length *Giselle* was presented with Markova as star.

Alicia was superb. The audience shouted their rapture all through the performance even though she was a home girl, but on second thought, of course, in the lobby, she was seen not to be compared to the Russians — to Toumanova, Baronova or Danilova, for instance. Rambert thinks otherwise. Rambert bases her opinions, not on current comment, but on exactly what is before her eyes, and her eyes are among the sharpest and clearest in England.

"You see," said Mim, "she can do *glissades* — I tell the children in class if they can do simple *glissades* well, they can do anything. Alicia listens to me." Alicia, of course, had been the pupil of Cecchetti and the Princess Astafieva, who trained her in everything, including *glissades*. "Now Betty Appleyard can't jump — no back — watch her now, she's going to let her back

go on the next jump — There! Dreadful! Is that not dreadful?
She should come to me."

"Alicia," said Mim in the dressing room, "you've come of age
— now be sure to spend the whole day with your feet up before
the next performance — one whole day."

Afterwards, Liza Hewitt, Mim and I had hot chocolate at
Lyon's (I paid). Mim talked nonstop of coming glory for Markova.

Giselle is to be followed by the *Nutcracker* and the complete
Swan Lake.

This letter reads like a professional bulletin — but I know
you're interested because you know them all. Family gossip in
next installment —

Devotedly,
A.

CHAPTER 11

THESE trips to theaters were not just recreation to me, nor even just encouragements, they were light in the gloom. I was not alone — there were others equally purposeful, and certainly as dedicated. There were others, gifted, but also bewildered. Antony struggled, experimented, and missed; taught stupid children, janitored, stage-managed, wandered around London (I seem to remember a cane) looking at things he couldn't afford, but Antony was finding a style. Two years later, he produced *Jardin aux Lilas* and the first totally new balletic voice of our time was heard.

Antony derived from Fokine, but between Fokine and Tudor, Proust had happened, Verlaine and Rimbaud, the Freudian school, and the new cacophony of music. Tudor tells stories about men and women dramatically, and therein he departs from Petipa and is linked to Fokine. His ballets, like the master's works, are succinct, compact and brief. Antony's ballets are all of a piece and cannot be broken into set dances, and the style is not interchangeable but particular to its own drama. Most of the Petipa ballets are in four acts and play in as many hours. They follow the same formula of separate *divertissement* and narrative mime. The Petipa pattern was discarded by Fokine, as well as the Petipa deportment, the eighteenth-century balletic stance and decorum. Fokine adopted the broken knee, the asymmetrical posture of classic statues, the free use of arm and back. As an inheritor of Freud, Tudor went the whole range of emotional impulse and susceptibility. He had at this point never seen Graham nor any of her pupils, but in his *Planets* he closely approached her technique and her psychological attitudes.

Just before I arrived in London, he had seen Uday Shankar and been enormously impressed. He was to go through his Indian period that summer in a matter of six weeks, but the sense that the arms and hands are an extra voice and not merely appendages to the spine remained a hallmark of his style; the visual effect is watery and permeating. Embraces and filigrees of arm movements, faint rubbings-out, like little sighings or half-heard exclamations, seemingly whispered in the air, are never mere decorations but evocations and echoes. In the same sense that Proust's digressions are the aura of his story, just so are Tudor's gestures overtone extensions. Each physical statement sets up a rippling of contrary suggestions, and each step is wreathed with doubts, regrets, aspirations, until the dancers seem literally to be moving through the human mind. He uses accompanying figures to expand or comment on the soloist's statements, producing through an accumulation of subtle choreographic devices a climax at once emotional and decorative. In effect, Tudor has translated emotion in all its contradictions and suggestibility to the terms of visual movement. This is magic and this is unique.

His ballets remain through the decades without any dimming; and even though the great shock of his idiom has disappeared, the delight and the strength remain. Tudor has been enormously influential and greatly copied. His disciples must, however, content themselves with producing vagaries and a few of his pretty devices. They cannot approach his impact; a brain cannot be copied.

Tudor has never stopped working, but he has produced in thirty-five years only nine lasting successes. Why after nine straight masterpieces did creative energy wither? It is a strange life pattern. One can only compare it to Rossini who, at thirty, just stopped, gave himself up to a lazy social life, with spaghetti parties for the gilded elite. But Antony has never been very rich; Antony has had to support himself with the drudgery of daily teaching. Lately, companies have hesitated to commission new works because they had no guarantee they would get a vintage Tudor. The later Tudor was flawed. Why?

I think the answer is simple. Hugh was Antony's friend, housemate, and artistic instrument; all the male lead roles were created on him. He was a limited dancer, but a good actor, a sensitive comedian, and a theater artist of unblemished taste. And he was crucially influential in the forming of Antony's style. (Indeed, I believe Antony's special use of music derives largely from the fact that Hugh had absolutely no rhythmic beat and could move only in long, vague melodic phrases.)

But he was more than this — in my opinion — he was a choreographic collaborator, with structural ideas, dramatic solutions, and merciless criticism. He helped. No one who had ever been in rehearsal with them could doubt how much. All good dancers assist through their bodies, but Hugh made decisions, Hugh balked, yelling at what he did not like, denounced openly in the rehearsal hall to everyone's acute embarrassment, and went home with the choreographer to find the correct and satisfying answers. This is collaboration.

When in 1948 Hugh got married and separated his artistic

life from Tudor's, performing only in the old roles, partici-
pating merely as a casual critic in the new works, the tone of
Antony's work changed. His beautiful movement remained,
the form blurred. In September 1963, in Stockholm, he
found himself again with *Echoing of Trumpets.* He was
alone, but so strong was his antiwar conviction that the passion carried him through to a new and splendid work.

Frederick Ashton made the more immediate success, although not of a financial kind. His brilliant invention had
been immediately apparent and he had had the blessed good
fortune of three extraordinary women as tutors: his teacher,
Marie Rambert, his designer, Sophie Fedorovitch, and presently he had Ninette de Valois as his patron and boss. As
soon as she was able, Ninette enticed him away from Mim and
set him up as chief choreographer for the Vic Wells Ballet, and
there he had the added advantage of association with an ex-
Diaghilev soloist, de Valois herself, and the superb men she
surrounded herself with, Constant Lambert, Lord Berners,
Thomas Beecham, Arthur Bliss, Rex Whistler, and Maynard
Keynes. The quality of these minds had, unquestionably, a
beneficial and shaping effect on the young hero of Notting
Hill. Mim let him go, although she minded to the point of
desperation, because she knew he deserved wider opportunities
than she could provide. With him went Alicia Markova, Pearl
Argyle and alas, Arnold Haskell, who had been so useful, and
who now switched, if not loyalties, at least focus and burning
hope on the rival theater.

Freddy was to be the champion for English choreography.
And he prepared himself with brisk British attention; there
was no muddling here. Now he was able to study the classics
because they were being revived with the help of Grigoriev
in Ashton's own theater. Ashton became a disciple of Petipa.
He learned how the master brought dancers onstage, got

them off, developed a *pas de deux*, and Ninette was able to advise him, because although lacking the daring and perception of Mim, she had actually danced in big repertory and was a very respectable choreographer herself. She knew the craft, and it is above all his great craft that distinguishes Ashton. In his case one must use the word with reverence. This word, this idea, has a special importance today when people accept accident and happenstance as part of their working technique; he does not, nor has he ever. His is the kind of technique that develops the instruments which steer vessels, that grinds microscopes and telescopes, that balances watches. Even in his ornamental pieces, in the pure decoration that he puts so lavishly on the stage, one finds a craft like Cellini's, like Fabergé's. Each dancer and each phrase is set as a master goldsmith sets a gem.

There is, in addition, the masterly skill of apportioning the formal pieces and the storytelling pieces — I, who have failed often, know how brilliant is his expertise in this. He has given to the formal *pas de deux* a new stature, and this is, perhaps, his best signature. He cannot achieve the unfathomable mystery that Tudor sometimes attains nor the majestic impersonality of Balanchine. But in Ashton's duets there is a kind of human love, and he has used the word himself in describing his own work.

His range is unmatched. For, in contrast to the story ballets, is the abstraction of the César Franck *Variations*, absolutely without peer in its kind, and the beautiful decorative frivolities: *The Birthday Offering* and the dances in *Midsummer Night's Dream*, where sheer prettiness is raised to such a pitch of finesse as to approach the celestial. His humor is entirely his own, as I suppose all humor must be, it being the one absolutely individual trait in human character never shared like the other universals, anger, fear, or hate. Ashton's *Façade, Mme. Chrysanthème,* and *Wedding Bouquet* could have been done by no one else. The last is silly; it is frightening; it is hugely funny. It reminds us that one of the strongest and most important books of the nineteenth century was written by an English mathematician who thought he was composing a comic nursery tale for a little girl.

Ashton's invention seems to be endless — like a mountain spring. Over the years many people, including international names, have helped themselves shamelessly to his goodies. Indeed, recognizing the thefts becomes a connoisseur's sport. It is unlikely Ashton cares. He promptly invents something new. In this nonchalant resourcefulness, he suggests Rossini, as lazy as prolific, who when composing in bed, his knees serving as music desk, let fall occasionally an aria to the floor and promptly wrote out a new one rather than put himself to the effort of getting up and retrieving the dropped pages. Ashton troubles about nothing, theft, imitation, piracy. He simply works on ballet after ballet after ballet.

That season I had lunch with Freddy in Mayfair (Kirk Askew was paying for it. Naturally neither Freddy nor I could afford a Mayfair lunch.) Just before we came to the sweet, which I greedily wanted, he said, "Well, good-bye. I have to go." And I said, "That's too bad. When will you be back? You're coming back to finish your sweet?" And he said, "No, I think not. I'll be back in two or three months." "Where are you going?" I asked. And he said, "Oh, out to New York. Virgil Thomson has sent for me." And over he promptly went to choreograph *Four Saints in Three Acts* to enormous acclaim. Between that abrupt departure and today stand one hundred and fifteen finished Ashton ballets. ("Oh," he said, "I should think so, easily, easily, and several moving pictures and operas.") Of this, probably twenty to twenty-five are authentic, enduring masterpieces. Fokine left only eight and two solos.

Freddy may seem to work with facility and speed but there is nothing complacent about his efforts. He still, after all his enormous success, spends the day before beginning a new work in the Brompton Oratory on his knees. He is not a Catholic, but he does not wish to pass up any chance for available help. He "vomits his way to the first rehearsal." After one *pas de deux* is outlined he begins to believe he can make it. At least, this time.

The woman who provided the framework for Ashton's career, supplied him with a stage and a company, was no mere handmaiden, but a giant in her own right. Although not an artist in the sense Ashton was (she says so herself with candor), she was vital; without her he could not have continued to amass, undeviatingly and uninterruptedly, his one hundred and fifteen works.

Ninette de Valois played no part in my London life, for the simple reason that she did not wish to waste time on me. (She felt the same way about Antony.) Also, I was American and she was a Buy-British-Irishwoman. Therefore, she had no foreigners in her company. But I must speak of her because she is in great measure responsible for the growth and widening of the ballet world, and the polarization of these two fanatic females — Rambert and de Valois — on opposite sides of London produced a heat of creativity that generated genius. I was not part of this, but I was there working in the periphery, and I felt it. It was of blast-furnace intensity.

The story of the Sadler's Wells Ballet must gladden the heart of every type of dancer, indeed of every member of the theatrical profession, and for that matter, of every teacher.

Basically, it is a tale not restricted to one art, although the Wells's splendid contribution to choreography is involved; it is rather the history of a plan and its enormous implementing.

Dame Ninette de Valois, the director-in-chief of the company, was born in Ireland, Edris Stannus. A bonfire had been built on the family hill for the expected birth of a male heir. It was not lit for the girl child. The rage engendered by this slight guided her youth and determined her to build her own bonfires and light them. Determination became her *métier*. Early on, when she made up her mind, dozens, then hundreds, of other people fell into pattern. It was her expressed conviction that any alternate point of view was "nonsense, darling." She believed this as she believed in God or her Country.

The detailed blueprint she worked out for herself was both audacious and comprehensive. It was also practical, and this kind of planning is rare in any field; it changes history. Her bonfires now blaze under many heavens.

In 1929 (two years before Ballet Club) Miss de Valois, an alumna of the Diaghilev company and presently head of a small dancing school in London, remarked that there was no national English ballet company to receive pupils after training. She thereupon decided to found one, and her notions of a ballet company were not paltry. There never had been a national one before so she was not restricted by precedent. She had less money than Mim; nevertheless, she did not think in terms of an eighteen-foot stage. She envisioned a great company for which she would somehow obtain private financing until the government should take over the job, as she was certain one day it would, although the English government had shown small interest in musical theater since the days of Handel. She decided that this company should employ the services of several native choreographers, not one of whom at that moment had yet identified himself; that she would hire only native ballerinas, none of whom had yet begun schooling, and harder still, find native male stars; that she would commission scores, sets, and costumes; that she would inaugurate an academy to feed the company and hold auditions for applicants drawn from every quarter of the British Commonwealth; that she would set up pensions and insurances and establish tributary schools and companies, and yes, even foreign subsidiaries. (There is a flourishing one now in Turkey.) She had all this clearly in mind when she had hardly the shillings for a hat — well, for three hats.

And she did it. The company stands. It is internationally known, the hallmark of high excellence. To be a performing member of the Royal Ballet means today through the world precisely what being a member of the Comédie Française or the National French Opéra meant one hundred years ago.

Unlike our companies, it is rooted securely and will not soon be upturned or cut off. Her original blueprint has been reinforced by government edict, and staffs of guardians and teachers and business executives are trained for its protection and expansion. De Valois accomplished all this in twenty-five years, six of which were spent under enemy bombardment.

There is, I think, no story comparable in the history of the theater. Similar organizations have been achieved before, but by kings with the full resources of a royal treasury and over a period of a hundred or so years, not by a lone dancing teacher with no money. And although at the gala celebration of the ballet's return to Britain after the first American triumph she cut through the ovation tendered her with, "Ladies and gentlemen, it takes more than one to make a ballet company," it was she who did it. And everyone recognizes this. For all her disclaimers, the winning ingredient was her own organizational genius, her amazing good sense, and her faculty for making everyone she needed work for her to the death.

She began as she could begin, courageously, with a small class of personal pupils and a class for business girls held after hours. This last, dreary and discouraging as it must have been, was for the purpose of building a knowledgeable audience. And at the first chance of getting her pupils on a professional stage, although only occasionally, and way out in the suburbs for a working-class audience, with virtually no reimbursement, she jumped to pledge her time and her strength. She was guaranteed nothing, no office space, no wardrobe space, no proper rehearsal facilities (the dancers had to practice on a cement floor), no first-string press response, no balletomanes. With the tirelessness of water, she worked her way through the months and years, task by task, expanding where it would lead to something rewarding, abandoning what was of no ultimate service. Her industry, the sheer dogged strength of her effort, makes praise silly.

She has never rested nor spared herself, not even after the great success. And although Dame of the British Empire, she still concerns herself with the housekeeping stints of dancing. She delights in teaching classes and teaches in any good school anywhere. She enjoys training replacements and substitutes, enlarging casts for bigger stages, reducing them for smaller, altering, adapting, and suiting for new requirements like a dressmaker. She has a zest for theory and has evolved extraordinary ones about the skeleton and musculature in relation to the dynamics of personality and type of movement.

No theorizing abated the slogging work. At one point she was coaching and choreographing simultaneously at the Abbey Theater in Dublin and the Old Vic in London. It was long before the air shuttle and Dublin meant the Irish Channel and all night on a train. Rambert was astonished at her energy. "I couldn't do it. I haven't that fanatic determination nor that strength." But Mim was older and Mim had a family. De Valois tried everything — nothing was too tiring. But she never for any consideration tried what did not lead to her goal — i.e., she never detoured into the English commercial theater, movies or foreign productions, although she probably had many offers. In the course of her other activities, she composed for the Wells company thirty-three ballets. Nor was she merely prolific. Her works contained, even the less successful ones, the seed of real discovery, with invention and dramatic daring that have had a marked effect on her colleagues.

The captaining of this enterprise, the financing of it, the administration through the years, the direction of its artistic and personal life, would seem to suggest a woman of almost Hitlerian force. She is very feminine and she is small, neatly pretty with the comely trimness of an eighteenth-century figure, and in eighteenth-century Irish style, she is pale-colored with black brows and a rosy, small, voluptuous mouth. Her carriage is elegant and brisk, and while her entire organism is at trigger point the whole time, she has not the rabid sense of desperate compulsion that drove Mim.

Her captivating wit is spicy with the robust quality of an autocrat, her speech is straightforward, clipped, forthright and final, but not outrageous like Mim's. It was also not as unkind. She said quite honestly that she didn't think I had any gifts, but she said this to Mim. It was Mim told me. It is characteristic of her life that men, and powerful men, accede to her wishes with alacrity and pleasure. (My husband and Sol Hurok succumbed totally years later when they arranged the American tour.)

With all this, she has been all her life fragile in health. Arthur Bliss, when working on the score of their joint ballet,

Checkmate, told me she ran a constant two degrees of temperature, day and night. It never abated. Her migraine headaches were legendary (as were Mim's, as are all women's who flout tradition), but bodily weakness was never allowed to interfere with her daily work schedule, nor with her private life. And she had one.

The officiating surgeon at one of her operations fell instantly in love with her. They married and at least two days a week, she became a country doctor's wife. There are stories, well substantiated, of Madame (during the war) rushing from rehearsal in Covent Garden to her country home and her husband's surgery on the char's day off and of herself scrubbing down his floors, then opening the door quietly and sympathetically to patients, and then taking the milk train back to her morning rehearsals, writing out the day's choreography all the way to London. (She wrote all her choreography out beforehand. She works entirely from notes, one of three people who do, Massine and Birgit Cullberg being the other two.)

But the bulk of her strength was given over to the building of uniform style in performances and repertoire, the development of artists through unbroken directed activity, the possibility of great production schemes through long-range planning. "A young choreographer needs to produce not one isolated work but at least two productions per annum in the same environment and with the same artists for a considerable period of time." She saw to it that her choreographers got just that. And that is precisely why hers became a great company. She is an evangelist. She preaches, and the more unredeemed the heathen the more irresistible the challenge. Any place is suitable for a ballet school, and any person a potential student.

In 1939, the Vic Wells Company became the Sadler's

Wells and moved to the theater of that name. The Old Vic
Theater had been offered to Mim, who was better known
than Ninette at this point. But Mim, with less than her usual
acumen, had rejected the plan. "I wouldn't touch that place
across the river!" Mim was a snob. In 1956, the Sadler's
Wells became the Royal Ballet, England's first (but not the
Commonwealth's: the Royal Winnipeg was the first granted
a royal charter) took up official residence in Covent Garden
Opera House, with adequate state endowment and royal patronage.

In 1963, Dame Ninette handed over to Ashton, now Sir
Frederick, one of the three or four highest-ranking companies in the world. He maintained it for seven years without
diminution of any kind, flourishing, potent and with the
happiest influence in all spheres. In the history of dancing
there has been no record that betters this — and in the history of national government, very few.

The weakness of the plan — its only one, I believe — lay
in its autocracy. The Sadler's Wells, in its beginning, like
any great state theater, suffered from the defects of monopoly. If the trustees and staff approved one type of dancer and
put their resources at her service, the differing types might as
well hang themselves, there being, alas, in England no alternate company of any scope, and the commercial theater offering small chance. The artistic dictatorship wielded by
Madame, however enlightened, was nonetheless a dictatorship, and although later not determined by a single individual's taste, it nevertheless represented a unified view. This
was at once its great undivided strength; it was also its limita-
tion. There ought to have been other good companies for
dissenting opinions and differing styles. There were none
adequate.

And mistakes have been made. Antony Tudor was forced

from the Wells because he, perversely against Ninette's advice, wished to choreograph. He had to go to foreign soil to find recognition.

It is obvious that what these four great talents shared, Rambert, de Valois, Ashton and Tudor, was a remarkable sense of direction. They knew where they wanted to go and they deviated in no way. Occasionally Tudor or Ashton took a commercial job, but it was only in order to eat. They did not consider the venture seriously. Their purpose, their style, their taste, their passion remained quite unmodified, developing, never warping. And so they wasted no time.

I marveled at them. I wanted to be in the theater — in every kind of theater, in all its diversifications; my path meandered.

They created in recognized and accepted forms. I wanted a new theater, unknown as yet and only dimly guessed at even by me.

CHAPTER *12*

3 Paulton's Square
March 5, 1934

Dearest Mum,

What do you think? What *do* you think? Uncle Ce has crashed through. Honest to God, at last, formally!

I have just learned that Paramount has been trying to reach me, because Uncle Ce wants me for dancing in *Cleopatra*. At $250 per week — and transcontinental fare but not transoceanic. The job must last five or six weeks at least — $1,500. Can you believe it? More details I can't give you. You will know them doubtless by the time you read this. Paramount had called Cochran's office to ask my whereabouts and been told that the office did not know, and that fifteen minutes after I'd been talking to the boss's secretary to beg an appointment.

Am I pleased that (when I bid Cochran good-bye) I can say that I've been sent for nine thousand miles and am hesitating whether or not to accept the movie job because of another offer here? Because that's the latest! Thompson wants me to stage dances for a show he's putting on at the Savoy. I'll learn more tomorrow. Don't fret. I want to get out of this town. I'm fed up with Cochran and his theater friends. (Everyone in the *Nymph Errant* company had been asked to the Noel Coward dress rehearsal, not I, and I had pleaded with Romney not to forget.) I won't change plans unless this one is a remarkable opportunity.

Jesse Busley comes with me. Stipulated that she wouldn't be on the same boat with XY.

I'll be seeing you ten days after you receive this.

Devoted love,

A.

p.s. Mim's youngest, Lulu, who had been wandering around all our classes for days feeling poorly, nearly died last weekend — appendicitis, measles, and inflammation of the throat. Poor Mim spent a wicked two days. The doctors haven't dared operate yet, but the child is, thank Heaven, very much better. I sent Mim flowers, which she was rhapsodically grateful for. She is a very dear woman when she is not being professional.

The London job was to do two ballets for a revue, *Why Not Tonight?* produced by twin brothers, the Thompsons, directed by Romney Brent, and starring Gina Malo, Greta Nissen, and Stanislas Idzikowsky — a minor Nijinsky from the Diaghilev. I had only two weeks to prepare before leaving for Hollywood. One ballet was to have Idzie as the wind in a blue wig in a garden of flowers (girls — natch); the other was to use Idzie and Greta Nissen, a Norwegian beauty with a freeform dance style that had nothing whatever in common with the Russian's. "For God's sake, help me!" I said to Ramon — "write me a ballet for those two unmatched egotists." So he did and it was *Three Virgins and a Devil* — the original score was to be composed by Walford Hyden, Anna Pavlova's musician in residence. Ramon had learned much. His script is lasting and the ballet is still performed.

I had been compelled to depart with both ballets half done. Antony Tudor took over for me and with love and care finished the job and pulled the curtain up. No one ever had better help.

I had been advanced some money and I could buy clothes.

"But Mim," I wailed, "when I had the time to get clothes, I had no money. Now I have money, I have no time." "That's life!" yelped Mim. But I did get a very attractive Bond Street coat, and two new Gardenia hats.

Ramon was startled at my sudden departure. He had always known I'd have to leave for home and jobs, but when the moment came, he was pitifully apprehensive. I reassured him the best I could. I gave him a growing garden which covered his bedside table and which he could watch blossom through the lonely spring. I promised to be back.

He wished me Godspeed. He said he would be good and would write. He was to write five times a week.

Obviously the accounts that had drifted back to California contained mention only of my more recent triumphs and no hint that same had cleaned me of my last copper. So I was pleased but not flabbergasted when Uncle Ce's long-hoped-for cable had finally come. No money for fare was mentioned. But I flew; I raced; I leaped to accept.

With my hastily assembled Bond Street wardrobe and a satchel full of Egyptian pictures from the British Museum, I climbed merrily aboard a train in Paddington Station. Ramon hung me with orchids and I was photographed Hollywood style by the Paramount photographers talking to the engineer. "Good-bye," I shouted to my friends, "I'm off to dance with a crocodile."

But the laugh froze on my lips when I read the script in New York and discovered that I was in very truth slated to danced naked on the back of a live bull. In fact, I broke into tears of pure dismay.

"Forget Shakespeare and Shaw," admonished Uncle Cecil's accompanying letter written, for some unexplained reason, on cloth, like the *Book of the Dead*. "I am giving these lovers their first human chance." It struck me he was giving me my last, but my viewpoint may very well have been undermined by the trip home. Two days at sea I broke out in a virulent case of measles contracted from Lulu Dukes, and I sweated out in sickbay storms that delayed the boat three days. I was escorted off the boat by my family doctor and given my first taste of a wheelchair. My sister, Margaret, took over responsibility for the trunks. She had her own method of cutting through red tape. "How many children do you have?" she asked the customs officer as he rummaged.

"Four, why?"

"Well, I just thought you might like to examine this bag of dirty linen as well. The owner has a virulent case of measles." Customs examination terminated within twenty seconds. The trip to Hollywood was perforce postponed and when finally I did go I traveled, too weak to walk, flat on my back, and this, of course was expensive. I traveled in a stateroom at Paramount expense, which seemed to them uncalled for.

I traveled with great eagerness but a certain apprehensiveness. I was bewitched by Cecil (we all were, all the family) but certain aspects of his later style dismayed me. It was Cecil's picture, of course, and it all had to be in his style. I was young. I was stubborn and foolish. I should have known that I either would have to adapt my tastes or quit. Instead, I was about to attempt, in my green arrogance, in my London snobbery, to put something over on him. Cecil had built a world reputation on his style, and many, many millions of people thought it was just wonderful. I came from a London basement on his money to say Pooh! As I read these letters now, an older woman who has found young rebels (Jerome Robbins, Sybil Shearer, Eliot Feld) in her own rehearsal hall, my sympathies are entirely with my uncle.

Cecil de Mille moved in legends. The first, and one that he

struggled very hard to promote, was that he was the world's greatest moving-picture director. He was certainly the best known, more widely hailed than even Griffith or Eisenstein! I heard his name in Russia, years after his death. Albert Speer uses it again and again in his autobiography as a synonym for grandiose, overblown opulence. "De Mille Style" seemed to the architect of the Third Reich the only way to describe the type of work he was himself then doing. The second part of the legend was the continuing presence of yes-men around the master, the entourage of sycophants and courtiers that he maintained from the first flashes of success until the end. These were not friends; they were reassurers; many of them loved him, all were loyal, but they never disagreed. He could not tolerate contradiction. And this was because — as with so many autocrats — and indeed with so many artists, and even some great ones — he must basically have been unsure of himself and his tastes. De Mille was a man dispensing millions of other people's money, bound by contract to deliver something that would pay back and make profits very quickly. His training in the arts had been negligible, his taste remained unfastidious; his theater experience was checkered at best and essentially haphazard, old-fashioned (mostly with the Shuberts and Belasco). He proceeded like a hunter by his nose and his ears and by signs and tracks. He persuaded himself that he was guided by inner passion. He may have been, I think, at the beginning. As the risks grew greater and the stakes higher, passion diminished and cunning and craft supervened. He was a tremendous craftsman, and the fact is that whatever his inner motives he was the most successful of his time.

Now, when a man who is not a genius and knows in his bones he is vulnerable attempts to maintain a world position which he also hopes will be immortal, the strain is considerable. Cecil worked like a man at the galleys. He had to believe he was infallible, and when someone questioned his conviction he felt his entire balance threatened. A refusal implied that part of this heroic legerdemain was pretense — or even accident.

I have always remarked that great artists can be uncertain. Of course they are while struggling to find solutions. Tolstoi's scripts are almost indecipherable. Emily Dickinson provided four or more alternates for every word; Beethoven wrestled with endings to the point of exhaustion; in our day Jerome Robbins and his lack of decision are a byword in the dance profession. But all of these knew very well what they did not want, and what they did not want was the current coin, the well-worn usage. What they wanted was something newly experienced, and therefore unknown and hard to attain. Cecil wanted what was most readily understood and universally accepted. There's a difference in the point of view and in the search, and most certainly in the goal.

Yet Cecil's pronouncements were given with total certainty: Kipling's "If" was the greatest poem in the English language; the best composers were Wagner and Tchaikovsky; Alma-Tadema was one of the finest painters, although he also liked Rubens. He stated the evaluations with less hesitancy than I have ever heard from professors, critics, or historians, his aplomb being unmarred by any wide exposure to the spectrum of achievement. Differing views were unthought of at his table.

Cecil was not outwardly pompous. He had wry humor and could tell jokes on himself. And he had wonderful charm. But he always got his way. No member of his family had ever gainsaid him except his older adopted son, but that was private and far from the set. No other members of his family wanted to. He was a king. He was known to his staff as "Chief." His wife, Constance, called him "Cecil," his brother and sister-in-law "Ce"; but no one else took liberties. His sons- and daughters-in-law called him "Mr. de Mille" to his death and after.

CHAPTER *13*

Dearest Mum,

I'm in Bullocks Wilshire being marcel-waved.

Aunt Con met me at Pasadena with chauffeur Ulysses S. Poe and a group of newspaper photographers. They held the train while I was taken on the steps, getting off the steps, getting back on the steps, resting beside the steps. A curious ring of passengers gathered about the cameras. Imagine their disappointment when I stepped into the center of the circle.

We drove straight to the studio, Chauffeur Poe proudly pointing out the flowering lupine to me.

The Boss stopped murdering Caesar to give me one of his really best embraces. I had just time to recognize with disappointment that Calpurnia was one of the regulation de Mille cuties when he halted again, and coming up to me surveyed me from top to toe with his quizzical jeweler's eye and then said, "Lift your skirts, baby. I want to see if your legs have thickened."

Now, my legs are and always have been all right. I passed that test.

Then he said, "Now, when the great net is dragged up from the Nile full of naked dripping women and they extend their hands toward Antony, in their hands are shells. But what is in the shells?"

"Babies," I said.

He only just smiled. He does not like his ideas joked about. I failed test two.

"I want to do dances for the camera and not for the proscenium arch," I said rather too smartly.

"What's the difference?" he asked.

That question he failed. Our score was now even. Uncle Cecil got back to the Ides.

I don't know whether it was the lights, the excitement, the nervousness caused by his staring, but I suddenly decided if I did not go home I would probably faint. Aunt Con and I went precipitously. She stretched me out on the sofa and flung hot tea at me, coming in every so often from a children's hospital board meeting to make soothing sounds. She was interrupted in this kindly office by an emergency call — a child had drowned in the reservoir across Los Feliz, a child she didn't know, but the police called her; people always call her; she's the lady that takes charge. She went to the victim's home — hysteria everywhere. She quieted the mother, gave her a sedative, then herself chared the victim's house and left promising there'd be some hot food sent over.

She returned to my side, took a sip of tea, and went looking for flies for Richard's horned toad and baby alligator. Then she dressed in lovely pastels for dinner, a rope of fire opals hanging to her waist.

Dinner was as always in this house, good eating, family-lusty and minus master. Sample of dinner conversation:

JOHN: Agnes, you seem to be taking a terribly long time to get started. (John obviously believes if one hasn't made a success by twenty-five — which his father certainly didn't — one has totally missed the bus. One is doomed, or at least faded beyond help.)

AGNES: Oh, I have a few good years ahead of me.

JOHN: But Agnes, you've got something you can sell. If a Barnum would get hold of you, you'd sweep the country.

AGNES: There isn't any Barnum today. I'll have a success. Argentina makes big money, but she didn't start to until she was forty.

FRANK: Gosh! Must we wait another year for you to come into your own?

KATHERINE: I hope, Frank, you'll live to see it!

FRANK: Kathie, it's dangerous of you to turn on your only public like this!

Between bouts I learned the gossip on de Mille Drive! One item will please Mag — the piano teacher's dog has been barking all night to the great annoyance of Hamlin Garland. So he wrote her a disagreeable rebuking letter but he signed his daughter-in-law's name because, as he explained, he certainly had no intention, even as scolding, of "giving that woman a literary signature."

Dinner lasted a long time and then they all drifted off to various pursuits and Aunt Con picked up her gauzy skirts and went to the wine cellar to find Uncle Ce a special bottle of Liebfraumilch.

Aunt Con is idolized by the whole group. She doesn't give herself a minute's attention.

And they all speak rhapsodically of the kind of girl you turned out to be. And you should hear Chauffeur Poe on you. "If there were more like her!" and he fetched the deepest sigh I've ever heard him emit. Literally, from John up you seem to be the pattern in the communal opinion of energy, enterprise, courage, stamina, wit, intelligence, adventure, and fun. Believe it or not you spell a kind of glamour to these mundane souls.

I was really wilting but I had to wait up and get some matters settled with the Boss. He came home at his usual hour — eleven. Aunt Con had his little table before the living-room fire and his dinner hot in double boilers and his German wine cold. And I, who was both hot and cold, tried to make sense. He listened very kindly and attentively — away from the set he's a different man.

He was delighted with my ideas, or professed to be, and then I told him I would like not to do a dance of a man whipping half-naked girls dressed as leopards. He said he'd been absolutely ravished by my *Ouled Naïl*, and he wanted something like that with the bull.

I said, "But that's a belly dance from a café, a dirty, angry prostitute, spitting betél-nut juice all over the stage."

"It was pretty effective."

"In its place it was, but it would not be fit for a queen on a barge like a silver shallop, nor for Mark Antony, who'd seen a lot everywhere. He should have something mysterious and exotic dished up for him." I was thinking of Martha Graham's *Aztec Suite*, and I told him about it with fervor.

"Well, I haven't seen her Aztecs, and I have seen your desert girl."

"Oh, I should so love to do something mysterious, beautiful, new. Beautiful movement, not belly grinds and bumps. I can do those as you well know, but I do them with a point of view, not to be seductive. *Ouled* is a raging, filthy whore."

"You use strong language, baby."

"Sure, but I don't dance dirty."

"I don't want you to. Anyone can do that; that is why I sent for you from London."

"Oh Uncle Ce, we'll make history together."

"All right, baby, but some of the things that have already been done are very, very effective."

Then I said he must decide who was to be in command, Le-Roy Prince, his regular dance director, or me. He said he understood my point and would clarify later.

Aunt Constance has installed me in the west wing, where she can watch over my convalescence. Once more I look to the mountains over arbors of waving roses. Once more the tall, beautiful, Norwegian Frederik serves me breakfast in the Italian patio and flatters and reminisces and gossips. This is very nice for me personally, but may not be good professionally. I enter the house as a distinguished European artist. How long will it take Uncle Ce to realize I'm only his niece? Three days? Will he recognize he's got a little nepot who can't earn a decent wage and is not certain she is the best choreographer in the world? But it's so seductive here, and such fun — and I'm so tired!

And I must save money! But I do hope I'm not making a mistake in policy.

Tuesday: The morning after I arrived I showed Ramon's medical charts to Dr. Sidney Burnap, who studied them carefully and said the disease was of too long duration to permit of any cure. The body has been invaded and taken over for ever. Ramon's dopplegänger is multiple sclerosis and he must live harnessed — until his death. The illness is not progressive, but it is incurable.

This sad interview readied me for the studio, where trouble has already begun. The resident de Mille dance director is a man with the aristocratic name of LeRoy Prince, a fibrous toughy with a Renaissance past. If he has not himself been a gangster, he has mixed with the worst in Chicago, has been taken for a Ride, has had his arm deliberately broken against the front right wheel of the car, and has witnessed more bloody, murky trafficking than most survivors. He has the quieting air of an Italian bravo and something of the gallows humor. But aside from the fact that I believe he will stop at absolutely nothing he is a likable enough guy. One of his amusements is to watch my eyes grow round at his stories of debauchery and horrid brutality, which Cecil affects to believe he invents. I believe he invents very little. He has photographs to illustrate the worst of his tales — lynched Negroes, drilled bootleggers, knifed prostitutes — and several hours, which were better spent in constructive work, have been whiled away in storytelling. But he does not let amusement or good nature dull his wits. He has survived gangsterism; he is not going to be cowed by de Mille's niece.

When I saw Prince on the set today, he said, after elaborate greetings, that we must keep together so that he could tell me what I had to do. He also informed me that he begged Uncle Ce to send for me, that Uncle Ce did not know where to find me, and LeRoy told him London. It's transpired subsequently that I'm to do the dances I suggested, and, I think, a bacchanal in falling rose petals at the finish, though I haven't been officially given this last one yet. But I'll be called in to help, I know; Le-Roy does Uncle Ce's ideas: the clams — the girls in the net fished from the Nile; a dance between a man with a whip and two women dressed as leopards; a dance in which a goat butts young naked girls around the hall. There seems to be a dearth of clothes in this dance production.

I get along beautifully with the staff. They are all cheering me on. "If only C.B. will let you," they say. Apparently they're all raring to go and they're held back only by the Boss's technique of work. He asks everyone's opinion about everybody else's business, and afterwards does what he's made a custom of doing during the last twenty years. This is the Belasco method, I've been told, and C.B. copies Belasco in very many things — the entire manner, the show for any audience around, the style, the "act." It's sort of nerve-racking for us little pros who would just like to get on with our own business. Yesterday, he asked me about Cleopatra's litter — the designer's business, surely. I told him what I thought. Then he asked everyone else on the set and eventually did what I'd suggested; it was however, two prop boys who had convinced him.

The musician, Rapp, is cheap and commonplace, but he sighed wistfully when I told him I wanted alternating bars of 3/4 and 4/4, and two rhythms at once.

"He won't let you," he said, "and I can't have the instruments I want. But we'll see what we can put over on him."

Then there's a Russian on salary for his opinion, which is seldom heeded, who is frantic to have the dances done in an unusual way. If I can only persuade C.B. to let me have one print cut the way I want as an experiment, I know I could persuade him.

Friday: Well, Prince this afternoon gave the Boss an ultimatum which was duly relayed to me over Cecil's midnight supper. Cecil asked me very levelly if, in the event he let Prince go, did I think I could handle all dance movement to his satisfaction. I was not sure: to my satisfaction certainly, but not necessarily to his. He acknowledged my candor and decided to keep Prince on.

So, we enter the job in double harness, outwardly friendly and gay.

Uncle Ce keeps a killing schedule. Up at 6:30 A.M., he has breakfast at 7 with Aunt Con in her beautiful east bedroom, the sun pouring through the climbing roses. Off in his own car at 8:00, he drives through the Paramount gate at 8:10 and in on the set between 8:30–9:00 — lunches at 12:30 in the commissary. He is the only producer-director that doesn't demand a private dining room. Of course, his table is in the center and on a raised platform and all his staff sits with him.

Back on the set at 1:30 — shooting until 7:00 — five straight hours of the most intense concentration and unbroken responsibility. He does everything (sets every camera angle, for instance, carrying a light gauge around his neck and a portable lens. His cameramen, although the best, take instructions from him.) He breaks at 7:00. Rushes — the daily laboratory prints — for an hour or so and decisions as to selection for the cutter (Ann Bauchens), who keeps right up to the daily shooting with her rough cuts. The office conferences and business decisions until 10:30. Home alone at 11 P.M. — dinner (kept hot by Aunt Con in double boilers) in front of the fire and conversation with her until 1:00 A.M. This is the time he catches up on family business, and he does. He knows about everything and cares very much. He personally locks up the whole house, speaks to the night watchman, and goes to bed. I think he reads a little before sleep. Sometimes new scripts, more often the Bible — there's one by his bedside. He never gets more than five hours' sleep.

It is a working program which would kill a young man of twenty-five. He never smokes, and he takes only a little wine,

German preferably, at his late supper. He needs no exercise, for he is on his feet all day and the energy he gives out is that of a general in full battle. He amazes me. No wonder his staff calls him "Chief." And I think I understand the yes-men phenomenon. They're his protection. If he wasted energy in self-questioning, he couldn't keep up the pace. This is the unflagging zeal, the undivided strength of the prophet, the fanatic — or alternately, the absolute monarch.

They all send love constantly — most particularly Uncle Ce —

Devotedly,

A.

1010 de Mille Drive
April 13, 1934

Dearest Mum,

Things get thicker and thicker, but not, on the whole, more satisfactory. I wear my feet out tramping, tramping, tramping over the cement from the costume department to the makeup, to the music, to the business offices, to the still galleries, to the stage and back to the costumes. I suppose this is unavoidable with affairs in such confusion, but the waste of energy is distressing and exhausting.

I don't know who countermands orders, or if Cecil knows what is happening and watches to see if I can fight my way through, or whether he is too busy to notice. But I've been most deliberately served with procrastination. I've been sent to rehearse in the studio carpenter shops, where the electric saws splitting wood make it impossible to hear a piano. On my protesting strongly, I was put in an empty set (by Prince) with no piano and no space. The costume sketches have never been prepared, the scenic designs never attempted. No music is forthcoming. I've worn myself out walking all day from one department to another, on cement walks, upstairs and down, and always I've met with great courtesy (except from the business manager, Burns, an ex-waiter, and the Boss) and always nothing had been done.

The crux of the matter is that C.B. trusts no one and does not seem to take the deciding voice with expedition and certainty. Yet he insists on okaying every single item from hairpins to the still photographs that are released for my personal publicity, also all estimates of cost. You can imagine the entailed amount of waiting. He must be shown. Cecil always has to see everything finished out and completed: every eyelash drawn on his costume sketches, every muscle, particularly muscles. And if showing him necessitates the use of drapes or props his businessman, Roy Burns, holds up all outlay until C.B.'s o.k. is obtained.

As far as the cooperation of the other subordinates is concerned, I am being treated like a beloved sister. I get willing, enthusiastic and friendly help at every hand. But the producer's attitude is not protective.

After our first talk, I have never been able to get his attention sufficiently to make him understand my ideas or get a decision. He has ignored my presence on the set, using the script girl for the setting of business or positions while I, a trained dancer, stand by offering suggestions to deaf ears. He has deferred right over my head to Prince on everything to do with action. He has forbidden me to hire any girls for rehearsal so that I could work out and show him the dances. At the same time he has continually announced his doubts as to the suitableness and effectiveness of my projected numbers, not in private, but in front of any members of his staff who happen to be present when his fears assail him. The psychological effect on me I needn't go into, and on the staff, which has been quick to take its tune from him.

And so we come to last Monday. On Monday afternoon Ralph Jester, the designer, brought a colored girl on the stage in one of the Lastex dresses we made as an experiment. It was not a successful one, and both of us knew it. I begged him not to show the costume, but C.B. insisted, so it was exhibited. Well, he didn't like it a bit (nor did we), or the idea which had prompted me to suggest it (which we did — I wanted something that looked carved in granite, a frieze against which I would be absolutely gorgeous). He knitted his brows; he gnawed his fist; he rocked back and forth in his chair; he snapped out questions at me. What did I think the girls could do in such a rig? He could visualize nothing. I wanted to reply that if he could visualize all they were going to do there would be no need for me around. He cut short all my explanations and continued, "It has neither beauty nor richness nor seductiveness. What will they carry in their hands?"

"Nothing," I said, "they are dancers. They use their hands for dancing."

Well, he bit his lip and shook his head and his face went stone. He demanded to see what they were going to do right then and there. I said he couldn't. I hadn't had one girl to rehearse with, not even for half an hour. (They are paid for rehearsals $5.00, by the day.) Then he ordered me to have the dance ready to show him the next day. I said that was impossible. He was angry. I stood my ground.

Christ, he said, how long was he going to be kept in the dark about what I was up to? I told him he was unreasonable, that no dance director in the world would show his work without rehearsal. Well, he said, jingling the money in his pockets, come over on the barge set and tell him about what I wanted to do there. Over there, he frowned and shook his head before I had completed the first sentence. It wouldn't be effective. I said I was convinced it was excellent else I wouldn't have suggested it. He said he wasn't, and that he was the director. Maybe I'd have my chance someday. So in desperation I myself showed him the steps. "That looks rotten," said Roy Burns, who always stands at the director's elbow whenever I wish to talk to him. "It looks dangerous," said Cecil.

I thought it did, too. It was to be a carpet of naked rolling girls through which stepped daintily the bull on whose back was to be me — naked and rolling. So far have I progressed into the spirit of things.

Well, he asked everybody's ideas on the subject until someone suggested youths pole-vaulting over the back of the bull. Then he'd had enough fun with the conversation and he went off to projection. And yet he says on all occasions that Isadora Duncan and I are the only dancers who have interested him.

I told Burns to get me ten white girls the next day so that I could show the Boss what I meant. He said I could have two girls. I appealed to C.B. He said I could have two, no more (that's $10). And that I could show him any kind of a dance in the world with two girls. "And what," I asked, "if the ten girls all did different things?"

Show them to him separately and he would visualize the assembled effect.

I sat in tears of exasperation and fatigue. Ralph Jester, the designer, kneeled on the floor beside me and begged me to alter the dance to something C.B. would know how to photograph, that he simply had no conception of what I was after. I realized that as I couldn't possibly get what I wanted I must work out something quickly that would suit his needs — and his tastes. Ralph took me out to dinner and was understanding and kind. I stayed up all night and did a new dance.

A frivolous footnote to the above distressing scene was the moment when Cecil, in the middle of the argument, had suddenly yelped, "Ouch!" The leopard which lay beside Cleopatra's bed, drugged on perfume, came to and playfully closed his jaws on Cecil's calf. The beast is kept so doped we all grew careless. Only the thick leather puttee saved Ce's leg. Even so, the teeth grazed the skin. Cecil was amused, but the keeper sternly rebuked his charge and hastened to administer another large dose of Arpège.

Friday: Well, now Colbert is playing sick (or so C.B. claims — indeed she may not be playing; in fact, the poor girl may be gravely ill), but the entire company has to lay off until she is ready to work again. This illness involves a possible loss of $10,-000 (as C.B. crossly and ungallantly expresses the situation, "She always was a bitch"), the complete rearrangement of the shooting schedule, and a two-day holdup — which I feel may be good for everyone's nerves. They might be more relaxed by the time we get to the barge.

Yesterday on the set, LeRoy Prince called me over and said, "Agnes, can you find out what goes on about the barge?"

"No," I answered, "I cannot. Not anything."

"Well, shake on it," and we shook. "It's not," he continued, "as though you could call what I do dancing." ("That will be the general criticism," I almost put in, but didn't, Mom, didn't.) "But I do like to know what I'm expected to have ready." ˙

I've made the acquaintance of the bull. He lives in the back lot, tethered in a pen. As I have always been unreasonably afraid of cows, I could see that this chore was going to present unusual tensions. At first I contented myself with hanging over the fence, making sounds that were soothing and, I hoped, bovine. But as matters have deteriorated up on the stages and workshops, I take to going to the back lot for comfort. And, yesterday, before I was aware, I was even climbing up and down his sides and leading him around (Ralph Jester had the courage and kindness to show me how). Since then I've been clinging to his enormous neck daily in a kind of animal sympathy for the strange predicament we both find ourselves in. He is a great dark tawny brute with a strangely subdued manner. It was suggested that he may be an ox. I am no expert, but as far as I can tell from a casual nonagrarian survey, he is indeed a bull, but perhaps he has been in pictures before; I think he's lost his spirit.

Yesterday, they made a camera test of me. Cecil directed. I mustn't move my head to right or left on account of my nose. I mustn't open my mouth on account of my teeth.

My bald Russian pianist (Chaliapin's accompanist, and don't you forget it) has pasted together bits of Rachmaninoff and Rimski-Korsakov and I've finally assembled a dance. I don't believe it's very good, but like the bull, I have lost my viewpoint.

A.

Kenmore Drive, Hollywood
April 21, 1934

Dearest Mum,

Plenty has happened since last I wrote, and that's the reason I haven't written. It's like this —

I'm out of the picture. Walked out. And thank God, too! Never in all my life have I been subjected to greater rudeness, humiliation, ignominy, and indifference. Cecil has been unlike Cochran at his worst only in regard to money because, while not generous, he has been scrupulously honest.

Yesterday, the time at last came to show him the number — in full panoply, like a performance, at half-past eight in the evening, after the shooting was over. Two hours before the audition, the makeup department went into high gear. Ignoring bones and organs they started from scratch and worked up something quite new. As Cecil thought of things during the afternoon's shooting he phoned up his orders.

"Pull out her eyebrows." I was straightaway rendered as bald as an egg.

"Grease her hair black." (Roy Burns very shrewdly had withheld authorization for a wig until he learned whether or not I and my dance were to be retained.) "Change her lower lip." Two women and two men worked, sweating, in the little makeup room, with grim mouths. Suddenly the head cosmetician, a Westmore, said, "My God, the body makeup is streaked. Strip her and do it over." He looked stricken. "My God, if de Mille sees that!" The photographing, you will remember, was not to take place for another five days. This was only an audition I was being groomed for. Westmore looked up from my legs with a brown sponge in his hand. "You mustn't mind me, honey. Think of me as a doctor. This has got to be done. I'm the best at it. And there's no time."

There was a good deal of me to be repainted. The costume was extremely brief and affixed to me at strategic points by surgical tape.

"Hurry up. Send her down," came the call. The dressers moaned and swore and hurried. Their hands began to shake. I felt as though I were being prepared for an electrocution.

The costume was beautiful, eight yards of pleated white gauze that fanned around my painted legs exactly like the great skirts on any lotus girl in a sunbaked relief. The skirt was affixed to a jeweled halter around the groin, a wide, flat Egyptian collar and very large eyes completed the outfit. For obvious reasons, the collar had to be rendered immovable, and this took some doing. Three times the dressers wrenched the jewels off my resisting flesh and adjusted it anew. The third time gouts of blood sprang out all over my back and shoulders. (The trained nurse took this last taping off me. And today I had to be given treatment for second degree burns. All's well now. I add this detail because I simply can't resist it.) But "Hurry" rang the phone. They wiped the blood away without apology and glued to fresh exposure. And I thought only of pleasing a man who found me not beautiful enough to permit the turning of my head or the opening of my mouth.

Done at last and breathing imprecations and prayers, we bundled over to the stage, where the day's shooting had just ended. Cecil sat in Cleopatra's great black marble throne at the top of a flight of steps, the Sun of Horus behind his head. On his right sat Claudette Colbert, most rebukingly lovely. On his left, the public censor to remind him not to break the decency laws. In serried ranks on either hand, behind, below, ranged the cast and staff and technical force — about fifty. Better so, I thought. Fifty is an audience. No audience I have ever faced has remained altogether unfriendly. The prop boys wheeled a Steinway grand onto the black marble floor. I walked to the end of the great hall and spread my white, winged skirt behind me. It was reflected white in the polished black marble. I knew I could walk beautifully. That's one thing I can do better than almost anyone. I can walk greatly. I started toward the throne and made the first abrupt gesture.

Twice the jeweled collar broke and I had to stop for repairs. The costume department had no conception of the strength in the muscles of a dancer's back.

During the second halt, Cecil spoke quietly through the stillness. "I think the costume department owes you an apology."

"Forgive me, darling," whispered Ralph Jester, who was working at my shoulder with safety pins.

On the third try I got through. I mounted the steps to Cecil's knees and dropped the hibiscus flower I was holding into his hand, Mark Antony's hand.

Then I waited and looked up. An audience? I have faced them in four countries, in every kind of theater, big and little, intelligent and dull, but here I faced a jury. This was a new experience. No one moved. No one breathed. No one held a thought. They all suspended, waiting, a row of plates on a shelf would have made a livelier assemblage. Suddenly, the line of disks stirred, the unfaces focused, the core, the nucleus had gathered life and moved. Like ripples on a pool they circled back the decision.

Cecil was shaking his head. "Oh, no! Oh, no!" he said very slowly. "I am so disappointed! This has nothing. It may be authentic, but it has no excitement, no thrill, no suspense, no sex."

"It had beauty," said Jester, quietly. Cecil wheeled to the censor, "Would that rouse you?"

"It sure wouldn't!" said the censor heartily.

"It wouldn't rouse me," said Cecil, "nor any man. What about the bull? What's happened to the bull?"

I was standing naked under army searchlights and angry.

"What I would like is something like the Lesbian dance in *The Sign of the Cross*," he continued.

"Boy!" said the censor, "If we hadn't had the Christians singing hymns like crazy all throughout that dance we never would have got away with it."

The dance in question was in my mind a piece of the cheapest pornography. I felt I had taken enough. I blazed. "That dance was one of the funniest exhibitions I ever saw."

"That is then precisely the kind of humor we are after, baby," said Cecil, climbing down from the throne, and then remembering, he stopped and threw back over his shoulder as he left the stage, "LeRoy Prince, take this number and make something out of it we can photograph."

With that sentence he broke my contract. Five minutes later I was off the payroll. Thank God I have a prepaid berth to go home in.

LeRoy Prince moaned, "Oh honey, honey, that belly dance!" Cecil also said, very levelly on the edge of the stage: "We'll have to be very careful about the press release. This could be awkward. Try not to talk, baby, until I do; you can hurt yourself."

So the announcement in the *Los Angeles Times* today read that we had disagreed over the length of my number, and that what he had in mind was a beautiful naked woman dancing sensually on the back of a milk-white bull.

And, Mom, that just wasn't true. The bull is not milk white.

In justice to truth let me repeat that the dance is not my best. It may be lousy for all I know. I'm bewildered. He had meant to help me and I had let him down publicly. One thing I am sure of, it could have been fixed with a quiet discussion. I knew very well what he wanted, but have tried perversely to give something that interested me. Something that Martha Graham or Arnold Haskell would have praised.

Then the heavens opened and Bernie Fineman came to take me to dinner. "Good God, Agnes," he said. "You're naked! If your father could see you!"

This morning I told C.B. over breakfast that I was getting out of the picture. He said that if Prince could not furnish the dance he wanted he would call on me again and stage the number himself. So against this contingency, I went to the studio and made up another dance which I knew was a skillful handling of what he wanted but which was also filthy. I called Jester in to watch. He said he knew it would please C.B. but that he hoped to God I wouldn't do it. I told C.B. I had a dance. He's never asked to see it. I didn't think he would. He'd described the dance he wanted to a member of his staff as an orgasm, a copulation between an animal and a girl. Only he wanted it with "class" and that's why he'd sent for me.

Today, I received congratulations. "You're well out of this, Aggie. I've never seen such an exhibition in my life. He was shameful to you," said Ralph Jester.

"I'da liked to've punched his head in," said Wally Westmore, the makeup man. "The way he talked to you! That dance had sex all right. I sat up and took notice! Only it wasn't dirty. If you ask me, it was too good for him."

"You won't do it for him, will you, honey?" said the wig girl. "You won't be that vulgar. You got class."

"He wasn't fair," said the assistant director.

"The bastard!" said Bernie. "If your father had been here!"

I'm no longer in the west wing — I've left his house forever. I'm staying with Dr. Lily Campbell while I decide what to do. Write me there —

My love,
A.

Poor man, he was never to get the dance he was after. They hung my bull with silk carpets and ropes of roses and led him staggering under the too-hot lights through the path of rolling girls, while naked women pulled his ears and fondled his muzzle and rubbed against his flanks. At the height of proceedings he just shut his eyes. At no point did he show the slightest interest. "It only goes to show," said a visiting Englishman, "how good a cow is."

The next night after my fiasco, I went to the back lot in search of a pair of work shoes I'd left in the bullpen. I was alone and I hung over the rails and stared at my late partner.

There he sat, darkly couched in sweet-smelling hay, giving an odor of male assurance. He quietly chewed something healthy and simple.

"Good-bye," I said, as I picked at a splinter. The tears stuck on my enormous false lashes. "And good luck with the sexy girls." He chewed and breathed out a great snuffle of warm air.

On the edge of the lot stood a young man I had known for years. "I hear there's been trouble," he said. "I've come to take you to dinner. The gang's waiting. And we've got a bottle of wine."

"You know," he put his arm around me in the car, "this is all not very important and what he said is not accurate."

I came to believe him.

The next day I took my new money and bought a very pretty dress and two fine hats, had my hair and nails done, then paraded around the Paramount stages. "How well you look!" everyone remarked. "Why, you're pretty!"

I met Roy Burns outside the commissary. "Well, so long," he jauntily said. "Good luck!"

"Roy," I answered levelly, "I came here from London a trained professional and with hits in a Charles Cochran show. I came in all eagerness, mad to please, adoring my uncle and believing in him; I have been flouted and cut off on every side deliberately. I go back without a foot of film shot. Figure out what I have cost all around and what you got for it and tell me if that's good business. And then figure out the utter wastage of talent that many people think first-class and ask yourself why."

He threw his arms around me. "Forgive me, I'm nervous. You don't know the Boss. I couldn't help myself. You're well out of this."

"Good-bye, Roy, I don't wonder you're nervous. Does anyone have any fun in this place?"

He shook his head. "I'm getting ulcers."

"Back to London!"

He kissed me. He did look regretful. He did get ulcers. What Cecil got was not the dance he wanted.

He also got a very bad press. I don't know about the financial returns. Claudette Colbert got big stardom.

Thereafter, Cecil was always unhappy and self-conscious about this episode. He stipulated when my first book was considered for a movie that *Cleopatra* never be referred to in any way (It hadn't been mentioned in the book). He had sincerely wanted to help me and he had truly been very rough. Much later, after my six Broadway hits, he greeted me fulsomely with, "Baby, you are now the greatest choreographer in the world."

"No," I said. "I certainly am not, but just possibly I am one of the best paid."

"Ah, baby," he said, looking at me with great spirituality, "there's more to it than that. You must think of other aspects. You can't take it with you, you know."

Before I left Hollywood I treated myself to a superb fling with a wonderful young man. I had earned it in blood. And, although no one except he and I know anything about it, I want to say in these words, which he will probably never read, that I owe him one of the very fine times in my life — unforgettable, dazzling.

CHAPTER 14

THE following summer can be looked on as convalescence. I had been badly mauled. It wasn't just the loss of opportunity and money, for had I pleased de Mille, I would have been launched in Hollywood. It was the stunning fact that at last my family, my powerful world-renowned family, had offered practical help and then thrown me away as trash. Never mind that the chance had been vouchsafed under impossible restrictions. I had been offered it and had failed. If one had to please Cecil in order to get before a camera, that was the requirement, as a trained instep and soft flexible heel are the requirements for getting into a ballet line. And surely pleasing Cecil was easier. The latter requires seven years of effort. No, there was an element of stubbornness and self-righteousness in not conforming.

Mim later asked, "Whatever made you think you could collaborate with this kind of taste?" He was my uncle who had excited me all my life and I thought I could. I believe had I been a man I would have been given a second chance. Men give men second chances, never women, except as an act of courtship. Cecil liked a show of spirit in a girl, but only as a gambit in flirtation; he liked sauciness, the devout preparation for his attention and then the taunting. That was high coquetry. One could say "no" if one was irresistibly gotten up. I've seen his daughter and my sister tease jewels out of him. But I met him eyeball to eyeball in football regalia and said like any man, "I won't budge. My soul forbids it."

My work marched on its own feet. But not very far, alas! I should have been able simply to dress better and to flirt. It was not simple. To me it was basic.

Mary Austin, the writer, had once said to me, "In all the history of art I have never heard of a man helping a woman because of the quality of her talent, not once. If they helped, they were seduced into helping the woman first and if needs must, secondly the talent. Men's talents are, of course, something else."

I let him know I was offended.

He hit back on a male level: "No sex appeal." A remark perfectly unanswerable, and given my situation, deadly. He had told me to my face, naked and in public, how he found me, one of the menfolk of my tribe, my kinsman, and the great expert in these matters. I think he was only dimly aware he tore open wounds not of his making. In any case, he was far too busy and set upon to take heed of what resulted.

I had admired Cecil. I had a lifelong crush on him. When Oscar Hammerstein read *Dance to the Piper* he said, "I don't believe you realize what a shaping influence your uncle had on you. It was as great as your father's — possibly greater. You must never underestimate it." Cecil's influence was, of course, the pull toward commercial success and the bitter sense of failure because I did not have it, and the belief that my work lay properly in the theater and not in the ballet.

Mother and Margaret were pained but their affection and admiration for Cecil were in no way dimmed. I told my father in New York what had happened. He smiled wryly

and said, "I know! Ce can be tough — particularly with
family. I've had some dealings that weren't pretty." Father
was Cecil's older brother and had been his close friend and
collaborator all through their young professional careers.

"One thing explain to me — did you yourself think the
dance was good?"

"Not very — at the end — after —"

"Never mind why. You wished to be a professional. He
treated you like one. Now you know. The pressures on that
man are overwhelming. His methods of handling these situations are not Lord Chesterfield's." Pop sighed deeply. "Still,
in the long run, it's the work that counts."

Parenthetically, I must add that Pop's kindness with actors
was a Hollywood legend, and that his patience with the
nearly-good and the stumbling eventually cost him his career.

I wanted him to champion me. He never did. In my whole
career, five men have jumped into the breach for me; Richard
Rodgers in *Oklahoma!*, Oscar Hammerstein in *Carousel* and
Allegro, Walter Kerr in *Goldilocks*, when he threw the star
off the stage for insubordination and insolence, José Ferrer
for the same reason in *Juno*, and Robert Lewis in *Quamina*.
When such things happened I felt as though the sun had
risen in the west and that it was beautiful. It was never on
any occasion dancers who were rude, it was actors. The men
of my own echelon, the writers, composers and directors, I
took on unaided. I came to be known on Broadway as a
terror, a really tough, intransigent woman.

I had overheard my sister remark to her husband, "Of
course Agnes is a neurotic girl." This struck me as the most
bizarre description possible. I, with my good, clean jump, my
exact response to rhythm, my nonsmoking, nondrinking
habits, my keen appreciation of all outdoors and fine china,

my witty conversation. I, neurotic? Impossible! What an odd, bad-tempered thing to say! It did not make me wonder a bit. I wasn't; although, come to think of it, they might be a little disturbed, and her husband's, Bernie's, reply proved it: "If your parents had only brought her up as a normal girl and put a stop to this career nonsense!" They must be mad to talk so!

It never occurred to any of us de Milles to seek help from a psychiatrist. That was not our style. There was nothing wrong with us. In time of distress, which were all other people's doings, one pulled up one's socks, one tried harder; as Mother put it, "One behaved oneself."

That summer, I went into exile, all my fires banked, and tried to find the means of believing that my work mattered, that I had a destiny. I returned to Ramon a cripple with — oh! — so much less courage.

I asked myself why I went back, why I stuck. It wasn't unselfishness — that I'm sure of — nor a suicide wish. I'm tough and I fight for happiness. Sharpe had kept saying throughout, because he knew it disturbed me deeply, that I was morbid. I think not. Simply it was, I believe, that I had been deprived very deeply and Ramon supplied a strength, a courage, an intellectual and humorous attitude and an acknowledgment of the importance of my work that I felt I must have or cease to exist as a personality. Let any artist try to live for long without recognition, even private, and see how soon the basic nerve fails. And I had to have this recognition from a man.

Also, demanding as his situation made him, he asked nothing compared to what an average husband would have exacted: "Give up your work, follow me. My work takes precedence always, and so does my will."

Ramon adored and served, a spoiling experience for me. I could accept it only from Ramon because he was apart from life, the Archangel Michael, a Visitor. In addition, it was Ramon's life I was fighting for and Ramon's character and what he meant to me.

CHAPTER 15

12 Paulton's Square
July 5, 1934

Dear Mum,
   Ramon looked up a room for me, across the square from his
house and four doors down from Mrs. Laing, who did my
Cochran publicity. It is not so nicely furnished as the one I had
before but the closet space is ample, and it is scrupulously clean.
Also, the landladies are not so genteel and therefore more willing
to do favors, and they are not so relentlessly economical as Mrs.
Daviel, given as she was to using the bread wrappings for toilet
paper. I am on the ground floor; my large window looks onto
the street and the square with its beautiful trees and it boasts a
window box. A peddler was crying this morning while I ate
breakfast.

> *A lovely lot of ro-ses!*
> *Have you got a bunch of ro-ses?*
> *All morning fine ro-ses!*

   Thousands of mourning doves hold wake in the two-hundred-
year-old oak trees.
   Mrs. Laing (who's a real darling) and Ramon have become
close friends while I've been away. She supports her husband.
He spends his energy drinking and abusing her. I had tea with

her the other day in her back garden. Husband was present in a soiled open shirt, filthy fingernails, and tobacco-stained teeth. He was, I feel, her major mistake.

During the course of the party, it struck me that she doesn't generally have enough to eat. (I took her over a cake tonight bought from my American shop as a homecoming present.) Her interesting clients practically never pay her. Shankar, for instance, gave her a rose instead of the check, explaining he had no money. The Hebrew Theater gave her £7 for a month's work. She continues merry and sends affectionate messages always to you. She's marvelous with Ramon. They drink beer together and gossip for hours.

Monday I took my first lesson. I proved to be infinitely stronger than I dared hope. Mim says I stand correctly at last and that the expression of my entire body and face is wonderfully better. I expect to make big progress this summer.

In Alice James's (sister: William and Henry) journal, which I am now reading, she speaks of the colored boy who prayed: "Lord God, make Thy servant conspicuous!" I'd like to wire this to Cecil.

You'll be interested to hear that the inside reports from Germany foretell an imminent Communist revolution.

Love always,
A.

P.S. Ramon has rented a house near Chester for the month of August and has bought a secondhand car. The Ballet Club will be closed during that month so I'm not missing lessons, and it will be nice getting out in the country. Cousin Joan may not be able to stay during the entire time but there is a female housekeeper goes with the place so, don't fret, I shall be chaperoned. The boy is really delirious with anticipation. We go up on Thursday. Ramon has had the front seat cut in half and the back of it hinged so that it lets down to form a bed for him. The Automobile Club has furnished him with a most beautifully worked-out route, complete with maps and all the towns we pass through. He lies in bed studying it. His anticipation of the trip you can imagine.

12 Paulton's Square
August 2, 1934

Dearest Mum,

Tomorrow at dawn, or literally very early, we motor north. The address will be

BRYNHYFRYD

PONTFADOG

WREXHAM

DENBIGHSHIRE

This is not a cable code. It is a Welsh address recognized by the Royal Automobile Club and the post office.

Sharpe and Ramon and I go up tomorrow. Joan follows later. I've been tooting all over London the last few days to get used to the car. It runs beautifully.

I must go to sleep now. We set off at nine and it has to be prompt. Ramon can only travel a certain length of time. So we run to schedule like a train. He's in good health and has been kept flat for two days with special food. Also, he's so happy with anticipation he ought to weather the trip nicely.

I do hope you won't feel so depressed now. Your last two letters have saddened me. Write about Judy. I miss her so.

Devoted love,
A.

Brynhyfryd
Pontfadog
Wrexham
Denbighshire
August 6, 1934

Dearest Mum,

I can hardly bear it that you're not here. The place is so exactly what you love.

Brynhyfryd, Wales

Just listen: We are on the side of a steep hill. Directly below us are fields full of cows and pigs and beyond them in a line of trees the river Ceiriog which once ran red with blood in battles between the Welsh and Normans. (The Welsh stayed put, I might add.) There's a church with a steeple and bells, and singing on Sundays, and roofs of the village showing in the trees and then precipitous mountains, again heavily wooded and very green. When you stand up and look out our windows you can only see trees, but when you lie down you can just see the top of the hills against the sky. Our hill is so steep we have to back the car up. In the early morning the hills go golden-green and the white houses set in their sides literally sparkle. To the left are high meadows checkered off with hedges and spotted with oaks, but all smooth and neat and quiet, worn still. On the right are more hills and meadows and steeples. Behind us are woods more like Merriewold than anything I've seen in England, but with great banks of moss cushioning down the slopes, ivy up the tree trunks, and the unfamiliar gleam of holly. In the open places are bracken and gorse, blackberries, and oddly enough, moss still, and the smell of the place in the heat is like a feast.

Our house is commonplace in furnishing, but possessed of tremendous charm in outlook, garden, and kitchen. The last is a marvel, with a dresser stacked with blue and white plates, a long deal table and an old fashioned oven in the side of the wall with the kettle singing on the open coals. We have tea there and I write at the table. Mrs. Humphreys, the housekeeper, being English, shows no surprise or curiosity at anything I do, so I find it possible to write for hours while she gets the meals ready around me. Next the kitchen is a scullery and behind them, her room and Mr. Humphreys', who gardens and keeps the bees and is, besides, the Pontfadog postman. My room is overhead, a grand big room with dormer windows, enormous bureaus and running water. Next to mine is Joan's room.

Along the hall and up a flight of stairs is Ramon's room — huge and with great windows; beyond his, Sharpe's, and their bathroom. Downstairs in their wing is the living room and library; both dull.

Sharpe has detached the mirror from a great wardrobe and taken it into the living room for me so I can practice there all morning. We sit on the terrace in the late afternoon after tea. Ramon reads while I sew. You can only just imagine what it's like: the mist rising, shepherds calling, river rushing, pigs squealing, hens cackling, and the clump of boots as some farmer trudges between the stone walls at our feet. Now and then a car passes down the road by the river, and twice a day a toy train bringing the mail in.

We started off at nine on Friday. Ramon had to get up at six to get ready, get through his physical routine. There is no way of locking the car and the garage men had turned the gas off so as to ensure its not being taken. I was a bit vague about how to turn it on and succeeded within ten minutes in running down the batteries, and this two hours before the garages opened. Well, I enlisted the help of some truck men, started the engine by pushing the car, kept the motor running while we loaded up, put our trust in God, and started off. On the outskirts of London, suddenly Ramon shouted, "Look, honey!" And there was the enigmatic, beckoning, limitless sign, "To the North," which we followed.

We made Kenilworth by lunch, drove into an inn for the meal, and whirled around the castle afterwards. We drove with the top down and Ramon lying flat. He showed no signs whatsoever of exhaustion. We had tea at a little place along a country road, weathered a couple of showers, and passed through Chirk into Pontfadog at sundown. Ramon, having completed the longest ride he's taken since he's been ill, was brighter than any of us at dinner. He's been up every day since, except today when he's running a small temperature. But there's color in his face for the first time since I've known him.

The drive was miraculous, through Leamington Spa, Shrewsbury, Weston-Under-Lizard, Crackly Banks, and such.

The presence of Automobile Association men all along the road removed most cause for worry. All the highways are regularly patrolled.

I must go into Oswestry now to do the marketing, and I've got to get there before the banks close.

Devoted love,
A.

Brynhyfryd
Pontfadog
August 13, 1934

Dearest Mum,

On Sunday we took our tea to the top of the hill. Monday and today we have stayed pretty well indoors because of the wind and a driving mist. I work steadily and am getting things done. But the amount of time tends to make me slow in pace, and the temptation to gossip is constant.

There's little to write about here. One day is like another except for the drives. Every other day or so we take one and my heart breaks that you're not along. Slate quarries, ruined abbeys, reedy lakes with swans sliding about, bald, bracken-topped hills noisy with wind and sheep that sound exactly like rusty swinging doors; little spiral towns glittering on the plain beneath noble eighteenth-century skies, old trees dripping and swaying like banners over timbered houses, thatched houses; haymaking with great long scythes, the sky dizzy with rooks, folks walking out on Sunday in their best black with umbrellas. Hell, this is no Baedeker! But I wish you were with us. Someday we must do this country. I'll send you pictures when they're developed. Ramon usually forgets to turn to a new film when he has exposed one.

Devotedly,
A.

It was at dusk after one of these drives that Sharpe, standing with a spanner in his hand, gave me the evilest fifteen minutes of my life. He had carried Ramon upstairs and I had settled on the terrace with a book. He returned, started to fiddle with the car, then picked up the spanner and found me. He could have killed me. I think at that moment he realized he wanted to. He didn't move. He just stood there looming and spoke. I've forgot the exact words because I could not endure to remember them. The gist was this: Get out. I was killing the boy. What I wanted from him he couldn't make out. What was there to love? He could feel nothing, he had none of the sensations of a man, and he was therefore incapable of passion. Why then did I hang around exciting him? What unnatural, ugly appetite kept me in this sickroom teasing and torturing? Was it greed for money? Could I, a young, healthy dancer not get myself a proper guy? He'd never met such a monstrous thing in the whole of his medical history. He grew specific and vile. Never mind if Ramon said he needed me. He didn't know what he needed, he'd get over it. He was doomed. It was a game for me! For him not; but Sharpe would get him back to where he had been — calm (and, of course, helpless) and somewhat contented. He'd get over it. He'd have to because he had no choice. It was his whole life and then after a while, his death. But the household was now in turmoil. Get out.

I went to my room, locked the door, and gave way to despair. The night before Ramon had said, "I'm happier than I've ever been since I was a child. Oh happier than that! I know real happiness now. I'm not afraid to die now. I've stopped being angry. Let this last for a little while — just a little."

Actually, I didn't hate Sharpe. I don't suppose he really hated me. We got on in a way. It was just the terrible, corroding jealousy that ripped through every so often, and Sharpe's abiding resentment of the fact that I was a lady, that

(ABOVE) *The top of our Welsh hill: Agnes sewing Ramon's gros-point chair set.* (BELOW) *Tea at a roadside inn: Agnes, Cousin Joan, Ramon*

I'd had an education, that there were regions Ramon and I entered he could not follow; mainly, I believe it was class resentment; he raged at being a servant. But beyond this Sharpe was fighting for his entire emotional life. He had once said to me, "When this case is over I'll never take another."

How much of this Ramon was aware of, I do not know. Sharpe thought nothing. I'm not sure. Ramon was as instinctive and subtle a human being as I've ever known.

Then Sharpe did a volte-face and decided to be my crony and my professional adviser. If Ramon could do it, why not he? And during my Welsh morning practices he took to sitting while I did my barre in the living room and commenting. He also volunteered to help count the Stravinsky *Sacre* — something that has defeated orchestra men. I suffered the last patiently, although it was both galling and distracting. It was at least something I could give without major damage.

The days went by — passing, passing. My time of opportunity and hope. A dancer's life is very short — fifteen years or so, and I had begun late and maladroitly, in an amateur, bungling way. I was ten years behind as it was, and no circumstances worked for me while I rested. I couldn't take three weeks off and let people get busy for me on the strength of my notices.

Beside the green bewitched cradle, lulling the magic boy toward death, I gnawed my heart in the night, and woke, with the white house across the hill shining like a sign in the morning, to a new day full of small events, and each day was one lost to my youth. While I stitched and read, poured tea, other people were getting the jobs, other people were getting married. And Ramon looked at me with a new world behind his eyes and said "thank you."

There was one evening on the top of our hill — we sat on

the gorse on blankets surrounded by tea things and looked out over miles of heather country burning down and away to the west country, crossed and recrossed with hedgerows and stone walls and in the middle distance every so often, as in Velvet Brueghel, was a church, its tower neat and tiny and spire-sparkling; over all was Ramon's sky — his English sky.

And suddenly a pink moon rose like a little blessing. We gasped to see it, the promise, the tenderness of it. It came from the troubadours for us. Sharpe arrived and ordered us home. The dews were falling, he said, and there was danger. But Ramon begged and Sharpe granted forty minutes more, threatening, "You'll pay for this" and "Mark my words." We didn't mark them — we looked at the enveloping sky and the deeply burning lands and the smoky gorse. The thread of evening mist closed in and the little lost moon mounted inevitably toward its brief arc. The colors pulsed and shuddered around us. The earth lay waiting.

"We have this," said Ramon.

He did pay. There was gangrene.

> Brynhyfryd
> Pontfadog
> August 18

Dearest Mum,

I find it difficult to drive myself up here. There's so much time, but I do manage an hour of technique every morning, from two or three hours of dance composition, and writing in between. I've put together two dances and am working on two more. I'll have four at the end of four weeks.

On Wednesday last we went into Oswestry and dashed home late to meet Joan at the train. I sat on the meat coming home so that my waterproof was splotched with red beef juice, very embarrassingly. I discovered this as I stepped up to the spotless and effete Joan, who marched down the station platform in natty black and white, a porter trundling Elizabeth Arden cases behind her. She grows more beautiful every time I see her. The meat, I was assured on returning to the house, had been partially cooked.

Joan is a peach. She's young and untouched, but thoughtful and sensitive to what she has not yet herself experienced. She expresses herself amusingly and has been places. She is wonderfully even-tempered to live with. She adores Ramon.

The last week has been marvelous. We've toured nearly all over North Wales. On Sunday we went to Snowdon, the highest peak south of Scotland. The country is rather like the Auvergne around Mont d'Or but better, it seemed to me, because not French. It is vigorous as our West in contour, but small, of course, and domesticated in texture. Its texture and coloring are exactly what one would ask for if one were designing a comforting land, ground to lie on, no prickles, soft, fresh grass of unmatchable greenness, water to bathe in, clear and sweet, trees to cast shade, air to refresh, sun to warm, but not to burn. Everything comforting, sustaining, delighting. A made-to-order place. The country I have been looking for all my life. Enough grass for the first time and soft and green, and enough water. The grass ran with it ceaselessly, myriads of threading rills. And every valley hummed faintly with the running and splashing. The rocks gleamed where the light caught, the foam too high and far away for sound. We were fortunate to cross the moors at sundown. The splendid gloom, the haunting excitement, due I suppose, to the vast, lurid stretches of heather and their reflected glow. The intensity and the sense of remembered tragedy I can only intimate. It beats anything of the sort I've seen.

We have eaten like lumbermen. Ramon says he has to. He expends so much daily in emotional enthusiasm. The scenery exacts so much in physical reaction that he has to eat enormous quantities frequently in order to meet its demands. At any rate he did eat like a pig. So did we all.

Last Saturday we went to sheep-dog trials — parked our car on the side of a hill among seated peasantry and watched dogs, under the guiding whistles of their shepherds, go to a far pasture, fetch three sheep, lead them through a series of gates, and finally pen them. The scene was extremely pretty. The grass gay with people, the "county" sitting in their cars, lemonade, tents, flying pennants, and rams, sheep, and plow horses washed, polished, and done up in ribbons, waiting on the sidelines to be judged. All the human participants talked Welsh. A surprisingly large number of the folk had white skin and red hair: true Celtic stock. Their voices are soft and cadenced. But the language is like sinus trouble.

I have no more news, except that I think I've caught fleas from somewhere.

This letter has grown short-story length. I'd better stop. I've already missed one boat.

Devoted love,
A.

August 20

Dearest Mum,

Yesterday was Ramon's twenty third birthday. We sent his presents in with his breakfast tray, done up in brightly colored tissue papers and ribbons. Then I worked, but during the morning I heard yells of delight when a package arrived from Fortnum and Mason's: six large crystal glasses from Joan for beer drinking. There were birthday letters and checks from Joan, the stepmother, and the father. His father wished him happy birthday and demanded to know what he meant by sending a telegram saying he had arrived safely, instead of writing (a telegram here costs one shilling, you remember). Had he come into a fortune, he asked, or was he making a large salary from his writing? Stepmother Joan wished him happy birthday and enclosed a list of the belongings in his room, which she was about to confiscate and transform into a nursery for her expected baby.

His christening silver he would want sold, she imagined, and some childhood china, but he would undoubtedly have use for six drawsheets and should she send them on? Of course, they're both psychopathic. Our Joan was appalled. She knew they were horrid, but not that vicious!

After lunch we drove to Shrewsbury to the flower show and country fair. We took the chair with us. So Ramon was wheeled around among onions the size of squashes and dahlias the size of sunflowers. The flowers were very fine, but arranged quite differently from the New York exhibits and difficult to see because of the crowds, which differed not at all from Coney Island, or Santa Monica, or Chicago, or Hampstead Heath.

The orchid exhibits were remarkable and fairly quiet, folk preferring to look at only what they might conceivably grow in their own dooryards. We struggled for a view of the circus, gave up, and made for the car. I fetched the car. Joan shopped. Sharpe went into an enormous wine shop to buy champagne — full of farmers and sheepshearers hitting it up. Ramon was left outside in the care of a policeman who, having other duties, made off up the hill and left him to the tender mercy of tipsy pedestrians, street urchins, and traffic. Oh well, we had tea at an inn beside the road, bought nine bottles of beer, wedged ourselves in with these, and drove home clanking.

We all had dinner downstairs and afterwards champagne and birthday cake with Ramon's name written in pink flourishes over the top. Mrs. Humphreys' face absolutely gleamed with gaiety. Her sister, Hester, who helps with the housework, couldn't stop giggling. But Mr. Humphreys — ah, there's a man! — leaned back in his chair, puffed at the enormous cheroot Ramon had given him, and let go in ancient Welsh songs. Most musically. Most beautifully. Most lovingly. Then we had gin all around, and absolutely teetering with tipsiness, I got up and danced as I seldom have, improvising, with form and meaning. The spectators sat in a ring and clapped. Ramon wore a wreath of nasturtiums. When I finished he said, "Cecil de Mille was wrong! Start on the beer!" Then Joan blew a fuse, put a large red flower in her mouth, and danced, her six-foot-two slender body swooping and swaying perilously over us. It seemed to all of us that she danced with extreme grace. Then, roaring and clapping, Ramon was picked up and borne to bed. Sharpe literally waltzed under his burden and had to try the door three times before he made it. And Ramon didn't help much. Singing at the top of his voice he clapped his hands behind Sharpe's neck and wagged his head until the nasturtiums showered down. Joan and I panted with laughter. How they got up the stairs in that condition or into bed, I don't know, nor do they.

Joan and I sat in bed for an hour discussing modern painting in an attempt to sober up.

A.

Brynhyfryd
Pontfadog
August 21, 1934

Dearest Mum,

You keep urging me to use the Ballet Club girls as "pawns." You forget Mim. She does not permit half an hour's rehearsal to take place unless she has fully approved of the idea. And she does not permit the choreographer to work in peace, but erupts into the practice with meddling and criticism long before the work is even defined in the creator's brain. She drives people nutty. She breaks their spirits. I have submitted two ideas to her, both of which she has rejected, preferring what Ramon calls her "charades." Ashley thought the idea of *Salome* hackneyed and I'm not going to beg to do it, though I am convinced it would be distinguished. I sent Mim to my revue (bought tickets) to see the *Virgin* ballet. She thought this pretty, but not important enough for the club. She's wrong, of course; it would be charming at the club. It's exactly right for their purposes. But I think I shall have to be more in demand outside before she listens to me. Her attitude toward me is a peculiar mixture of admiration and condescension, and I'm sure we'd fight mercilessly if we tried working together. But she'll probably come 'round some day soon. She no longer has Freddy to do her ballets and she needs new ideas and inspiration dreadfully. The tempo of the club is getting drearily steady. And Ashley has almost bankrupted the place with his last bad play.

The Thompsons may have me do some Negro dances for their new revue in September, importing girls for the purpose. It's too vague to speak of yet.

I have a hundred left and this ought to carry me well into September, when I'm hoping for the Thompson job, but in case something goes wrong, could you send me another two hundred? Or one would do. I'm being as careful as I can. I had planned to earn my lessons this summer, but Mim made that impossible. Of course, if I can get a professional engagement that pays me a salary anywhere in the world, I'll throw everything to the winds and go to it. But I'm not counting on anything like that.

Devoted love,
A.

12 Paulton's Square, London
September 1, 1934

Dearest Mum,

The enclosed heather has faded. The dark purple is bright magenta when fresh.

I'm back and more or less settled. Joan left early by train. We motored down yesterday, suffered one blowout and a couple of wrong turnings, but met with no other misadventure. The weather was fine, clear and blowy with great buoyant clouds in the sky and we made good speed. Miss Deere, my landlady, had my house beautifully clean, chrysanthemums in a vase and hot milk and toasted buns on a table in front of the gas. The box of mushrooms I sent her was a good investment. She has taken meticulous care of me all summer — polishing and whitening my shoes, mending, ironing, and washing, running errands, taking messages, all for 17/6 a week. I am constantly surprised and grateful. I can't make out whether she's impressed by my relations with picture stars, or seduced by my personality, or just naturally kind and good. She doesn't look the latter. She smells on occasion heavily of gin — so maybe it's that.

A.

12 Paulton's Square
September 12, 1934

Dearest Mum,

I've missed a mail again, I'm afraid, but I've been jumping around so fast all over southern England that I've hardly been quiet in London except when asleep or at the barre.

On Wednesday of last week we all piled down to Joan's house in Sussex. She lives in a half-timbered Elizabethan house, surrounded by most lovely gardens and orchards and overlooking the rolling Sussex meadows that stretch away to the sea about ten miles distant. The timbers of the house are painted black, inside and out. The walls are plastered white. Each room is on a different level, floored with glossy footworn planks. The fireplaces are dressed with shining brass kettles and pots, and the tables, cabinets, benches and beds are like something out of a legend. We carried Ramon's chair on the back of the car, so he was able to enter the house for the first time of his life. Joan's mother (Mrs. Farrant) is extraordinarily beautiful, possesses the poise of Aunt Constance and something of the warmth and magnetism of Geraldine Farrar, without of course, her brilliance or glamour. She was a great charmer when young and together with Ramon's mother, who was also beautiful, made local history, to the bewilderment of their ridiculous twin husbands. Ramon's share of the twins just gave up and became a hypochondriac. Joan's half began playing around and is now on his third wife. Joan's mother married a pleasant but more than accommodating Englishman who threw up his Hong Kong business to settle in the home country with her and the children and

The ballet version of Fokine's Les Sylphides *with corps de ballet of twenty-four reduced to six. Margot Fonteyn and Frederick Ashton in the center*

has never found a job since. He gardens. While we were there he rushed about picking boxes of apples and plums and sweet corn for Ramon, who had never seen or tasted corn before. It was a grand day, and it's a family you must meet. While Ramon was being put in the car, Mrs. Farrant confided in me that she had no use either for Reed *père* or his second wife, that they had not wished Ramon to live when they found out how hopeless his case was, had, in fact, rather neglected him purposely, and when he stubbornly persisted in living, had lost interest.

After we had gone they happened to phone the Farrants, were dumbfounded to hear that Ramon had been down there, and then added that they supposed he looked awful, that his hair needed cutting, etc. I'm crazy to meet them in situ. They sound like museum pieces.

The Thompsons, producers of my last dreadful revue, have been babbling about another, colored. As I was leaving their office I said, "Someday you should have me in a revue."

"Why, honey," said Jack, "we didn't know you wanted to be in one. You can be in this one. You can have anything you want, except a large salary, but carte blanche with the decor and action. We'll tell you how much time you can have and you go ahead. Come back Friday and we'll talk about it." I left the office dizzy. Of course, they don't know yet whether or not there is to be a revue. They expect to know Friday. If I do this, and I'll only do it if I get exactly what I want, you must come over for the opening.

I've seen *Cleopatra*, which got ghastly reviews. The only really moving moment was, to me, the last, the queen's dead figure. That I felt showed power and solemnity. The dances do not merit comment. Diana's, however, in her very best Cockney, is worth repeating — "An or-ghee, a proper or-ghee, a girl cleaning a bull with her feet!"

Devoted love,
A.

CHAPTER 16

12 Paulton's Square, London
September 19

Dearest Mum,

Your letter has just come telling me to come back quickly and get jobs. Now listen, doolie, I'm coming home very soon, but I do feel that a definite job here is better than the vague courtesy of the people you've been talking to. Obviously, they haven't seen my work and are not going to give me anything until they do see it; it, not me. Nobody ever gave me a chance on the strength of my offstage appearance.

Don't dare to give up time in Merriewold to sit by the New York phone. Nobody who really wants me is going to let a weekend absence interfere with plans. Take it easy. If we can pull off the schedule I have outlined I shall be very well satisfied.

Romney just informed me that the Thompsons are bankrupt, that they have been sued by any number of people for nonpayment of salaries, and that he, Romney, was offered the furniture in their office in lieu of a fifty-pound payment which they did not seem able to meet. Having seen the furniture he declined to accept it as settlement. They are foolish, untrustworthy, unreliable, and reckless — not dishonest, "not smart enough," Romney says. The chorus went on opening night in Manchester in odd shoes because the management neglected to pay the shoemakers. Many of their checks have turned out to be bad. Romney says not to put foot in rehearsal hall without a cash settlement in advance. The news somewhat dashed me.

12 Paulton's Square, London
September 26, 1934

Dearest Mum,

The Thompsons folded up just as Romney prophesied. Of course, they gave only vague and untrue reasons for not going through with plans for the new revue, never hinting for a moment that they were hard put to it to keep out of jail.

As a matter of fact, the *Virgin* ballet that I did for them has done me good service. Even Ninette de Valois, the head of the Vic Wells Company, chief English choreographer and my most bitter scorner hitherto, is reported as highly admiring of this piece.

I work very hard, a class in the morning, then rehearsals for two hours afterwards, then shopping, then tea, an enormous one, then preparing the next day's rehearsal, then dinner, and if there is nothing special on, writing while Ramon reads. Afterwards I sew and he reads aloud.

The arrangement with the Ballet Club is better than before. They take the first £10 out of the box office at every performance. I have the rest. They furnish theater, three stage rehearsals, the studio room when it is not being used and a room in which to store and renovate my costumes, circularizing and advertisements in the three leading papers for two days. I pay for the dressers, pianist, assisting artist and any extra newspaper publicity. Billy Chappell has agreed to do three dances at each performance for £5 the lot and help in the designing of new costumes, which is a real blessing, as they will be cheap, ingenious and lovely. Mrs. Laing, although I haven't yet approached her, will work for very little. I'm sure £5 or so. I haven't talked to Norman yet either. The music problem is still a delicate one. Too many people dislike Norman's playing.

It rests now with the Ministry of Labor. I can't do more until

I hear from them. In the meantime I'm rehearsing hard and will be in fine shape for New York whether or not I perform here. I expect to sail a week or so after the concerts. I should be home in time for Mag's birthday. Will she come to New York as she suggested? My God, it would be fun if we could all be together again so soon!

Ramon's stepmother was rushed to London last week, where she gave birth to her baby two months too soon. It died. As the child was the only thing in life she wanted and as she has been trying to have one for ten years she is now prostrated with grief in a nursing home.

Mag says your new apartment is grand.

I gotta rush to the school.

Devoted love,
A.

12 Paulton's Square, London
October 15, 1934

Dearest Mum,

About the recitals and my career. I don't expect the New York managers to give me work until they've seen me dance, and as I don't propose ever again in my life to give tryouts they must see me in recital, and as I know the way their minds work they must see group work if I am to expect to get group commissions from them. *But* my group has to stand comparison with the Humphrey-Weidman group and Graham's, and I can't possibly get any girls into that slick shape without six weeks rehearsing. The important thing is that my compositions be first-rate when they are seen, not that they be seen right away. I would rather wait indefinitely than spoil my chances by over-hasty preparation. So, don't try to urge me to appear before January. I'm working steadily here, and well, too. No time is being lost.

Interpolation by Ramon to my mother. Suki was the nickname used by all my contemporaries.

Chelsea

October 17, 1934

My Dear Suki,

These new dances are in my opinion going to be very great. There will be five new ones in the first recital: the *Witch Dance* (Stravinsky), the Mozart minuet, a southern American dance called, provisionally, *Lazy Dance*, the Palmgren nocturne and the Elizabethan dance — in the second recital will be added the *Dance of Death.* Agnes showed Paul Fielding and myself the two most important the other day: the *Witch Dance*, a witch's spell danced to music from Stravinsky's *Sacre du Printemps* is really magnificent. It is a great tour de force, has quite new and significant gesture, is worked up with great tension to a climax that is astounding. The minuet is a very beautiful piece of work: full of tenderness, pride, gracious power, excellent in design, full of new and extraordinarily effective steps. Both dances show an advance into the region of pure dancing as opposed to mime that is important and fortunate. They are serious, significant and deeply sincere pieces, created and executed with great artistry. Paul was as enthusiastic about them as I was. Agnes's technical improvement is terrific. She is really dancing superbly. This addition of technique to the profound maturity of her movement will make her recitals a very great success, I think. . . . Her southern dance, too, is going to be very fine; full of comedy, but comedy achieved through the medium of dancing rather than mime, for which I am glad.

That, I think, is all the news to date. Agnes is working steadily and well. She is keeping good health, except for a slight cold last weekend, which Sharpe made haste to help cure her of. Working at the Ballet Club is not altogether easy; people will wander through during her rehearsals, the children there are not very good mannered. Madame, very fussed about her own productions, is inclined to be a little inattentive; but when the time of the recitals comes she will doubtless be as helpful as she always has been. Norah Stevenson is acting as pianist during

Agnes's rehearsals, a very good pianist and an ideal person to work with, Agnes finds, because she confines her attention to the piano. She is a very nice person, too.

Fondly,
Ramon

12 Paulton's Square
November 6, 1934

Dearest Mum,

I'm distressed at having sent no personal word in the last two weeks, but when you hear how I've been kept running you'll understand. Briefly, I'll tell the history of the first performance. Diana turned to and devoted two days to serving me. Did everything. Sat in on rehearsals, coached, advised, shopped, mended, ran errands, comforted and inspired.

Every aggravation was compounded by the fact that Billy Chappell dropped out at the last moment (notifying me through the mail) and I had to train in a new boy found for me by Mim.

Wednesday came. I worked until tea time, rushed home, cleaned up, and went over to Ramon's, who had supper waiting for me in the living room in front of the fire. He was lying in bed suffering from stage fright that gave him cramps in his tummy. Naturally he did not tell me until the ordeal was over. Well, friends or no friends, the house was sold out, an audience in full dress and quick in their response.

I don't know what happened during the Mozart except that I panted from the first step as though I were strangling. They say I danced badly. I must have. I can't remember. Paul said the necklace on my throat was jumping with nerves.

Then *Stagefright*. As I ran on the stage I felt a piece of glass in my left shoe. It was not until halfway through the dance that I could work it from under my heel to the instep so that I could put my foot on the ground. Then the instep of my right shoe broke. It doesn't seem possible, but it's so. My foot crumpled every time I rose to point.

Antony said as we stood on the stage for *Branle,* "Come on now, everything that's going to happen has. Get started."

He was wrong. Everything hadn't happened. The new boy went into a funk, forgot the dance, and improvised the most appalling slapstick performance I have ever witnessed. Mind you, he had played well and straight in rehearsals. I have never been so ashamed on a stage. I did the *Hymn* in a state approaching unconsciousness.

At the end of *Hymn* there were six calls and cheers. I couldn't possibly tell you why. Diana says it's because I danced not only as well as I ever had but as well as anyone has danced. I don't know.

Then I did the Stravinsky fairly well. I'll do it better next time. It's a heller both emotionally and technically, but it's going to be my best. Ramon thinks so, and Paul and Romney. The end of the dance is a fall. I fell outside the curtain at the end. The curtain is set across the middle of the stage and is difficult to gauge. Instead of leaving me there and drawing back the curtain for me to jump up and take a bow, Antony, if you please, reached under the curtain and rolled me back.

The rest of the program went off beautifully. The new American dance, *Mountain White,* went well but this is an English audience and the real test will come in New York. I did the research and notes for this with the help of James Truslow Adams, who lives on Campden Hill nearby. The Elizabethan number will be good and now is pictorially effective. Also the old galliard and canaries which I perform in tradition are very lovely. *Nocturne* completely made over is good and my partner in it, Hugh Laing, is excellent.

The furies were not especially against me; accidents always happen. That is why we have dress rehearsals, several of them, and many assistants, dressers, stage managers, electricians, prop men. But adequate safeguards cost time and money, a great deal of money. Martha Graham, Doris

Humphrey, Marie Rambert ran all the same risks. They re-
lied on the pupils of their schools for professional help. If
these people do their jobs, the performer can keep his mind
and energy on his one proper business: performing. Today
the number of assistants would be enforced by union ruling.
Today my series of Mercury concerts would cost between
twenty and thirty thousand dollars, and foundations, private
or governmental, would probably foot the bill. There were
then no foundations; no government aid. Marie Rambert in
England, Mary Wigman in Germany, Martha Graham and
solo mavericks like myself in the United States, we built the
theaters the young, brilliant choreographers walk into today,
grumbling and complaining because they have to keep asking
for grants of fifty thousand dollars at a time.

Afterwards, people streamed up on the stage. Doris Zinkheisen
raved! And what's more went home and called up an important
manager, who is coming tomorrow. Frank Collins apparently
liked the show. He is, you remember, Cochran's right-hand man,
my birthday twin, and the chief casting director and adviser for
C.B. Anthony Asquith was there, bought his seat. Oxford comes
tomorrow.

Besides the flowers I've listed I received an exquisite bunch
of violets from Muriel Stuart (ex-Pavlova company, my teacher
in Hollywood this spring) and roses and lilies from Ramon. I
went to lunch with Romney on Sunday. He and Blanche Yurka
worked over my makeup. He's been wonderfully kind, brought
three people last time and three this and has mailed out quantities
of notices.

I took in £11 as my share of the box office last week. I may
be able to pay for my costumes. Which, by the way, are damned
lovely. Andrée Howard designed and helped make the very
spectacular Elizabethan dress all covered with "Ye Tudory
Roses," and Margaret Watts dyed and made an extraordinary

garment for the Stravinsky *Witch Dance*, which she claimed made me "look as though I had been pulled through a hedge backwards." These are the first dresses I've had designers' help on, but I'm going to continue to have help. It is help. I'm a damned good designer but I don't know everything. I have no *fantaisie*.

It's been a terrific job and one day last week, I was so tired Liza made me lie down on her couch at the theater and poured brandy into me. The recitals have been a success, but it's been constant work. Ashley and Mim do nothing whatever and no one has offered to give me a party or drum up trade in any way. And because I had to dance when I was unwell, I was nearly floored for several days after. But on the whole, I am better than I've ever been after recitals, and I only tell you so's you won't think I've been callous in not writing.

Liza sends love — and by the way, there's a girl has proved herself a most loyal and full-hearted friend.

My love,
A.

12 Paulton's Square
November 16, 1934

Dearest Mum,

Just a line before the mail goes.

The third recital was jam-packed. We could have sold the house three times over. Next week is nearly sold-out already. The folks all bought seats at the box office for future shows. Arthur Bliss came around in the intermission and raved about the Stravinsky, saying to all and sundry that he thought it was better than the Diaghilev *Sacre*. So I feel fine. He thinks it shows great advance in my work.

Mim's attitude gets slightly better towards me as my success continues. Ashley beams, of course; he's found a golden-egg-layer. As for me, I adore Liza and let it go at that.

Ramon is in fine health, comes everytime, sends me bouquets, and is a great help. His parents came and were dumbfounded.

First, that I was good, and second, that he was surrounded by so many gay and glamprous people. They've been considerably more gracious to him lately. Lady Oxford's presence impressed the father no end. And speaking of that one — she said to Mim — I'll tell it this way: Mim said to her, "Well, how do you like it?" "I don't," she answered. "For instance, the Arabian one, what does it mean?"

"Why," said Mim, "I think it gives a good impression of an Oriental bazaar. And how do you like the *Hymn?*"

"It's too like a bazaar," said Oxford vaguely. "That is," noticing Mim's surprise, "a curate's daughter at a bazaar."

To someone else she said, "The *Hymn* used to be good when she danced it in a long, black-velvet gown. Since she's changed her costume, it's no longer attractive." I've never changed the costume from the cream gauze for one single performance — Do you remember she advised me always when dancing Bach to wear black? — This was at the lunch she gave at which she ate nothing — her regular proceeding, I'm told, particularly if she has to manage a large and/or dull party. Once she started off a party in which she was not at all interested, saw that the guests were under way, and retired to her own apartments, where she had a card party all set up. The next day an officious climber met her somewhere and rushed on her saying, "Oh, Lady Oxford, I was at your party last night!"

"Were you?" said Margot. "Thank God, I wasn't!"

Apropos of Oxford: Arnold Haskell says that she told him how much she knew about dancing, adding, "After seeing Pavlova's *Swan* I gave her one or two pointers. And, do you know, she resented it! She was never the same to me." You see, she's nuts. Senile and scattered. She accepted press tickets, she always does, but this time hasn't written me up. Perhaps it's just as well.

I must quit.

Love and love,
A.

P.S. The Check for £ 10 has come.

Rehearsal, Jardin aux Lilas (Tudor). Left to right: Elizabeth Schooling, Frank Staff, Peggy Van Praagh, Maude Lloyd (back turned), Hugh Stevenson (designer), Hugh Laing, Ann Gee

Jardin aux Lilas (*Tudor*) *with
the original Hugh Stevenson
decor on the Mercury stage:
Antony Tudor, Maude Lloyd,
Hugh Laing, Ann Gee,
Elizabeth Schooling (Photo by
Dunbar)*

12 Paulton's Square
November 27, 1934

Dearest Mum,

I'm in a sweat to catch the *Berengaria*. I'll do the best I can. The recital (4th) last week on Nov. 21st was the best I've ever given. I danced better than I ever have before: this is unanimous opinion. "Even the *Gigue*," said Paul. The house was not sold out; a dense fog having been predicted in black letters all over the front pages, people were chary about risking an all-night stranding at Notting Hill Gate; so they stayed home. But the small audience was warm, clapped me on the curtain rise, something they've not been doing, and so heartened me that I stepped out and danced brilliantly. Madame led the cheers at the end of the *Dance of Death* and came backstage to throw her arms around me and say such things as she's never said before. Things like: "You've begun to find new movement; a really important way of moving. The new costume" — Maggie Watts — "is lovely too, and most effective in motion."

I'm well, extraordinarily well, and happy. I must arrange things in future so that I can dance once a week in surroundings that are sympathetic and helpful. I feel alive for the first time in about six years.

But I'm looking forward to New York. I don't think I'll be ill again. And if things don't turn out, I'll just damn well not bother to force them. Now that all my young men are getting married, the personal problems are becoming simpler, and as for my career, I'm starting to do grown-up work and if no one there likes it, I can always come back to where they do.

Plan something cheery for Christmas.

And would you make inquiries through Lincoln Kirstein about what classes I can take at the Balanchine School? I don't want to lose a day, if I can help.

Can you send me some money? Would two hundred do you in? I don't think I'll need it, but I've got to have a margin. I've

paid for eight costumes and a season's lessons. I'm living as
cheaply as ever I can.

Is there any chance of Mag's getting on after Christmas?

Devotedly,

A.

This parting was going to be for months, but Ramon said
he'd follow me — how? He would; obviously he did not
wish to hold up my work. If New York did not prove fruit-
ful, I was going to push on to Hollywood, where Margaret
and her family were back again. Having spent all their savings on the farm in Goshen they found themselves suddenly
without funds, so Bernie was busy once more at Metro-
Goldwyn-Mayer in order to pay for the largest barn in
Orange County, New York. One should not go to Hollywood
and look around for work; one should be sent for. I knew this,
but there was no choice. Very well, Ramon would go to
Hollywood — how? Why, quite simply on a fruit boat
through the West Indies and the canal and up the Mexican
coast. His eyes glistened.

"Is this possible?" I asked Sharpe.

"God knows," he replied. "When he makes up his mind,
no one can change it."

Ramon had a nightmare at this time; a very small Siamese
gentleman was trying politely to catch him and put him in a
small square box. Ramon knew that ultimate escape was impossible. He was doomed. Ramon said the horror of that tiny
box and the Oriental's persistence caused him to wake sweating. This dream recurred.

So I was going away and Ramon would join me in America, and then I supposed we would come back together. . . .

But then something happened.

CHAPTER 17

At my last two London concerts, red roses, great bunches of them, came across the footlights, and not this time from Ramon. The cards were signed by someone unknown to me — Edgar Wind, a German name. The cards were ardent and disturbing. I was on the point of departure and wished to leave behind no further complications — so I did not reply. But the gentleman contrived a meeting.

A meeting at his cousin's house, Belle Moskowitz's daughter. I was asked for lunch unsuspecting. And there he was, the young professor I had met months before at the Franklins' lunch party, the one who was moving the Warburg Institute from Hamburg to London. He was very tall, quite large, black and white as a penguin, with a brilliant smile and twinkling glasses; a presence.

"Forgive me for being a pig," I said. "I should have thanked you." And he started laughing. He was compelling. We left together.

I remember laughing on the bus top passing the Albert Memorial and his comments on that. (Which, if I recall, he didn't altogether dislike.) We chattered in high excitement. "What exactly are you?" I finally asked.

"A philosopher."

"What's that?"

"Nobody really knows."

He arranged not to have anything to do for three days. He came to ballet class and saw me do my triumphant thirty-two *fouettés*, which impressed and amused him (Ramon never had, of course). Mim was most theatrically helpful that day; she sensed romance and showed me off. We went to the Sadler's Wells Ballet. We went to the Queen's Hall.

We went to the National Gallery and he spoke of each painter as of a personal acquaintance, but of Michelangelo and Hogarth as intimates. In fact, after half an hour I began to wonder exactly what century we were in at the moment. His own living friends of this century were Sir Kenneth Clark, Jacques Maritain, Erwin Panofsky and a slew of Germans that I wasn't to hear about for several years, but who all made their mark on the times. Dr. Wind seemed to know, with lively understanding and zest, and encyclopedic memory, everybody dead or alive, and everything they did or had done. I was bemused. I had never met anyone like this before.

To his great amusement, I changed my mud boots into high-heeled shoes in the Elgin Room of the British Museum and he suddenly shifted his remarks from the front of the Parthenon to my feet, and then to my dances. And he talked with respect and incisive evaluation.

For the first time in my life a man of position, of stature, of achievement, was courting me, was offering me support and guidance. Subsequently, I have heard him classified by Rudolf Wittkower, his colleague, the head of art history at Columbia University, as the one true genius of his acquaintance. A man who needed no help, who stood on his own, a man of power was courting me.

I asked him about Germany. He had handed in his resignation to the University of Hamburg on the day the first student had been disqualified on grounds of race. He and his colleagues had salvaged the only complete cultural institution from Hitler. It was now located and functioning in Thames House. Many of his friends and intimates had been left behind. Beyond this he would not speak. He understood European politics and prayed that some nation, France or Great Britain, would call Hitler's bluff. It was a bluff, he said. The longer the delay, the worse the reckoning. He was very emphatic about this. The taking over of the Ruhr had been the time for immediate action. He asked me, "Have you read *Mein Kampf?*" Of course, I hadn't. Wind knew the philosophers and writers who had influenced Hitler and he was alarmed.

He spoke four living languages interchangeably, and two dead ones, and he played the piano with Schnabel's pupils. All this came out as we chatted. He talked very little of his personal life. He talked about me.

And he was fun.

I told him about Ramon. But I had such a need for hope, I simply fell head over heels in love. I can truthfully say I was infatuated. And this he recognized.

The evening I left, he brought a cab to my lodgings and waited with the bags outside Ramon's flat. Ramon was prostrated at the thought of a six-months separation and all the uncertainties ahead. I came back downstairs shaking.

"But," said my suitor, "how long has he been ill? Surely, he is now reconciled."

"As he grows older," I murmured choking, "he realizes what he has lost — I don't know what to do."

There are many things he could have said. What he did say was, "We'll find a doctor — I'll look after him while you're gone. I'll do all I can for him."

Then he took me in his arms and kissed me. It had been a long time since an able man had held me in his arms. This kiss held peace and promise — "I shall love you, Agchen," he said, "and you will love me — be patient."

So I went to New York.

It was good getting home. Outside the windows was the perpetual roar that drives foreigners crazy, but spells to a born New Yorker the familial blood-beat. Energy was gathering all night; all night, adventure was happening and preparing to happen, and the next day would be ripe with excitement, and confrontation.

Mother's apartment was warm, every corner of it; the water ran hot; the phone was free and at bedside; breakfast was brought with love; and the apartment bustled with business and news and concern, private and public, and with energy and warmth. Everyone was up and marching and everyone was interested. And outside, the city hummed like a dynamo building up nine-million-lives'-worth of intention. It wouldn't be quiet — it continued day and night. Everything continued with energy.

The concert in New York was put together with spit and string. We had no money — Mary Hunter managed the business and the stage. Alden Stevens helped with publicity — everyone addressed notices, including Muriel Stuart.

I had to get new partners, one of whom was Robert Lewis, the director. There was no money, but we proceeded anyhow.

Over the footlights came a sheaf of flowers signed by twenty London dancers and choreographers. The concert was all right, but nothing came of it — no business offers, so I pressed on to Hollywood.

In Hollywood the same effort was repeated; I stayed with

Margaret, two concerts sold out, fine press, praise at parties. We did not do too badly. We got the theater for $75 a night, and as the crew was nonunion the nightly house expenses ran about $125. The lighting rehearsal cost $15.

You'd think somehow, someone would find something for me to do — but no. This was the era of Busby Berkeley, Fanchon and Marco, Albertina Rasch and their spectacular musicals. People thought only in terms of fifty revolving pianos on spiral staircases, or lines of girls made to look like threshing machines, or naked girls swimming in patterns like starfish.

At last, there came an offer from the Hollywood Bowl, a single night's performance at a fee of $2,000. I'd never had such money, but with it I had to organize and costume a company of about sixty. The Bowl was very large, seating about twenty thousand. I suspected fine pantomime wouldn't do. Indeed, after the fortieth row, one could hardly tell man from woman.

I had about thirty dancers. They numbered among them Lester Horton's pupils, Bella Lewitzky, and Mary Meyer and also Donald Sadler from Carmalita Maracci. Warren Leonard was once again my partner and assistant. The dancers were paid $15 each for a month's work, which was considerably more than they were used to getting. (Martha Graham did not pay her girls for years. No rehearsals — and they could last for six months — were ever paid for by anyone. The great body of dances, technique and choreographic achievement built up in the second quarter of this century was voluntary, unrecompensed, an act of dedication. It was one of the creative acts of the time, and those portions we have been able to preserve prove the statement. Very few have been preserved. Of that extraordinary prewar period hardly any films exist. None of the young Graham or Humphrey and strangely enough, none of the young de Mille, although family connections might have suggested otherwise. Every Hollywood producer was exposing yards of footage on his dogs and his tennis and his children. We dancers were simply not valued at all by those in the business. What would films of the young Wigman or Graham, or for that matter, Duncan, be worth now? Where were the equivalents of our record companies? Where are they today? Where, for God's sake, were our museums and libraries?)

The Bowl rehearsals in midday sun were punishing. I wore what I always wore, my black English woolen tights, a black wool bathing suit and a black sweater, ends crossed and tied at my waist (the standard European ballet-practice clothes), a black Czechoslovakian handkerchief tied over my hair, on top of all a broad-brimmed black straw hat for the glare, and, Bella insists, white cotton gloves. I was mortally afraid of sunburn. The gloves made a strong impression on the dancers. I did more running through the audience to inspect angles and site lines (four or five acres of seats) than dancing and twice I nearly had heatstroke. When the sun had turned, the musicians came back to their sheltered acoustical shell and complained of the annoyance of having to move a bowing arm before the afternoon really cooled.

The stage was huge, a two-hundred-foot proscenium, so different from the Mercury. The dancers would have to be bold, plain, large and panoramic without, I hoped, being vulgar or trite. I learned a lot in those hot afternoons. There were about thirty dancers, men and women, for the *Harvest Reel*, an expansion of my solo, which was built of accumulating rhythms and windlike rushes, and ten in my *Dance of Excitement*, the finale of Gershwin's "Piano Concerto in F," and sixty performers in the Czech *May Festival* to the music of Smetana. My original thirty dancers were augmented by members of one of the Czech ethnic organizations of Los Angeles who brought their own native dress, thank God. Mother hunted them up and obtained the original lyrics from *The Bartered Bride* in the public library and copied out by hand about thirty vocal parts *in Czech* for them to study. So that at the climax of the May rites, after the burning of the old Maypole, the new pole, decorated with Czech colors, would be borne on the shoulders of old men and women and led by small children, all singing at the top of their voices in native tongue. The dancers' costumes were designed by Robert Tyler Lee and made as a work project by the students of UCLA. They were hand-dyed cotton and decorated most ingeniously with yarn and tinsel and buttons from Woolworth's. The wreaths and headdresses were all of colored paper. They were going to be perfectly lovely and they would cost between fifteen and twenty dollars each. It was a stylish and very pretty spectacle.

The music was supplied by the Los Angeles Philharmonic with their number-three conductor, who said he would officiate only at the music interludes. He would hand over his baton to the concert master whenever the ballet took stage. This is usual and reflected the prevalent attitude of musicians toward all dancing. The concert master would prove, I believed, not a whit worse than the conductor.

All the time I kept writing to Edgar. *The Dance Observer* had spoken of me disparagingly as "an entertainer." "They don't respect me," I wailed.

He promptly replied. "Get on your knees and thank God for the epithet; it also applies to Mozart, Verdi and Shakespeare, not to mention all great performers. These critics are stuffy pedants. You just go on being entertaining and see who lasts longest."

"I don't have any faith in myself," I wrote in my Uriah Heep manner.

"Neither did Cézanne," he rejoined, "if that's any comfort to you. And why don't you?"

"Well, I really don't, but anyway John Martin of the *New York Times* says he always gets a lump in his throat when I do my American pieces."

"The little lump of sugar in John Martin's throat makes me impatient. You're better than that, don't rely on nationalism or nostalgia. You just do the work clean."

I signed off one fourteen-page epistle with "love or our temporary equivalent." He wrote by return post four words, "There is no equivalent."

I would not let him take our relationship as an established fact. He said he truly loved me. But I distrusted the declaration. It had been made too quickly. I'd been mistaken before. Did I love him? I'd seen him four times. His impetuousness disquieted me. It also, of course, excited me.

He said he would wait, that he knew he was in love and would wait. But could I leave a passionate chanticleer uncoupled for so long? He was more than attractive. Men, I had been assured by everyone, were not constant, could not be. Any man that proved to be was in some way crippled. But the letters kept coming, reassuring, intense, loyal, sympathetic, and above all hopeful.

And, what a lovely thing hope was. I'd almost forgotten. My headaches ceased for the first time in my life. And my skin cleared to the dazzling complexion my sister was known for, the skin my mother had bequeathed us. Everyone took notice. "What's happened?" they said.

And then, finally at last, Ramon embarked, as he had promised, on a fruit boat. Edgar cabled they were safely en route. They were fogbound in the Channel and had two bad nights of cold and mist rolling in place while the foghorns wailed. The upshot of that was not pure ennui. The upshot was a spot of gangrene (as Sharpe made haste to tell me on their arrival). But he rallied. On, on down through the big waters toward new skies, new air, new trees, new life, a sun he'd never seen, winds he'd never felt, voices he'd never heard, and space, the space of the swimming earth. Every breath he drew was new to his lungs, fresh living, fresh trying.

The boat was Dutch and small, the cabin cramped, but the mate and skipper were old hands, the sailors jolly. There were two or three girls aboard of casual nationality and indeterminate morals whom Sharpe found reassuring. And each day the winds blew from the other side of the world.

Ramon grew brown in the new light — he had stepped into a Maugham story. The sailors talked to him as best they could. He learned how the ship ran. His news was no longer just the cat and Ethel's buns. The elements were now his daily concern.

He stopped at the Virgin Islands and Kingston, Jamaica, and Curaçao, and while he could not disembark with the other passengers, he lay on the deck in the golden day and watched the banana boys hauling up their loads and heard their shouting and singing and laughing and talked to them. And in the canal he lay watching the pageant of palm barriers sliding by, so long and so propitiously, like a preparation in a musical piece. And then he was in the Pacific.

I'd rented a little house for him, entirely decorated in Mexican style, which had a truly charming patio with a well, potted geraniums, ollas, strung peppers; and I'd prepared the car. We were all waiting — all my friends who knew him but had never seen him, were waiting. This was his time.

My family was waiting. This was a kind of solstice in my life, too.

The day Ramon's boat docked in San Pedro, I drove his car the fifty miles to pick him up, but he was not let off the ship. He had to go through quarantine and special legal ceremonies, nor could I even wave to him on deck. Sharpe shouted from above that he was keeping him in bed against the next day's exercises. The next day I had to rehearse. We were only given certain hours on the open stage and my presence was obligatory. So Mother and Margaret drove the big touring car down again. It was a secondhand model with one-half of the front seat cut away to take a stretcher. The heavy oak chair would be lashed to the back spare tire.

They spent the day waiting in immigration chambers until finally Ramon, white under his new tropical tan, was rolled in, crooked as a cricket and crouching under the American flag. He swore not to contribute to the overthrow of the United States government by force, nor compass the death of the President, nor bear arms against the citizens. Mother and Margaret swore most solemnly that they would undertake not to let him become an indigent charge to the State of California. They signed papers to this effect and produced bank balances to bolster their pledge. Then he was released and loaded into his stretcher and Mag drove the four of them into the Promised Land, through fifty miles of gas stations, California cemeteries, vegetable markets, real estate offices, junky restaurants and cardboard dives under the web of electric wires that crossed out as though erasing the line of great blue hills that stood for all we loved and hoped for, that were so much farther away than they seemed, that were the highest hills Ramon had ever beheld, that meant America.

They took him to his little new house, bright and jolly and pert with Mexican ollas and painted furniture. He was

Margaret de Mille Fineman
(Photo by Clarence Bull)

put to bed laughing with happiness under a handwoven magenta Mexican blanket.

And when I arrived frantic from rehearsal we had dinner in Mexican earthenware and drank tequila to the new joy and the happy adventure unfolding ahead.

Ramon was being born again.

The Bowl concert sold very well. It was a full audience, eighteen thousand people, and we danced very well. I danced the *Harvest Reel,* I think, extraordinarily well, but since we had no stage managers and no telephone communication with the electrician, the lights were tragically turned down below visibility. And so, the first ballet was simply not seen. The Smetana — *May Festival* — was really very lovely.

The press was nasty, just that — taking delight in the failure of a de Mille. There were no picture offers, which was the object behind all these exercises. It was a bad blow.

But Ramon would not let me mope.

Now came the fun. He spent long hours in his enchanting patio in the sun and in the fringed shade of his palm shelter writing his stories, reading to me, playing records. The mocking birds flew around, neighboring cats visited, bees banged around in the hollyhocks, the cicadas whined in the drying grass outside his fence. At night there were lanterns and candles in tin holders and great moths and again mockingbirds, which would not stop for the dark. Friends gathered. E. E. Cummings (whom Ramon had worshiped for years) and Marian Morehouse, Elliot Morgan (whom Ramon had known in Oxford and who introduced us), my buddies David Hertz, the playwright, and his wife, Michael. There were dancers — Mary Meyer, Bella Lewitzky, Carmalita Maracci, my partner, Warren Leonard. There were picnics and drives through the foothills and to the beach and trips to the Hollywood Bowl, and on occasion, because he was this summer brown and strong, we visited the San Fernando Mission and wheeled through the eighteenth-century chapel and into the cloisters. We visited the Los Angeles Mission and dined in Olivera Street by candlelight; we shopped in Chinatown (and I ordered Chinese silk pajamas for Ramon, black, lacquer red and mandarin blue. I could afford three because he needed no trousers).

Ramon went to parties with me. This was the era of the great sedate and gorgeous Beverly Hills parties; not wild and drunken and forbidden as in my youth, nor hysterical café society, as later, but social grace newly discovered and served up without restraint, with harlequin dash. The three most enterprising hostesses were Tai Lackman, Ouida Rathbone, and Gladys Robinson. I never knew the first, but her faults and failures were recounted promptly by the other two. They kept a kind of tally on who got the best guests. The weather, being summer, was always good and it was before smog, so the festivities were not only in great rooms but spread over garden lawns, under bosky shades and beside greenly lit pools.

Edward G. Robinson was a Rumanian and one of the finest actors of his time. He made a fortune (*Little Caesar*) and he chose to spend it with old-world elegance. He was the first to collect pictures. Not the first on the coast — there was, of course, the Huntington Collection, which included *The Blue Boy* and *Pinky* by Gainsborough and *Mrs. Siddons as the Tragic Muse* by Reynolds, and there was the unmatched Arnheim collection of moderns. But Robinson was the first in the movie colony and with the advice of the family art curator he laid down several Monets, a Cézanne, two or three Renoirs, a delicious Degas pastel, the Degas bronze with the real tutu; also quite a few of the adviser's own works at a disproportionate cost. These, however, can be forgiven in the

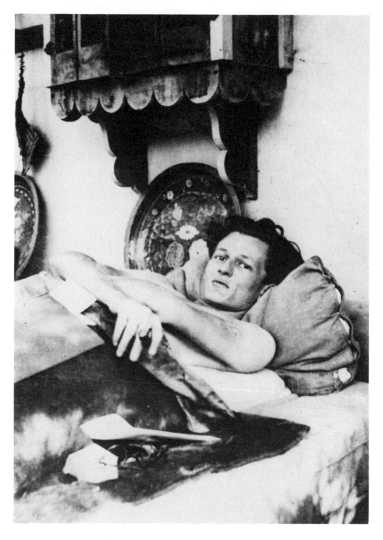

Ramon in his Mexican patio, 1935

general excellence of the rest. They were displayed in a jolly room full of sunlight, flowers, chintz and good, shiny Sheraton, and they made a very happy background to the wonderful parties which wife Gladys threw with dazzling éclat. Doll-like, bouncing and bonny, she took hold of the guests and the menus and the service with masterly energy. I never saw the like again until I went to the White House. She made a superb coup in obtaining Stravinsky for his West Coast debut. Many of the guests had never heard his name before, but they certainly had by the time the invitations went out. She obtained the services of first chairmen of the Los Angeles Philharmonic for quartets and such. "Just think," said Eddie Robinson beaming, "they haven't even practiced together. How professional!" She obtained Iturbi to play for hours and hours.

The parties often began with lunch under umbrellas on the lawn and progressed through all sorts of entertainment to supper, with music, among the Renoirs. Their son, Manny (aged six) would be brought down to sit playing chopsticks at the piano with Iturbi or Godowsky, while all the actresses and producers' wives gasped over his being able to use ten fingers at once. Eddie played poker stolidly in the rumpus room. Gladys never sat down, but watched over the least need of the least important guest.

Outside, by the door lintel, hung the mezuzah.

Into this strenuous and competitive relaxation wheeled Ramon and was engorged like a minnow in a tank of Japanese goldfish. He was obviously not a moving-picture power, but he was, as Kirk Askew had remarked, "pretty damned theatric," and he held his own in any conversation.

When Sharpe arrived late in the evening to pick him up, Gladys locked her arm in the nurse's and led him in to supper, waiting on him herself and introducing him all around.

*Edward G. Robinson and Agnes de Mille in front of one of his
Degas paintings.*

And was that something to tell the folks on the King's Road!

Ramon went to parties at my sister's which were smaller and quieter, but still fun. Mag and her husband Bernie rented a palazzo on Belagio Road in Bel Air, absolutely opulent, with rolling lawns adjoining the greens of the Bel Air golf course. (Mother used to run barefooted over the grass every night because she liked dew and then naughtily over the sand traps because she liked to leave footprints to stagger curiosity — size one. The green keepers could never guess what child was running wild in the night.)

Ramon came several times to Mag's parties. Sharpe would bring him but was not asked in and he grew very surly.

Mag seemed to be living in fine style, but actually it was a false front. Bernie was undergoing the ghastly experience of waiting for a renewal of contract and each day they watched for invitations as sure clues. Several mornings after a big bash I found my sister weeping over the bills and over the lack of important calls. Everyone knew out there weeks before an official word was spoken and friends shunned friends.

I was of no importance — no one's friend. I was asked very kindly as Margaret's sister and I sat in a corner and watched. Naturally no one spoke to me (except Gladys Robinson and Ouida Rathbone), but this did not disturb me at all. I saw Dolores del Rio bending over Louis Mayer, her rubies and diamonds falling away from her beautiful bosom. I saw every man in the room circling and circling about my old school-mate, Edith Mayer Goetz.

Cecil de Mille, who was still a monarch in that land, remained absolutely aloof in royal isolation from all these goings-on. He entertained, but not such as these. He entertained political and business figures; he was never a guest; he was a host. I was always close to Aunt Constance, and Cecil and I were cordial when our paths crossed, but that was seldom. My father was quite out of the business, and writing.

But I went to all the parties I could and listened and stared.

It was all most extraordinary. They were functioning with top energy the whole time and preening in the excitement. They were all terrified. I don't suppose since Versailles there's been anything else quite as focused, as dangerous, and as powerful. Mag and Bernie were caught in the undertow and being sucked away.

I was a pauper. I lived in my sister's house and ate at her table. I wore her clothes. I used the governess's car.

Michael Hertz called up one day and asked to borrow ten dollars, in order, she said, to eat. I did not have ten dollars. I couldn't ask my sister for this. I couldn't ask Mother. Mother was drained even of petty cash — I got it from Ramon. Sharpe was resentful.

Sharpe was getting more and more restive. He had to go home, he said. It was all very well for Ramon to be having this fling, but it was pretty poor pickings for Sharpe. I still called him "Sharpe." He didn't like this. Everyone else addressed him on his command as "Mr. Sharpe." He couldn't get a single girl to go to bed with him (I secretly cheered my countrywomen). Why didn't he go to a brothel, I asked? No, Ramon explained, he was too proud. He'd never stooped that low. Ramon had to recognize his misery and go home, where Sharpe could easily find girls — never mind that this was the first gaiety in Ramon's life.

We cajoled and temporized, not just yet — not just yet. Please!

At one of Mag's parties Ramon met Dr. Sam Herschfeld — a surgeon of whom another doctor remarked, "His hands cutting were like a lace-maker's," but as someone else added,

"Great surgery is knowing not only how to operate, but when to operate." Herschfeld couldn't wait. He just loved to cut. He was remarkable in other ways, too, it seems. For him the Ziegfeld Follies Beauty, Justine Johnston, left her producer husband, Walter Wanger, and became a laboratory researcher, achieving in this new field great professional renown.

Herschfeld proclaimed himself absolutely fascinated with Ramon's personality and Ramon's symptoms. "They all contradict each other," Herschfeld said. "If he had multiple sclerosis as he claims, he'd be fat, not rail thin. He's been wrongly diagnosed. If we got him in a hospital I'll lay my reputation we'll find something unprecedented and unrecognized. And there's a possibility we'll be able to rectify it, or at least better it. I'll give my services and so will every doctor I call in."

I told Sharpe. Sharpe was grim. "Does he think all the diagnosticians in England are fools? His father, I'll say this for him, had in every good man available. If they get the boy all stirred up again, I'll kill them. We've been through this too often. The agony of disappointment is unbearable. He must not be asked to live through that again."

But Ramon was eager. Ramon would dare anything.

As I kissed him good-night in the Good Samaritan Hospital he whispered, "Ag, I've begun to hope again. I'd forgot how it felt. I'd almost forgot."

Four of the greatest specialists in Los Angeles were called in, among them Dr. Ellis Jones, orthopedist. Ramon was there two days and then home. When I rushed to Sharpe for news he simply shook his head with tight lips and shut his bedroom door in my face.

Ramon was subdued but cheerful — "Oh, something will

come of this — you'll see! Let's have tea in the patio tomorrow. I'll get Sharpe to carry me out."

Dr. Herschfeld was suddenly unavailable for consultation except briefly on the phone. "It looks rather bad," he said. "That's not a diagnosis," I replied. "I could have said that myself."

"You go talk to Ellis Jones."

I'd known Ellis Jones since I was a child. He'd examined my sister's fallen arches and recommended ballet training, hence my career. He kissed me as I met him at his office door.

"Hopeless," he said, "absolutely hopeless. The English diagnosis was correct. It's not progressive, but the condition is dangerous, in a daily way."

"Why then did Herschfeld hold out such promises?"

"When I heard Herschfeld was in the picture I was appalled. He's a showoff. He's not responsible. I came to the consultation because of you, not because of him. The boy cannot be cured. He will have to make a life entirely of his intellect."

"This is a bitter prospect for a boy of twenty-three. He's never had any life."

"Look at Steinmetz," said Dr. Jones. "Look what he did with his life, a hopeless cripple."

"But how can I tell him? He's so young."

"Agnes dear — I'm a busy man. I have people waiting to see me professionally — you'll have to go now." On the way to the door he picked up a photograph. "These are my boys — they're very gifted, eighteen and nineteen. Handsome, aren't they?"

Ramon was given the medical conclusions and Ramon was permitted to read them. The papers contained such phrases as "ridiculous spinal curvature," which is not medical and not helpful.

CHAPTER 18

Four days later Ramon decided we'd better make a tour of California.

So we did Ojai the first night, then Santa Clara, Fresno, Monterey, the Redwoods of Muir Park — Sharpe growing angrier and more vicious all the time. "You're killing him," he said to me plainly. "He can't live through this. You'll answer for his life."

I had never been in the Redwoods before. They are just as John Muir describes them. I sat on the porch of our little cabin and noticed the wild purple foxglove (so rare a sight to a southern Californian!) standing in the light shafts between the gigantic red trunks, the deer, an antlered stag tiptoeing through the ferns, the doves circling through moted columns. Sharpe had not spoken to me for forty-eight hours, and there we were locked into the touring car as into an iron lung.

"Clothed in the armor of the Lord," said Mother, "you can't be touched if you don't intend to be." "I've brought you low," said Ramon. "Oh, my darling, just let me have this month."

And Sharpe did not speak to me for three days. When exasperation reached crisis, he tried to make love to me, and swore bitterly and brutally that I was the most unnatural girl he'd ever met in all his medical experience for rebuffing his attentions. None of this could I speak of to any living soul.

If there'd been a doctor in charge, or in consultation, but after the Good Samaritan episode, Sharpe spat on all American doctors. He wouldn't let one near.

"Ramon, get Sharpe to train a substitute nurse," I begged.

Sharpe, however, wished to remain Ramon's total claim on life.

I was due now to go to Steamboat Springs in Colorado to do my very first teaching at the Perry-Mansfield Camp. This was an extraordinary summer camp run by Charlotte Perry and Portia Mansfield to train girls in the performing arts. It combined camping, horseback riding, barn-dancing, local sightseeing, hearty food and the arts. And I do not know its equal. I had never taught. Not one single hour. I was fairly nervous about this.

Back in Fresno — the two travelers put me on a train for Colorado and I immediately fell asleep sitting bolt upright. I asked Ramon not to follow too soon, but he did, because he knew, I'm sure of it, that he simply had not time to spare.

Sharpe drove him alone across the desert and into the Colorado Rockies. Sharpe did all the nursing and all the driving alone, lifting Ramon's dead weight into the stretcher, strapping the great chair to the back of the car, and if there was a puncture (and a couple of tires blew in the heat), unstrapping the chair and toiling on the road in the dreadful sun — sweat making his hands slip. Nightfall meant the long, long medical preparation for bed, morning a repeat, and then the lifting and lugging and driving. But they arrived, Ramon with cameraloads of pictures, absolutely beaming with excitement.

I had barely got my breath. This was the first teaching I had ever done and I had to prepare carefully. Every morning

I did my teaching — every afternoon I made up the next day's work. It was as creative an activity for me as composing a dance — every single exercise was brand-new. Never mind all that. Ramon arrived.

Sharpe put him to bed for two days and stretched out under the aspen trees himself. One glance at the bevies of teen-age girls in their Colorado dungarees made him feel it had perhaps been worthwhile. They were very young. They were very pretty. Unfortunately for Sharpe, they were quite pure and totally chaperoned. But Sharpe could hope, and Ramon and I wickedly egged him on, knowing his lusts were quite useless except for our purposes.

This was the crowning point of Ramon's life; I think it must have been, there on the top of the Rockies, driving down the narrow road at the side of bright mountain waters, progressing slowly and carefully through those high magic meadows, through natural plantations of birch trees and aspens at the foot of the great steeps, the cloud shadows moving royally over, everything large and big and extensive. Ramon had come from narrow confines, tethered and hobbled in a small land, and here the barriers were down and the wind swept out; hills rose, and the sky yielded back. He was pushed or carried from the car most carefully by young hands and laid on his stretcher on a field tapestried with Colorado flowers, and there he rested, smoking and looking up through the dancing leaves and the unceasing twinkle to the Indian sky. The children brought him barbecued meat to eat, and coffee in tin cups, and sat in the sudden dusk singing campfire songs, and when the dew began to fall they helped Sharpe put him in the car and stood by their sleeping bags calling good-bye as he rode back to his cabin, his long thin arm waving a scarf out the window. They stood quiet for a minute as the motor receded and the cicadas took over, and

The California desert. Ramon lying inside car reading road map

*High in the Colorado Rockies near Steamboat Springs: Ramon,
Agnes, Portia Mansfield*

then nighttime prattle broke out and the giggles about bed arrangements.

There was one excursion too far for Ramon to attempt, a ranch far up in the mountains where a Saturday night dance was held for the hands. I danced with many of them and sat with their women between times while the men went outside for their smoke. There was absolutely no social talking or mixed standing around. We danced to an upright piano and a fiddle and the wonderful "calling" of a very old man. In the middle of one set, a cowboy put his head in the door and yelled, "Bull's out, boys!" and every male disappeared. In a quarter of an hour they came back rolling down their sleeves, their hands wet from the trough, apologized, grabbed their girls, and restarted. Charlotte Perry surreptitiously asked the musicians to strike up "Turkey in the Straw" and I cut loose, solo hoedown style, as she knew I couldn't help doing. They had to hang me over the rail fence to cool off. But I was fetched back. "Where's that little one? That little red-haired one? I want her. I reckon she sure can dance!"

I think *Rodeo* began that night.

Nearly every night the students lugged Ramon in his chair up the hill from his cabin to the big house for demonstrations and concerts.

"Watch it," said Ramon, "I think my foot's off the rest — that's why you're having trouble" — and I'd stoop and put his foot back, together with the hot-water bottle Sharpe had slipped into his bag. Nobody paid the slightest mind. They were fine, those kids.

He even took part in an improvised play. Charlotte Perry devised him a role as a tyrannical father who drives his daughter to suicide. I was the mother who cut down the body. We surprised ourselves, Ramon and I, we were just splendid. We should have gone on as a team. Ramon had an extraordinary incisiveness in his delivery, and power, and the little girl — she was a wonder! (What's happened to her? She was the daughter of a lawyer.) The whole school cheered us, and Ramon was for the first time not the center of pity but of straight admiration. Ramon could act. He was in no way amateur — he played with aplomb and complete control. He'd never been on the stage in his life before.

When my teaching weeks were over we rode down the spine of Colorado, Sharpe and I spelling each other at the wheel. Ramon lay flat, directing from the map (roads were not well marked in those days). Ramon had a phenomenal memory, and if he had ever passed even once along a road he recalled each turning.

Ramon wanted to see Taos and pay his respects to D. H. Lawrence's widow, Frieda, who lived in Taos and received homage, or at least, we hoped she did. So we set out from Santa Fe but were dissuaded because of the rains, and although Ramon was bitterly disappointed, we decided to try the Puyé cliff dwellings. We started off about three. There was a thread of water at the bottom of one dry gully. "Is that running?" I inquired apprehensively.

"That's nothing, honey," ordered Ramon on his back. "On to Puyé." But we stopped for directions at a gas station.

"I'm not going to tell you," said the man. "Look at those mountains. That's trouble. That's black rain. You don't go down there. You turn around and head for home as fast as you can. He's ill, isn't he? Hurry!"

So we turned — the thunderheads gathering up behind us.

We were at the top of a decline when I saw it. Sharpe didn't, apparently. He was at the wheel and he kept right on without slackening. "Sharpe," I screamed, "water!" Our trickle was now a roaring flood.

Sharpe put the brakes to the floor and the car swerved

Cowboy dances in Colorado

around and headed sideways right to the brink. "Christ!" said Ramon. The car kept sliding.

Sharpe frantically gave it some gas and turned the wheel. The front wheels lodged in mud, the engine flooded and died. There was no sound but the water rushing through the arroyo. Our left front wheel was now well over its hub in water. Ramon was tilted painfully on his side. I put out my arm to brace his weight. A car approached on the other bank. We waved and hollered but they heard nothing, turned, and went away. Another came beside us, looked, and grimly proceeded without stopping at four miles an hour to emerge on the other bank. Well, that showed there was a bottom.

The storm had now hit us and the rain was heavy. "He mustn't get wet," said Sharpe. He took off his jacket, I found my sweater — anything we could wrap around his legs and shoulders.

"For Christ's sake, I'm all right," said Ramon. "Stop fussing."

The waters were rising. I don't think Ramon could see, but he could hear.

A carload of nuns now drew up and popped their coifs out in terrified dismay. "It's all right," said Sharpe. "You can get through. Take it very slow and steady. Send help. The young man's paralyzed. Our engine is dead. Send help fast." The nuns looked and nodded; one smiled at Ramon. "Good luck," we called. They went through and we were alone in the rain.

"Don't be frightened, Aglet," said Ramon, patting my hand.

"Frightened? I can open the door and climb the bank any time I choose."

"And Sharpe can lift me, though, by God, he won't want to," Ramon laughed. "There'll be a lot of pretty grumbling after this, I can tell you."

It was the rain, the wet, the gangrene, we feared.

"Hulloa! Hulloa there!" called Sharpe, New Zealand style. He was wet to the skin and his glasses blinded. A car had arrived at the far bank. It crossed. A tough but sturdy mechanic got out. He had chains.

"Oh boy!" he said, and then he and Sharpe got down in the mud and the swelling water and fastened the chains.

He dragged us through and escorted us home. As I paid him, I said, "I think you saved a life today."

"Yeah?" said the man. "What's the matter with him? He's young."

"Yes, he's young," I said.

Sharpe was gathering Ramon in his arms. The chair stood in the rain on the sidewalk. "Now," said Sharpe, "the real work starts. Everything up to now has been child's play." But he was wrong; with his new stamina Ramon showed no ill effects.

We proceeded south — our object Gallup and the Indian ceremonials. As we drew into town we passed the Santa Fe station. It was one-thirty P.M. and the "Chief" was due — "You've only seen those little toy English jobs. I want you to see a real virile transcontinental snorter."

And it came right in on cue — roaring and puffing, venting steam from every orifice, its pistons and wheels grinding up life and geography. (Oh, what have they done to our trains?) As always, my heart beat until I thought it would burst. "Wow!" said Ramon. The engineer waved to us from his cabin window as he went by.

The engine stopped, panting, down by the water tower and the cars ground and shrieked and clattered to a stop. Out came the porters with their little footstools. "Gall-up," they yelled. And down the steps in princessly decorum came Martha Graham followed by Louis Horst.

"God is with us!" I shrieked. "Ramon, of all the people in the world, it's She Herself!"

I nearly knocked her down in my eagerness. She came right over to the car and leaned over Ramon — she, about whom I had been talking for two years.

We took four cabins in a row at a motel and washed our faces and prepared to go up to Zuni, where Louis had learned five minutes after arrival that there was to be a secret rain dance. How did Louis know? Louis knew everything necessary always.

He said it was there and we never doubted his word, but there seemed to be no sign of it and every stray Indian, mostly young girls, pulled their Czechoslovakian printed shawls over their mouths and stared at us silently with agate eyes. The more loquacious shrugged without speaking. So we parked Ramon and Sharpe under a tree and went exploring.

And suddenly there it was — in the central plaza, which was very small — about twenty men in Stone Age masks of wood and feathers, their bodies painted in symbols, stepping and shifting to the undeviating thump of two sticks on a sack of cloth. One man sat on the ground in the center and beat. For thirty-five minutes he never let up and he never accelerated, on and on, an unvarying unresonant thud. The dancers slowly reorganized the universe through their bowels and continued and continued. There was only one other white man present besides us three — the members of the Pueblo stood about unmoving and attentive.

"They killed their Catholic priest nine years ago," whispered Martha, "and the Church has not replaced him. This is a very fierce place — one does not trifle here, they warned an airline against sending a plane over the reservation — the airline persisted — the first plane fell."

There was no sound except the light rattling of beads and

*Louis Horst and Martha Graham at Bennington College,
Vermont, summer 1935*

gourds, the sliding and whispering of deer-shod feet — the sound of breathing was muffled in the masks.

The beating went on. No watcher moved. When a girl shifted her shawl back, the freshening rain wind lifted her hair. I pelted down the street to the car. "This is worth the trip to America — get in your chair and follow me." Sharpe never transferred him so fast in his life and then began pushing him up the rutted and rocky alley, Ramon urging him on as though on horseback.

"Good God!" breathed Ramon. "James Frazier! here we come!" Martha and Louis had disappeared. Sharpe, Ramon and I were at a corner. We didn't move. Suddenly all the dancers, masked, rattled, beaded, and painted, converged toward us, literally on top of us.

Ramon looked up into the great hovering masks. I turned around incredulously. We had done nothing. We had made no sound or move. A young brown Indian laughed with perfect teeth. "He's crippled — he's got to go — we can't have him here."

"But he can't help that!"

The boy just laughed. "Go up to the roof," said my laughing friend.

"He can't climb." I explained compassionately. The boy laughed. "Up!"

Sharpe took firm hold of the chair and began to push it down the alley back towards the car rather faster and more bumpily than was medically wise. Three enormous masks kept right at his heels shaking rattles. But there remained five close around me. They said nothing, but their meaning was quite clear.

My anthropological delight turned to something more primitive. It couldn't happen, but it was happening. We were surrounded by savage displeasure and no means of communication, and we were five and they were nearly two hundred.

I climbed the pole ladder. The boy looked full in my face and said the most educational phrase I'd ever heard before or since: "You're white. Bad for the dance."

Martha and Louis were on the roof with the one other non-Indian and although the view was fine, rain made the adobe move under our feet; the dance below us was achieving the result it wanted. I grew restive — the effects were unvarying and I was concerned about Ramon. "Let's go!" When we left not a head turned. The beat diminished with distance, it didn't accelerate, it didn't retard. The rain accelerated.

We had forty miles to make over bad roads and the storm was now heavy, with lightning, thunder, and rushing streams. But we got through and Ramon came out laughing from under the clothes we had piled on him. We were all soaked, but after hot baths we had dinner and drinks and the kind of talk Ramon had waited all his life to hear and had come across the world to find and that night he had it.

The next day we left for the desert and California. The next day Louis Horst came down with pneumonia. Sharpe had predicted that, among other things, was what Ramon would get. But Ramon didn't. Louis did. Louis's whole trip was spoiled, and of course, Martha's.

We proceeded at thirty miles an hour through the stifling heat, thirty miles because of the chances of bursting tires. Mathematically we could figure out how many days it would take us to reach Barstow — too long! And after that the Mojave Desert and then to the coast.

A week later Ramon buckled himself into his car and drove down Melrose Avenue waving out the window. Ramon was going back to London and Edgar, but I wasn't. Sharpe drove him right back across the continent — deserts, mountains, plains, bogs, cities, wastes, rivers and lakes to New York City. He did it absolutely alone without help, and he did all the nursing besides. They rested a couple of days at a hotel in New York, which Ramon hadn't seen, and they took ship for London. Lincoln Kirstein and Mary Hunter visited Ramon and brought him books for the trip. The return passage was easier and less picturesque than the way out, but when they got home the boy was fairly tired.

He now faced the empty months ahead. But he had boxes of photographs, and he invited his family up from Sussex for an illustrated narration of his adventures.

"It must have been ghastly," they said. "Such vulgar people!" How could he have stood them? And what had the trip cost?

Ramon thereupon shut up, as far as they were concerned, forever.

Cousin Joan was at hand, and heartwarming; Sharpe found his patient and faithful girl waiting, whom he had so tirelessly and so fruitlessly endeavored to betray.

The household settled down, cat and all, in the fog and bus noises of the King's Road.

When the car had turned the corner, I threw myself on Ramon's unmade bed and slept without moving for four hours.

Then I tried to decide what to do.

I had to make some money. In London was Edgar writing, writing and begging me to return. There were no jobs there, however.

George Cukor had been Margaret's director when she was a stock-company actress, and George had remained a friend. He kept an eye on me. He was now one of the most powerful directors in Hollywood, and he was still Margaret's friend. Perhaps she phoned him; the family wished to keep me away from London. In any case, he offered me the dances for the million-dollar Irving Thalberg version of *Romeo and Juliet*, starring Norma Shearer. I would like to — yes — but first, I wished to race to London and clarify my emotional life. I was neither promised nor not promised to my astonishing correspondent. It seemed vital to get this matter cleared up right away — I had seen him only four times and letters could be deceptive. "You don't know you love me," I said.

"Yes, I do," he replied. "I've seen your work. I know you. You have genius and I love you."

Could he come to me? No, his work did not permit it. I made plans for a four-week dash to London. Four days across the continent, five days on the Atlantic — four days there and return.

I had to be sure he would not fall in love with someone else. I had to be sure I wanted him. The voyage meant borrowing again from Mother.

Margaret got very firm with me about this. She was appalled at the risk I was taking. "Let him come here." But he couldn't. Of course, he couldn't. His work would not permit absence, and as a German refugee, he didn't have the price of the fare. "Nevertheless," said Mother, "he should be doing the courting. He should be coming to you." He couldn't. He sent flowers instead.

"Don't go," said Cukor. "Stay here and prepare for your job. Go into this job for once rested and ready. He'll wait."

And indeed he said he would, so I stayed, but so tense, so worried. I would have to be gone from him sixteen months in all and what man would wait out this stretch? He said he would wait. He said Ramon would be okay — he'd look after him. Take the job. Earn the money. Make a success. Do what was good for me.

It made sense professionally, but I didn't know how I could stand the uncertainty, the waiting. I had to.

When I cabled that I was not coming to England, he wrote of his bitter black disappointment and his dismay. Maybe he didn't trust himself either. But he didn't say so. I was the one with the doubts.

The letter-writing intensified: He was starting on a major study of the Sistine ceiling. Carl Jung had come to study at his library ("The mind of a god; the nose of a dog"). He'd taken Ramon the typed transcription of Jung's lectures. He had taken Ramon to other lectures at the Warburg Institute; he had brought the lecturers to Ramon's bedside. He had found some books for me, promptly forwarded: Darwin's *Expression of Emotion in Animals and Humans* (which I used thereafter in all my classes). J. A. Symond's *Michelangelo* (so I could keep up with him. Good God!), C. K. Ogden's *The System of Basic English* (so I — well it was extremely witty). And there were flowers at intervals, beautiful ones, which I knew he could not afford. I had flowers where I was but, of course, I did not have orchids, and these he cabled.

I took German lessons, two a week. I had previously learned one phrase in German from Max Reinhardt, *"Noch einmal bitter."* I now learned another from the Berlitz teacher, *"Sie kommen zu spat."*

Romeo and Juliet was the first job in my life in which everything was opulent and everything was fun. I was getting five hundred dollars a week and no one was in a hurry. The job was to last for six months. I had my own office-dressing room, on a wooden balcony under the dripping eucalyptus trees. (It was the rainy season and fragrant.) I had free use of a secretary, researchers, musicians, assistants, anything I wished. My group was treated as a separate unit, given an assistant director and a prop man and an enormous rehearsal hall. I hired whom I wished. The cast included Bella Lewitzky, Mary Meyer (my lead dancer), Warren Leonard (my partner, assistant and leading male), Donald Sadler, and Paul Godkin.

I asked for muslin skirts cut like the great brocaded court robes, and we lived in these. The dancers became so habituated to them that they could do anything, run up and down stairs, back up, move around furniture, turn, bow to the floor. I made them rehearse with books on their heads. They carried their heads as though they'd been born wearing crowns. Whenever any courtiers were needed, the dancers were summoned instead of the more highly paid extras because the dancers could move like nobility. The men were taught to fence — not that they were going to have to duel, but because a man moves and stands in a certain way if he is used to handling a sword.

The dances were finished in three weeks. What to do? I had to keep a company of thirty-two busy, six hours a day. We gave classes in everything — always ballet, but sometimes modern (Mary and Bella were Lester Horton pupils and they obliged). I taught them the original preclassic forms learned in Haslemere so they would know where the patterns derived from. They began to get, every one of them, a most extraordinary sense of style. Bella Lewitzky was memorable. We were a very happy group.

Every afternoon at four, we had a large tea prepared for us by our prop man. And at five, we showed the dances to guests. A lot of foreign visitors. Our five o'clock demonstrations were one of the sights of the studio. After one such performance, the company business manager turned to me and said, "This makes me feel like living a better life. I've never seen anything like it."

Pavane from Romeo and Juliet: *Agnes de Mille and Hugh Laing*
(*Photo by Angus McBean*)

And indeed the dances were lovely. The madrigals by Byrd, Morley and Dowling were the finest counterpoint I had ever done. And the pavane, which was to be Juliet's introduction to Romeo, to a fifteenth-century French ballad, was really strong. (I danced this pavane in concert with Hugh Laing as partner for three years afterwards. The style and use of hands form the basic idiom of Tudor's ball scene in his *Romeo and Juliet*.) I was very proud. I was well pleased with my work.

George Cukor, the director, and his staff came early but not later, through pressure of work. Thalberg never came.

For the first time in my life, I had earned money. I did not spend it. I hoarded it — but I stopped borrowing from Mother. I was living with my sister, but I could buy gas for the car. I could take friends to lunch. I paid for theater tickets and after a while, I bought clothes, although carefully. Carmalita Maracci knew all about living well cheaply. Dollar Day on Hollywood Boulevard was just that — anything for a dollar — good shoes, for instance — and good pocketbooks. And I. Magnin had its annual sale. I had the money at last. I got five dresses for $210 — my very own, not Mag's. One, I recall, was emerald-green silk velvet, full skirted, which swept the floor, and a tight high-waisted bodice with little velvet buttons running right down to the ground — with my red hair and my white skin — wow!

I wore the gown to one of the first Academy dinners as Cecil de Mille's guest. (We had reestablished formal relations — my association with beloved Aunt Constance and the remarkable family had always remained unchanged.) It was long before television and fairly contained, as a trade affair held like any business celebration, in a hotel ballroom. The tables were covered with pink camellias strewn by the hundreds down the cloth. Margaret had given me a brown summer ermine muff. I filled it with the blossoms to take home. To whom? Ramon was not there — I had become a habitual scavenger.

I bought two suits custom-tailored at a place Gladys Robinson took me, with shirts of contrasting shades. The suits, English cloth and superbly cut, cost $60 each, the shirts $25. I remember all these details because they were land-marks; these clothes were my first personal indulgence, bought with my own earned money, symbolizing success and freedom. I hadn't a pang about getting them. I needed no costumes at the moment.

"Pay Mother what you owe her," said Margaret. "In a minute," I said. "First, a saving for the future so I can live free, and a few real clothes."

"Pay Margaret some board," said Mother. "She can use the money." "In a minute," I said. But I did send Mother presents. She turned them all right back at the store and had my account credited. She would not be repaid. Later, after *Oklahoma!*, I gave her checks. She promptly turned them over to the Henry George School. I found several so en-dorsed after her death. She let me pay for the hospital room she died in. That she let me do.

I did not pay back that winter. I treated my conscience like a royal guest.

I used to drive to the studio (in the governess's car) through the winter rains, through Fox Hills, now all built up, then green and with acacia-bordered roads. The grass in California is strong, energetic and succulent, not tamed and matted as in England. It springs from the earth in its brief season and it bears in its embrace blue lupine and brodiaea and invisible-stemmed painted Mariposa tulips. These flowers are my childhood flowers and they promise good things always, hope, happiness, power. The acacia trees were pearled and studded with raindrops and gave off an odor that was a cleansing. This was a Botticelli spring, and I was young and healthy and beautiful, and there was a great man in England, a very great man of enormous enchantment, writing me every week. And although Ramon's love and need burned like a forest fire on the horizon, somehow God in His wisdom would show me what to do about this.

And when I arrived at the studio, I said, "Good morning" to all I met as the boss says good morning and went to my dressing room, which smelled of sweet wet wood and eucalyptus, and found requests from Cukor to write transition scenes for him, which I promptly did *allegro vivace,* all of which were used with enthusiasm. And then, I put on my woolens and had a roaring ballet class with the kids. I was boss and was doing first-class work and was being appreciated. Whenever I was introduced, it was as the choreographer (from England) of the biggest picture of the year for the greatest producer in Hollywood, with one of the two or three biggest stars and one of the jolliest and kindest — and best — of directors. I was now in Big Time and everyone thought I was wonderful.

Every night I sat quietly at home, writing, writing to Ramon, and to the other. (Would Edgar wait? He said he would.) My life was absolutely hopeful.

Ramon kept writing the daily gossip: he had been out on his own to Notting Hill and had seen a new ballet by Antony, *Jardin aux Lilas,* and, wrote Ramon, "If the Rambert company can produce a couple more works of this caliber, England is going to lead the world."

I straightway called up Louis Horst's monthly journal, *The Dance Observer,* which in reality was a house organ for Martha Graham's company, and asked if they'd like an English critic on their staff, unpaid, of course. They would, yes.

But I said, the articles would deal with ballet, since there was no other form of dancing in England — out of the question; ballet must not be mentioned in their pages. They were trying to counteract Lincoln Kirstein and the Ballet Russe. "But you're missing real news and some very good writing."

No matter — no ballet — they were on a crusade and they were going to destroy ballet in America, or at least put it in its proper place, a top shelf in the corner.

Sancta Simplicitas!

Ramon did not get the job; he would have made a brilliant critic.

I was now living with friends. My sister, her husband and child, pursuing their waning fortunes, once more had moved and had now gone to London and were installed in Trevor Square with a wonderful nanny of quality, the sister-in-law of Sean O'Faolain. Bernie was trying to promote work in the British studios.

When it came time for filming *Romeo*, the set was large and magnificent, the costumes exquisite and functional, the music enchanting, and the time for shooting, eight days, more than adequate.

But although Cukor had seen the dances, he had no plans for photographing them. Thalberg was not interested at all, and the cameras were simply halted. The dances were either not filmed at all or in bits, the director and producer feeling stubbornly that the story pace must be maintained even at the cost of choreography, a point of view I naturally did not share.

Lincoln Kirstein came to town and I showed him all on a practice stage. He turned out to be the job's sole knowledgeable audience.

The disappointment was blasting, but I had eight thousand dollars in the bank; I could start to repay Mother. I had a

Norma Shearer dancing in Irving Thalberg's Romeo and Juliet.
Agr es alone at the left (Photo: MGM)

wardrobe and six months of self-confidence behind me. One can coast on this for some time. Now I knew that, given adequate cooperation, I could produce really good professional work. I knew this, and this knowledge was armor and ammunition. From here on I was impregnable — not successful, yet, but impregnable — I knew.

And ahead lay hope. A tragic decision with Ramon, but it had to be faced. It was time. I had now to take over my life.

CHAPTER 19

THE accident occurred around Christmas. Sharpe was changing a tire in the wet, slipped, and tore a tendon in his heel.
He had to go to the hospital. Substitute nurses were hastily
found, female, without adequate strength and sufficient training in the special requirements of this case. When Sharpe
came back, Ramon had in his system more toxins than his
body could throw off. The condition worsened slightly during the spring. It was Ramon's wish that none of this be told
me. Therefore, when I returned in May, although I expected
to find him the same, I returned with terrified emotional
misgivings. It was I who had changed. "He'll be all right,"
vowed Edgar in letters. "You will always be his friend. He
has known all along he couldn't hold you forever. You un-
derrate him. He's much stronger than you think." But I was
scared.

Edgar was on the tender in Plymouth and he took me
straight in his arms. It was as though the intervening year had
not happened. He met me as a lover, as a husband; he met me
as the absolute beginning and end of my life. The trip up to
London was magic with happiness.

"You will love me," he said. "And there will be no grief
with Ramon." And because he said so, I believed it was true.

Edgar kissed me at Ramon's door. "It will be all right," he said.

Ramon looked at me with wonder. And he knew without being told. But until I said the words, he held his breath and waited.

And the next day, while Edgar was playing Mozart ("I don't particularly like Mozart," I murmured. "You don't like Mozart, Agchen?" and he chuckled as though I had dirtied my pinafore. "I must teach you."), I suddenly knew that he was the answer to everything in my life, and that he was all I'd ever looked for, father, mother, lover, teacher — all — I'd come into harbor. I wept quietly as I breathed hope and certainty for the very first time. He would make up for all.

Two days later I received a letter from him stating that he had thought it all over carefully and that he could never see me again. No explanation.

I went first to Trevor Square to my sister, and then I went as planned for supper with Ramon. I was determined not to say a word, but as I entered the door, he looked at me and said instantly, "Aglet, what has he done to you? Oh, I knew this would happen! That inscrutable man! I knew this was happening. I couldn't save you. What could I do?"

I wept beside him all night. I didn't take my hat and coat off. "How brutal of me to do this to you!" I said.

"No, no. This is how I can serve you. This is the only way I can be of use. Steady now. We'll understand it all later. Have the courage to break with him."

And in the dreary days that followed, I let Ramon think I had. I never mentioned Edgar again. But what I prayed for was his return, with all my heart, with all my entire heart.

It was a widow sat beside Ramon's bed, and he was kind and cheerful. But his pride, which is part of hope, had died.

Mine had not, however, altogether. I was not passively accepting.

I demanded to see Edgar and he was gentle, but firmly resisted my accusation that there was another woman. "Absolutely not," he said. He would not explain further.

There was a second meeting, a longer one. And it turned out there was a woman after all; our absence had been too protracted. He didn't love her, he loved me, and had told her so, but he was obligated to her, and she was not giving up.

She was not being reasonable at all. She resorted to blackmail threats of suicide and drugs. He had so hoped everything would work itself out, simply and easily.

"He's not good for you, Ag," said Ramon. "You must never see him again. He'll damage you. This is no way to begin a love. You're lucky it's finished."

Nevertheless, Edgar and I continue to write, although unsatisfactorily.

Two weeks later, I returned from a shopping trip to my very pretty new flat to find hourly messages from Ramon. When I got him on the telephone and he himself spoke, he asked in a perfectly normal voice, "Could you come over immediately, darling? They can't get my pulse down." It was that sudden and that quiet.

I went over. He had blood poisoning, a temperature of 104°, and racing pulse. His eyes glittered. "We've been through this before, Aglet. But, it's so much easier when you're here."

Sharpe had at last in pure terror called in a doctor, not the family physician from Sussex, nor a London specialist, but a strange little gnome he'd found wandering around the ward of some hospital he'd once worked in. This was a creature of nostrums and demimagic, with pills and serums and a cure-all in a great needle which he administered lavishly, without sterilization, to Ramon's complete astonishment and Sharpe's demur. But he would not prescribe a sleeping pill, and Sharpe's mild paregoric could not reach Ramon's caged mind. Ramon did not sleep for seventy-six hours.

On the fourth morning when I went into the sickroom, Ramon's skull was all but through his flesh, his eyes had burned to the bottom of his head.

He took my hand in his hot one.

"Where does one go for sleep, Ag? Where does one lay one's head?"

The doctor finally arrived. "Give him some peace," ordered Sharpe. "Let him rest."

But it was not to be a pill. It was again through the arm and unsterilized. Ramon looked at me. "Will I be here tomorrow?" he asked.

"You will. Hold on! Hold my hand!"

But this was not like the other vigils. There was a Presence with us now, and we took note of the minutes. Pulse by pulse by pulse. I willed him to keep on. I willed him to be there. I willed him to continue. I am not talking in hyperbole. I gave him my will, and as he would not turn his face to the wall, he could use my will. He was there in the morning, and he had finally slept.

Sharpe at this point notified his father, who hurried to town and demanded to take the boy down to Sussex. Sharpe objected. But he promised to call in any consultant he was asked to. Percy Reed agreed to wait and departed without giving instructions. I did not know that he had even been in town.

"If we could only get away from here," Edgar said in one of our stolen meetings. "Somewhere peaceful. We could work everything out."

But, of course, I couldn't leave.

The little ward-hopper continued ministrations to Ramon, then turned his attention on me. "You're looking poorly," he said. "You need some pepping up." Arriving at my flat with his syringe, he invited confidence. It is proof of my near breakdown that I confided in the wretched quack. Nothing was safe with that creature. He was totally untrustworthy, and I knew it well, but I was not balanced at the time. I had to talk.

On learning that I was emotionally upset, he inquired why. Here was a doctor to talk to, even if unorthodox. I confessed my troubles fully. By way of a cure, he gave me an unsterilized shot in the arm; by way of comfort a highly unmedical pat on the bosom. He then proceeded directly to Ramon's bedside and recounted to both Ramon and Sharpe my intimate griefs and my continued relationship. "And this," Sharpe later said, "I could not forgive him. He tore the boy's heart out. The poor thing felt utterly betrayed."

Ramon now underwent a complete transformation. Between Wednesday and Thursday a stranger lay on the bed and whenever I entered the room his eye searched behind me to the door.

"No, Aggie. Has Sharpe given permission? You can't come in without his leave."

He no longer cared for what I was doing. He had become totally withdrawn. He grasped his last strength with desperation.

"You can't stay long," he would remark as he took my hand limply.

And then Sharpe's shadow would appear behind me.

Sharpe spoke barely a word to me. Just "He's very bad" or when he felt benevolent, "How are your troubles? You don't look well. I'll give you some paregoric for sleeping."

Indeed, I was not well. Edgar had suddenly shut all the doors. It was finished absolutely, finally. He refused to see me. He refused every form of communication.

I went down as though poleaxed. I thought I was going insane. I had risked Ramon's life for this. I did not have the energy to think, to care, to try.

I took class in a kind of reflex. I returned home and lay on my bed until supper, served on a tray, then lay not reading until paregoric time and woke to the exact nasty smell and the last dismal idea. With dawn came street noises and the realization that someone or other was busy, thank God! And eventually breakfast came and on the way to class I could inquire about Ramon. Ethel or Sharpe would meet me at the crack of the door and I would be told to come back for ten minutes in the afternoon or not to. And Ramon did not dare or did not care to protest. He was occupied just then, minute by minute. He was so sick he kept his mind on living through the nights. He was dying, he was going away.

I walked the square and the Chelsea streets and my room or just lay gnawing my fists, but it was at least in some sort of privacy. What had I forfeited by staying away so long? My whole chance at happiness. My proper wifehood. And for what? Dances cut to grotesque remnants. I had eight thousand dollars. I had sold my happiness for eight thousand dollars. After all these years to do this! Why had I not known immediately this was the man for me? Someone else seemed to be living my life.

And that day drew to a close. And the shades came down and the tea tray came in. And I knew absolutely the taste of destruction.

Cousin Joan, I think, was in Hungary. I should have found her and warned her. I should have notified her family in

Sussex. I should have got through somehow with the whole truth to Ramon's family. I didn't. To the day of my death, I will never forgive myself. I didn't because I couldn't do anything. I lay paralyzed.

Mother had come over and sat in the corner of the room reading. She never spoke to disturb me. She was just there and she was wonderful. My sister was in the throes of a violent divorce in Trevor Square and Mother lived with her, and when not with me looked after Margaret's Judith. It was an unforgettable summer for Mother. Margaret looked at us as we sat red-eyed from weeping around the Trevor Square dinner table one evening and remarked with a dreary giggle, "Three blind mice!"

I suppose Mother left her corner from time to time to tend to Single Tax duties. She must have seen the faithful, perhaps she even addressed meetings. I lay unasking. I could eat; I could practice; I couldn't listen to news, not even gossip. All I could do was watch the clock as it went round so fast and ask "Why?"

Mother recognized major shock and begged for help, not from a doctor, of course. There was never anything psychologically wrong with the de Milles. Elizabeth Bowen explained with great embarrassment why she couldn't have me at Bowen Court in Ireland. I had not thought of being invited there — Mother had. Rebecca West, under Mother's prompting, sent an invitation a month hence. The Folkes cabled from Denmark; I couldn't move — Mother should have reached the Reeds, but she didn't know them and her main concern was me.

Robin was living now with a sweet and pleasant girl in a pre-Elizabethan house in a village called Nasty near another village called Ugly. They invited me to spend the night and

I did go down to them and they were enchantingly kind and comforting. Robin was quite free of me now and had started a vigorous and zestful life. His girl was in love with him and deserved him. He was now like my brother.

In October, if October came, I was to do Leslie Howard's *Hamlet* in New York and that delightful man very kindly came to my bedside and interviewed me there. He wondered if I'd be well enough. I wondered too.

Minute by minute, hour by hour, the dreadful summer passed. Back from vacation, Joan phoned that Ramon had been taken down to Sussex, Sharpe with him. Their flat was to be vacated. The family physician had at last taken over. It was too late, of course.

Then a letter came from Edgar: be patient, let him work things out, he still loved me. He was suffering from a nervous breakdown. He asked me simply to wait. I had no choice. I had no will for anything else.

Late in September Joan phoned to tell me I must hurry to Sussex if I wanted to see Ramon. The family had given permission.

I drove to Sussex, where he and Sharpe were staying in a rented house near the family estate, where I suppose he had hoped to recuperate, but even under the circumstances it proved an accommodating arrangement, because the exercises of dying were too disruptive for Netherfield Place.

When I arrived there was a conclave of doctors in his bedroom and I had to wait about forty minutes in the living room. The doctors' notes lay open on the table. I shouldn't have read them, but I did. Some were in plain English. "This morning I drew half a cup of pus from his knee."

The chief doctor — I believe he was the family's regular physician — took me on the lawn for instructions. Ramon's father and stepmother, Joan, had persuaded him that I was after the boy's money, and he was extremely harsh, not softening any information with kindness but using blunt facts like fists. Ramon was dying. It was a matter of days. But then he saw my face, and he spoke differently — still brusquely, but not cruelly. "I'd get myself in hand if I were you, before I went in. Get rid of your tears." Later he was to say to Cousin Joan's mother, "She does care. She's not just a little Hollywood adventuress."

"You've been totally misinformed about her," said Joan's mother.

When I went in, Ramon was sitting up in bed waiting for his supper. They had not warned me. He was suffering from some sort of edema and his face was swollen, all his beauty flattened and puffed, unrecognizable — I couldn't have identified him if I'd been asked to. But the eyes were there, the great dark glowing eyes, and they turned again with love to me. He put out one of his long hands.

Across from the bed was a low window. He could look straight out into the Sussex woods gilding slowly toward autumn. He held my hand firmly and we talked trivia. He had difficulty getting his spoon in his mouth, but he liked his pudding. We talked until dark. We talked about my good new job.

"Ramon," I said, "I'll stay. I'll give up the job — that's nothing — would you like me to stay here? To be with you?"

He sighed softly, "No, Aglet, this that I have to do, I have to do alone.

"And Ag, don't worry about the work — it will be recognized, I know this." And again he added very quietly, "And darling, listen to me, dear — get some happiness. There is in you a terrible need."

"I'll stay."

"No. Look, honey, look out the window! Oh, Agnes — the hunter's moon!"

I kissed him good-bye — good-bye indeed, and went out into the crisping dark to drive home. I sent a frantic note to Elizabeth Bowen from the boat train: "Write him — write him, anything he can hold in his hand. There's little time."

There was too little time. She delayed too long.

The word came in New York during a rehearsal of *Hamlet*. Cabled from Joan — "Ramon died peacefully at nine this morning." I went straight to Mother. "Well," she said, "you expected this."

In rehearsals people asked from time to time how Ramon was. "Oh, fine," I said. "Fine. He expects to come back here for another visit next spring."

I sat listening to the lines for the first time, Ramon's copy of *Hamlet* in my hand, signed on the flyleaf by his long-dead mother, Beatrice Thrift.

This grave shall have a living monument.

Report me and my cause aright.

> *Let four captains*
> *Bear Hamlet, like a soldier, to the stage,*
> *For he was likely, had he been put on,*
> *To have prov'd most royally.*

At the funeral, which was in Sussex in the Netherfield church, the family took possession and played the bereaved and loving parents of a tragic youth. They snubbed Sharpe. He was a servant and possibly responsible for the boy's death, as he had been most certainly responsible for ten years for the boy's life. They had the Gothic nerve to snub him, and Cousin Joan's mother found him standing forlornly on the church porch and took him in to sit beside her in her own pew.

My love went down by train to represent me, but, of course, no one knew that except he and I. Margaret and I cabled a great sheaf of flowers. The family was astonished at the amount of flowers and the different places from which they came. They were astonished at the letters that poured in.

Afterwards, on the station platform, Stepmother Joan's old mother mouthed the complacent platitudes that after all, it was a good thing he'd at last died — considering how he had suffered and how useless and limited his life had been. Now, bless God, he was released, to everyone's relief.

Elizabeth Bowen, I am told, rounded on her. Elizabeth blazed. Standing quite quietly and in a cool Irish voice without stutter she cut that foolish old lady down to size. Ramon would have loved that moment. Ramon, said Elizabeth, was a splendid person, and far from being tragic was effective and gave joy to more lives than his family would ever know. And he knew joy himself at times, very fully. There were people, more people than the family could even guess, who would grieve.

There had been shelter; now there was none. There had been a roof; now there was blowing air. There had been one man whose life enkindled from mine, whose face blazed with vigor each time I went to him.

Steady, steadfast, undeviating, unafraid, he set direction like the fixed star. All fell away from the quiet progress. Clamor stopped. Demons howled to silence.

There were no alternatives in his style. He never considered compromise. "Do not settle for anything easy, Ag, or quick; settle only for what you really want, the best. The comprehension will come, and the strength." It was not possible he could do anything mean, or malicious. He never cursed his fate or railed against the inevitable. There was no thrashing. What energy he had husbanded from his half-life he gave to me, he was my servant and my help.

And now he was not. He was dead. He had stopped. But the steadfastness was still there, like the resonance of a bell. I had been loved not because I was pretty, or clever, or agile but because I was. Simply that. He was like my child, like my teacher, like my master-teacher. I, by being me, had won this. "Be still, Ag; quiet down, dear, talk to me. It will all straighten out."

Only the living change. The vibrations of the dead circle out and out, true and continuing.

The will was probated on November 19. It had been drawn up September 19, 1932, at 3 Paulton's House, Paulton's Square, while Sharpe was in residence. Undoubtedly, he knew about it and it was in Ramon's nature to reassure him by telling him the truth. At his death Ramon was worth £14,022.7.10.

He made a bequest of £6,500 to "Henry Arthur Sharpe as a recognition of his cheerful companionship and the unremitting care and attention which he has given me."

The rest of the money — after Sharpe's guarantee — went to his old nanny, Mary Louisa Toy of Cornwall. Sharpe got all the movables including the old car. He was entitled to them.

The furniture went back to the Reeds, I suppose, the Queen Anne chairs and the Venetian mirrors. Sharpe gave Joan her choice of records, including the signed "Porgy and

Bess" that Mag had obtained from Gershwin himself. Elizabeth Bowen asked for and was immediately given the complete Dryden set, museum caliber.

I asked only for the keepsakes I had given him. When I returned to London, Joan put in my hand the boy's wristwatch, taken from him at death. This, I kept. Sharpe gave me Ramon's French paperbacks of Rimbaud and Verlaine. "He loved them so much!" he explained. "He was never without them." These also I kept — in any case, Sharpe couldn't read them.

Sharpe put his money in real estate and when all was tidied up and he realized he was independent and free from daily work, certainly as a subordinate, he began calling me and inviting me out to dinner, suggesting that it was high time I had a little real fun. I asked Edgar to explain that I would not go out to dinner and to make it final. His explanation was apparently effective. There were no more calls.

In class, Mim said (it was during *Adagio*, I remember), "Ramon Reed's will has been probated. It was in the *Times*. Poor Eggie, poor, poor Eggie! Not a penny! After all that, and not a penny!"

Diana Gould spoke suddenly beside me, "I'm leaving class," and she did. But Mim had been kind and tender and had put her arms around me and held me while I wept. In class, however, she was someone else, the court jester.

Two years later I was driving through Sussex with my beloved pianist, Norah Stevenson. We stopped by the roadside to picnic and chose that particular roadside in all of Sussex and that particular hedge.

"Hulloa! Hulloa! Hulloa!" boomed the familiar New Zealand voice. "Come in, come in. See my roses!" And Sharpe escorted us into his country home, a charming cottage with ample garden and all the latest mechanical gadgets.

There was a pretty girl there from London who was ordered to make us tea. "She'll do for the moment," said Sharpe, as she retired rather sullenly into the kitchen. "But, of course, she's not up to me. No brains. I've got to get someone better." And those were the last words he ever spoke to me.

A month after Ramon's death, I finally met his father. Percy Reed called on me. It was the first time I had ever seen him, frail, tall, ashen, exquisitely refined. He had in his hand the gros point I had for Ramon's Queen Anne chair; he had in his hand D. H. Lawrence, James Joyce, John Donne. He held Ramon's hopes, and my love, and our laughter — days and hours of laughter.

"I have brought back the embroidery you did for him — and very pretty, too — if I may say so. Wouldn't you like something? A chair? For instance, the chair that belongs to the embroidery. A mirror? Something?"

I shook my head without speaking.

"We were, you know, very surprised that you inherited nothing. That you were not mentioned in the will. It seemed — well — odd."

I said nothing.

"But he was an odd boy. Selfish, strange, difficult, and then he grew so Bohemian! All those actor friends, and — and — musical people, and his hair long and Chinese jackets, so effeminate."

"I gave them to him," I said quietly. "I had them made for him in Chinatown in Los Angeles. I thought they were cheerful. Quite virile Chinese men wear them."

"So Bohemian, and his hair too long, and then his writing!"

"Elizabeth Bowen is going to see his manuscript through the press."

"Dear Elizabeth, so Irish, so charming! Of course, she

promised. I think she'll find she's too busy to do it. I can't believe it's very good. I've never read any — you see — his temper was so snappish — he didn't want to be helped — he didn't want our advice or our kindness."

Then I spoke.

"When a boy in his teens half-blind, paralyzed, and motherless turns away from his only living relative, I think that man should look in his own heart for the answer."

Mr. Reed stood up. He was shaking.

"One thing he kept to the end."

"Yes?"

"His beauty. As he lay in his coffin, I have never seen such a face."

"He was not beautiful when I saw him last. He was bloated pitiably, past recognition."

"I'm glad I did not see him then."

"But he was, of course, alive."

"You have nothing to feel badly about. It must be nice to have a clear conscience."

Mr. Reed found the door handle. He stopped at the door. "There's one thing he had — unconquerable courage." Then he left.

Two years later he was to blow his brains out. He simply could not bear being alive.

He is buried beside Ramon in the old Netherfield Church Graveyard, Sussex, the two closer than at any time in life.

Elizabeth Bowen had the manuscripts. There was that. I counted on her. But she informed Percy Reed (as she explained to me later) that the posthumous printing of an unknown must entail a certain amount of subsidy, and this settled the matter forever as far as the family was concerned. I imagine every page, poems and all, has been burned long since.

If it be now, 'tis not to come; if it be not to come, it will be now; if it be not now, yet it will come; the readiness is all.

"Oh, Agnes — the hunter's moon!"

The Years After

Ninette de Valois, Dame of the British Empire, has retired from the management of the Royal Ballet. She now spends her time teaching and advising. She is active on the Ballet Board of Governors, and the gratitude and admiration of her country for what she built and bequeathed and for her example of heroic continuity during the war move like a halo about her. She still teaches a spanking class. She is still the very best possible company.

She and Rambert have gone their separate ways, and her position is incomparably more powerful, but she defends Mim stalwartly on all occasions. Just once or twice with chuckles she tells a sly joke. She went to Mim some years back and suggested that they pay to Fokine, the most universally pirated man since Shakespeare, a royalty for the works they were all performing.

"Sairtainly," said Mim. "Sairtainly. It's only just. We should be proud to." And then looking Ninette very levelly in the eyes, she added, "How much?"

Dame Marie Rambert, now white-headed and widowed, still holds the fort in Notting Hill Gate. She still maintains what is probably the best small company in the world and still experiments with choreographies and designs. The list of her discoveries is a long one. In the early fifties, she saw Martha Graham and experienced what was in a sense a conversion. She has since produced ballets by modern Americans, Anna Sokolow and Glen Tetley, but she never invited me to work for her, although she was warmly enthusiastic about seeing *Fall River Legend*. She is cherished and loved, respected and watched.

When *Oklahoma!* first went to London in 1946, it carried an American cast on the understanding that they would be replaced six months later by British subjects. Lulu Dukes got "The Girl Who Falls Down." I saw her in 1950 when I went over to stage *Carousel*. "But, of course, Eggie," said Mim, "she is completely wrong for this. She has no idea of your style."

Imagine! Her own daughter! Mim had never seen anyone else dance the role, but she knew what I intended. I love Lulu, but I did not find her suitable. Mim was instinctively right and quite merciless.

On March 21, 1972, in the *New York Times*, John Percival, one of London's leading critics, wrote of her current season: "The total effect is not only original but entertaining, too, and confirms Ballet Rambert's position as certainly the most creative and intelligently directed of British dance companies." Her competition are the Royal Ballet, the Festival Theater and the Western Ballet.

Bravo Mim! At eighty-four and with nothing like the state help the others get!

In a letter to me dated April 14, 1972, she writes:

I am very lucky to have lived to see this day, or month, or year. It seems there is much more understanding of my work than I ever imagined there was. You, I am sure, know to what a degree my work was impulsive. I had no idea where I was going, but I had to dance or make others dance — and create or make others create.

Now, it seems, there are lots of people, in addition to you, who acknowledge it.

And as to Ashley's deeply hidden help to me, which I only realized now and about which I wrote in my little book (*Quicksilver*), I wish I had appreciated it in his lifetime.

Lulu had to leave Trinidad because of Black Power, which became quite frightening. They are now settled in Spain, where Lu teaches a little (she had left over three hundred pupils in Trinidad) and gardens and is a happy wife and mother. I love them all. And Angela, too, is happily married with a son and daughter both at Oxford by their own exertions.

I practice every morning: one exercise, less than a minute, and then five minutes in bed. And so through the whole barre. The object is to keep my balance, as I sometimes get giddy and must stand firmly on my legs.

And so I thank God for all that!

Much love

Mim

Sir Frederick Ashton is, together with Balanchine, probably the best-known choreographer and he is almost as prolific. He recently retired from his official post as head of the Royal Ballet. (The present incumbent is Kenneth MacMillan.) But although retired, Ashton has not stopped working. His ballets are performed across the world.

Antony Tudor has made his official home in New York since 1939, but he never acquired citizenship. He has taught for two decades at the Juilliard School of Music and supervises his ballets in Tokyo, Toronto, New York (both big companies, American Ballet Theater and New York City Ballet), Stockholm, Copenhagen, Essen. He is the president of the First Zen Institute of America.

Hugh Laing retired from a brilliant career as a soloist with the American Ballet Theater and made a name for himself as a photographer. He is currently acting as Tudor's chief assistant and restager. He also designs and supervises costumes with outstanding ability. He had originally intended to become a designer and was studying at the London Slade School when he first met Tudor.

Admiral Harcourt (Diana Gould's stepfather) became, after the war, governor general of Hong Kong, and Mulberry House having been badly bombed, with the destruction of one maid and a Bechstein, Mrs. Harcourt accompanied her husband east with less reluctance than she might otherwise have done.

Diana Gould, in common with thousands of young women, worked in factories during the war and then spent a dreadful stint in Davos with her sister, Griselda, who had contracted tuberculosis (this was prevalent after the long period of rationing). Griselda recovered and married the pianist William Kempner. Diana married Yehudi Menuhin and by him has two sons. The older one recently appeared as solo pianist in New York with his father conducting. They make their home variously in San Mateo, California, and England. Wherever they go they involve themselves in establishing festivals of fine music, in education, and in sociological works of high order. In 1945 in London I heard Menuhin across a dinner table persuade Benjamin Britten to go with him to play for the inmates of the Belsen concentration camp just opened by the United States Army. Diana still talks eighty-to-the-dozen and never a stupid word.

Andrée Howard created several memorable ballets for Rambert, *Lady into Fox*, in which Sally Gilmour starred, and *The Sailor's Return*. For the Royal Ballet she choreographed *Mirror for Witches* and *Fête Etrangère*. She died tragically on April 18, 1969, of an overdose of sleeping pills, which her friends are convinced was accidental.

Peggy van Praagh, who figured in most of Antony's ballets, is now Dame of the British Empire and, with Sir Robert Helpmann, head of the Australian National Ballet.

Walter Gore is an outstanding choreographer, William Chappell, one of London's best designers.

Alicia Markova, Dame of the British Empire, after an unmatched career as soloist for the Ballet Russe de Monte Carlo and the American Ballet Theater, returned to home ground with performances for the Royal Ballet at Covent Garden and the Festival Theater. She more recently took over the thankless post of ballet mistress at the Metropolitan Opera House and struggled for years to drag this ill-used group of dancers up to some sort of standard. She has finally, like all her predecessors in the unfortunate house, lost heart and left. At the moment of writing, she is Professor of Ballet and Performing in the College Conservatory of Music at the University of Cincinnati.

The costume designer, Margaret Watts, married Roger Furse and as Margaret Furse is now one of England's top designers, responsible for the lovely clothes in most of the great historical films, *Henry V* (Laurence Olivier), *Anne of the Thousand Days* (Richard Burton), *Mary Queen of Scots* (Vanessa Redgrave, Glenda Jackson).

Arnold Haskell, who with his white goatee now looks like a Chinese sage, is informally regarded as the dance critic emeritus of the English-speaking world and travels around the globe judging competitions and writing reports. His wife died in 1969. In 1970 he married Markova's middle sister, Vivian, whom he claims has been in love with him "since she was five."

Liza Hewitt lives with her architect husband in a small Kentish village and leads the quiet life of a retired English gentlewoman.

Peggy Laing, having married a second time, now runs her own half-timbered inn in Devonshire.

Arthur Bliss is Master of the Queen's Musicians and a truly august figure in British music.

Clifford Curzon has become one of the ranking pianists of the day. He and his wife, Lucille, adopted as their own the two orphaned sons of an Austrian friend. Their house at Highgate, Hampstead, is a most beautiful home that contains many fine paintings — and in a place of honor, a cast of the hand of Chopin.

Krishna Menon was for a time editor-in-chief of Pelican Paperback Books in London. He later became the right-hand man of Nehru and was sent as Indian delegate to the United Nations, where his stormy denunciations of the western powers, and chiefly the United States, made headlines constantly. He was in time recalled to India and made minister of war, but after the disastrous border conflicts with China and Nehru's death, his career declined, and although active in politics he has since lived in relative obscurity. He always remained my friend and because he loved little children was very kind to my small son.

Robin Lennox, who has asked to remain anonymous, had a fine career with the British Broadcasting Company and is now retired and living with his wife in an eighteenth-century brick and flint country house. He writes.

It's a cul-de-sac hamlet — just a few cottages and a pub grouped round a patch of grass.

I am only just beginning to emerge from postretirement lethargy. I suppose I have read more in the past two years than in the previous twenty — but that's not saying much. I dabble ineffectually in politics. I do a lot of walking (this house is at the center of a splendid network of footpaths) and I represent walkers' organizations at public inquiries about rights of way. Sometimes I go off on long-distance walks such as the Pennine Way (about which I did a broadcast last year) or Offa's Dyke. One day, if ever I can get enough commissions to cover the expenses, I hope to try the Appalachian Trail.

Do you everhear from Krishna? I saw him in Delhi in 1966, when he was very kind and helpful.

Arthur and Lily Madsen and Jessie Paul died as they lived, denouncing the economics of their country and crying out against stupidity. It was at the end of a Taxation of Land Values Conference in Bostall Heath, Kent, on Sunday, April 7, 1957, that Madsen, in reply to a proposal for government help, a kind of dole, in lieu of justice, jumped to his feet. "What!" he shouted. "Beg? On bended knees?" and dropped dead.

Elizabeth Bowen lives in Hythe near Folkstone, having sold her gorgeous Regents Park mansion and Bowen Court in Ireland after her husband's death. She writes less than she used to, which is a tragedy for all of us.

Rebecca West has become one of the immortals — going from strength to strength. Her last novel, *The Birds Fall Down,* is an achievement of the highest order. Widowed in 1970, she sold the fine estate in High Wycombe and lives now near my old stamping ground, World's End, London.

Charles Cochran died horribly, scalded to death in his bathtub. His wife, Evelyn — disconsolate for many reasons — followed him a year later.

Romney Brent, after continuing success on the English stage and screen, returned to the United States at the outbreak of war and joined the army. He served with the USO, staging performances at the great air base in Winnipeg, Canada. Subsequently he toured under the auspices of the United States State Department for many years in Spanish-speaking countries, directing and acting in plays sent out by our government. Under the same auspices he made a worldwide tour with Helen Hayes. He now lives in Mexico City and teaches at the University of the Americas at Puebla.

Cole Porter suffered in 1937 a terrible fall while hunting on Long Island and his leg was smashed under his horse. He sustained more than ten operations during the next two decades only to lose the limb eventually. He wrote the words and music for twenty musicals, several of them ranking among our greatest. He continued until his death to turn out matchless songs. Music scholars consider his melody the best-crafted of all of our contemporary songwriters.

Douglas Fairbanks, Jr., married an American and makes his home in the Boltons, London, in neighborly proximity to James Laver. Laver retired only recently from the Victoria and Albert Museum. The Fairbanks figure in every good list of Café Society which, since it ingested royalty, is probably the only Society there is.

The glamorous and make-believe life of Gertie Lawrence came to a temporary halt the year after *Nymph Errant*, when she suddenly declared bankruptcy. Her house and goods were put up for sale and a dozen or so small shopkeepers and green-grocers were ruined. What happened to the jewels I do not know. But Gertie bounced back more zestful than ever and went on from triumph to triumph in London and New York and to international honors for her services as troop entertainer during the war. In 1940, she married Richard Aldrich, but continued her career with mounting acclaim until, during her unforgettable run in *The King and I,* death, unexpected, unbelieved, cut her down with infectious hepatitis in 1950. She died at fifty-three, beloved everywhere. The lights of the playhouses of the two greatest theatrical cities of the world dimmed that night in her memory.

A couple of months after Ramon's death, Cousin Joan Reed came to me and offered her services and car for whatever purpose I could use them. She said Ramon would like her to do this. She proved of invaluable help and when Antony and I had our joint company the next summer she worked for both of us, perfectly free, of course, and very expertly and tirelessly, and like all of us paying her own way.

Just before the war she got married and moved to South Africa, where she lives with her rancher husband and two children in East Traansval. When she leaves the veldt it is to travel in Europe. She spends as little time as possible in England: "I do not like London at all and the people have become so dreary. I am sure I was not an Evelyn Waugh heroine, just a middle-class English girl who wanted to climb out of her environment — and I did, and you and Ramon helped me."

The chronic melancholies of Percy Reed deepened in the years after Ramon's death and he repeatedly threatened suicide. After lunch one day in 1942 he got up from the table and shot himself in the next room. He had, however, begot two children, and his wife, Joan, was able to look forward to continuity at Netherfield Place. She died in the late sixties. Her daughters are married.

Dan Folke became something of a national hero during the war, working in the Danish resistance. He ferried his wife, Lise, across the straits outside his house to Sweden and returned many times alone on secret missions.

Their two sons were born in Copenhagen when peace was restored. Dan and Lise died within two years of one another of cancer while still very young. He was at the time in line to become the head of his publishing house, Wilhelm Hansen.

Cecil B. de Mille's last picture was his second version of *The Ten Commandments*, made with the collaboration of the Nile Valley, Queen Hatshepsut's tomb, a sizable part of the Egyptian people, a Squadron of Royal Egyptian Cavalry (an Egyptian cavalry officer married Cecil's granddaughter, little Cecilia), and several scores of Hollywood stars and staff. "Did you deal through the State Department?" we asked naïvely. "Certainly not," he replied. "I made my arrangements directly with Gamal Nasser and his government. I don't like red tape and delays." The picture is revived frequently and seems to have become a part of our permanent heritage.

He remained a top drawing-card until his death, which is a very unusual achievement in Hollywood. When he died in 1959, three entire pages of the *Los Angeles Times* were given to his obituary. The event was headline news around the world. His death closed an era. He left a fortune.

My sister Margaret did divorce, had a distinguished career in the fashion business, and retired to marry George Doughman. She leads the life of a contented matron on the Eastern Shore of Maryland. She is the grandmother of two.

My father spent the last years of his life as head of the drama department (which he founded) at the University of Southern California. He was adored by his students. One of them wrote me in April 1972: "Through the years I've treasured my association with 'Papa' de Mille. He fussed, ridiculed and chided, saw me through several school romances; and when I introduced him to my future husband he said, 'Well, I like him. That's the best thing Agnes ever did. She also married a Texan.' "

Pop died in 1954. He was very proud of me because I was the first dancer ever to direct a big musical (*Allegro*) and he thought I did it very well. We were close at the end.

My mother died in 1947, two days after *Brigadoon* opened in New York City. She lived to see me the most successful choreographer in the commercial theater, to see me offered the direction of the Salzburg Festival by Reinhardt's widow, the direction of the Paris Opéra Ballet by a representative of the French government, a salary of $4,000 per week by Hollywood, all of which I declined. She lived to see me married happily and to know that my son, who had been desperately ill, would survive. The best press I had ever received was at her bedside when she died, together with a letter from the University of North Carolina Press, promising to publish the biography of her father on which she had worked so many years.

Edgar Wind did not marry me; he married someone else and they lived, I presume, with reasonable happiness. I saw them only once, some years after the wedding. He seemed embarrassed by my presence. His career during the war and later, as a lecturer in America, was distinguished and on his return to England in 1956 he became the first holder of the Chair of History of Art at Oxford, which he retained until 1967. On his formal retirement he was succeeded by Arnold Haskell's son. He died of pneumonia on October 12, 1971. He is survived by his widow.

I never heard from him except when he sent someone to use my library, a colleague who was writing a study on Henry George.

All inquiries have failed to elicit any information concerning Henry Arthur Sharpe beyond the fact that he was dropped from the Nurses' Registry in 1941 for nonpayment of dues.

All of Ramon Reed's letters were thrown out of my basement and destroyed by an overzealous janitor. Not one scrap is left me. His writings entrusted to others have disappeared.

The beautiful oaks in Paulton's Square were blasted in the war and never replaced. Otherwise, the square seems unchanged.

The Single Tax Movement has languished politically for lack of any great driving personality and because of formidable opposition. The men who own the earth do not intend to relinquish it easily. The idea has, however, made considerable progress in education. The American movement is now centered in the Henry George School of Social Science at 50 East 69th Street in

New York City. The school occupies all six floors of a superb town house and maintains classes daily and correspondence courses throughout Latin America. There are other schools in Boston, Los Angeles, San Francisco, Philadelphia, Toronto, Calgary, and a flourishing one in the Dominican Republic. Several universities give college credit for courses taken on George's economics and philosophy.

Important experiments have been made in the taxation of land values in New Zealand, Cleveland and Pittsburgh, but always within the existing tax framework, a handicap which does not permit the theory to work to full advantage.

The province of Alberta, Canada, however, has retained through its constitution all the mineral rights of the land and exacts the full rental value of these rights in taxes. The Crown owns ninety percent of the petroleum and natural gas — mineral rights — and administers these natural resources by lease to private companies of specified blocks. The Crown collects economic rent which is paid in free competition with others.

During the past twenty-three years the petroleum industry has paid $3.8 billion to the provincial governments of Alberta, Saskatchewan, Manitoba and British Columbia. It is generally conceded that Alberta's high level of prosperity is due mainly to this natural revenue. All inheritance taxes levied by the national government of Canada are rebated to the individual citizen by the provincial government.

A growing body of important men now openly advocates land-value taxation. Dean Richard Netzer of New York University is perhaps the foremost economist, and Senator Paul Douglas and Senator Edmund Muskie have spoken forcibly on its behalf. The last hundred pages of James Michener's *Hawaii* is straight Georgism and constitutes as brilliant and persuasive an argument as could be found anywhere. Michener speaks with loving admiration of the small group of London Single-Taxers who did such valiant pioneering work.

Perry Prentiss, vice-president for twenty-five years of Time

Inc., the second publisher of *Time* Magazine, and publisher and editor of *House and Home* and the *Architectural Forum,* writes and lectures regularly and tirelessly. He says:

In my opinion there is nothing so powerful as an idea whose time has come. The problem of our cities, and it is our paramount problem, is the property tax. We tax improvements harder than any other national product except liquor and cigarettes; and then we wonder why we don't have improvements. . . . The injustice and foolishness of our tax system has got to be faced now. Welfare is no answer. What people don't realize is that the income tax is straight socialism. . . . George came to his convictions through his concern with poverty. I came to the same convictions through my concern with the disintegration of the cities. Men are talking seriously everywhere along these lines. Tomorrow the legislatures and governments will act.

The Henry George bed is where my mother wished it to be, in the birthplace, now a landmark museum on South 10th Street, near to the old Customs House in Philadelphia.

To those who are moved by more than passing curiosity, I think I can do no better than to quote the essence of Henry George's philosophy in his own words.

The Single Tax
What It Is and What We Urge It

By HENRY GEORGE

Whoever, laying aside prejudice and self-interest, will honestly and carefully make up his own mind as to the causes and cure of the social evils that are so apparent, does, in that, the most important thing in his power toward their removal. Social reform is not to be secured by noise and shouting; by complaints and denunciation; by the formation of parties; or the making of revolutions; but by the awakening of thought and the progress of ideas. Until there be correct thought there cannot be right action; and when there is correct thought, right action will follow.

I shall briefly state the fundamental principles of what we who advocate it call the Single Tax.

We propose to abolish all taxes save one single tax levied on the value of land, irrespective of the value of the improvements in or on it.

What we propose is not a tax on real estate, for real estate includes improvements. Nor is it a tax on land, for we would not tax all land, but only land having a value irrespective of its improvements, and would tax that in proportion to that value.

Our plan involves the imposition of no new tax, since we already tax land values in taxing real estate. To carry it out we have only to abolish all taxes save the tax on real estate, and to abolish all of that which now falls on buildings or improvements, leaving only that part of it which now falls on the value of the bare land, increasing that so as to take as nearly as may be the whole of economic rent, or what is sometimes styled the "unearned increment of land values."

That the value of the land alone would suffice to provide all needed public revenues — municipal, county, state, and national — there is no doubt.

To show briefly why we urge this change, let me treat (1) of its expediency, and (2) of its justice.

From the Single Tax we may expect these advantages:

1. It would dispense with a whole army of tax gatherers and other officials which present taxes require, and place in the treasury a much larger proportion of what is taken from the people, while by making government simpler and cheaper, it would tend to make it purer. It would get rid of taxes which necessarily promote fraud, perjury, bribery, and corruption, which lead men into temptation, and which tax what the nation can least afford to spare — honesty and conscience. Since land lies out-of-doors

and cannot be removed, and its value is the most readily ascertained of all values, the tax to which we would resort can be collected with the minimum of cost and the least strain on public morals.

2. It would enormously increase the production of wealth —

(a) By the removal of the burdens that now weigh upon industry and thrift. If we tax houses, there will be fewer and poorer houses; if we tax machinery, there will be less machinery; if we tax trade, there will be less trade; if we tax capital, there will be less capital; if we tax savings, there will be less savings. All the taxes therefore that we should abolish are those that repress industry and lessen wealth. But if we tax land values, there will be no less land.

(b) On the contrary, the taxation of land values has the effect of making land more easily available by industry, since it makes it more difficult for owners of valuable land which they themselves do not care to use to hold it idle for a large future price. While the abolition of taxes on labor and the products of labor would free the active element of production, the taking of land values by taxation would free the passive element by destroying speculative land values and preventing the holding out of use of land needed for use. If anyone will but look around today and see the unused or but half-used land, the idle labor, the unemployed or poorly employed capital, he will get some idea of how enormous would be the production of wealth were all the forces of production free to engage.

(c) The taxation of the processes and products of labor on one hand, and the insufficient taxation of land values on the other, produce an unjust distribution of wealth which is building up in the hands of a few, fortunes more monstrous than the world has ever before seen, while the masses of our people are steadily becoming relatively poorer. These taxes necessarily fall on the poor more heavily than on the rich; by increasing prices, they necessitate a larger capital in all businesses, and consequently give an advantage to large capitals; and they give, and

in some cases are designed to give, special advantage and monop-
olies to combinations and trusts. On the other hand, the insufficient taxation of land values enables men to make large fortunes
by land speculation and the increase of ground values — fortunes
which do not represent any addition by them to the general
wealth of the community, but merely the appropriation by some
of what the labor of others creates.

This unjust distribution of wealth develops on the one hand
a class idle and wasteful because they are too rich, and on the
other hand a class idle and wasteful because they are too poor.
It deprives men of capital and opportunities which would make
them more efficient producers. It thus greatly diminishes production.

(d) The unjust distribution which is giving us the hundred-
fold millionaire on the one side and the tramp and pauper on the
other, generates thieves, gamblers, and social parasites of all
kinds, and requires large expenditure of money and energy in
watchmen, policemen, courts, prisons, and other means of de-
fense and repression. It kindles a greed of gain and a worship of
wealth, and produces a bitter struggle for existence which fosters
drunkenness, increases insanity, and causes men whose energies
ought to be devoted to honest production to spend their time
and strength in cheating and grabbing from each other. Besides
the moral loss, all this involves an enormous economic loss which
the Single Tax would save.

(e) The taxes we would abolish fall most heavily on the
poorer agricultural districts, and tend to drive population and
wealth from them to the great cities. The tax we would increase
would destroy that monopoly of land which is the great cause of
that distribution of population which is crowding the people too
closely together in some places and scattering them too far apart
in other places. Families live on top of one another in cities because of the enormous speculative prices at which vacant lots
are held. In the country they are scattered too far apart for
social intercourse and convenience, because, instead of each tak-

ing what land he can use, every one who can grabs all he can get, in the hope of profiting by its increase of value, and the next man must pass farther on. Thus we have scores of families living under a single roof, and other families living in dugouts on the prairies afar from neighbors — some living too close to each other for moral, mental, or physical health, and others too far separated for the stimulating and refining influences of society. The wastes in health, in mental vigor, and in unnecessary transportation result in great economic losses which the Single Tax would save.

Let us turn to the moral side and consider the question of justice.

The right of property does not rest on human laws; they have often ignored and violated it. It rests on natural laws. It is clear and absolute, and every violation of it, whether committed by a man or a nation, is a violation of the command, "Thou shalt not steal." The man who catches a fish, grows an apple, raises a calf, builds a house, makes a coat, paints a picture, constructs a machine, has, as to any such thing, an exclusive right of ownership which carries with it the right to give, to sell or bequeath that thing. . . . There must be an exclusive right of possession of land, for the man who uses it must have secure possession of land in order to reap the products of his labor. But his right of possession must be limited by the equal right of all, and should therefore be conditioned on the payment to the community by the possessor of an equivalent for any special valuable privilege thus accorded him.

When we tax houses, crops, money, furniture, capital or wealth in any of its forms, we take from individuals what rightfully belongs to them. We violate the right of property, and in the name of the state commit robbery. But when we tax ground values, we take from individuals what does not belong to them, but belongs to the community, and which cannot be left to individuals without the robbery of other individuals.

Consider the difference between the value of a building and

the value of land. The value of a building, like the value of goods, or of anything properly styled wealth, is produced by individual exertion, and therefore properly belongs to the individual; but the value of land only arises with the growth and improvement of the community, and therefore properly belongs to the community. It is not because of what its owners have done, but because of the presence of the whole great population, that land in New York is worth millions an acre. This value therefore is the proper fund for defraying the common expenses of the whole population; and it must be taken for public use, under penalty of generating land speculation and monopoly which will bring about artificial scarcity where the Creator has provided in abundance for all whom His providence has called into existence. It is thus a violation of justice to tax labor, or the things produced by labor, and it is also a violation of justice not to tax land values.

These are the fundamental reasons for which we urge the Single Tax, believing it to be the greatest and most fundamental of all reforms. We do not think it will change human nature. That, man can never do; but it will bring about conditions in which human nature can develop what is best, instead of, as now in so many cases, what is worst. It will permit such an enormous production as we can now hardly conceive. It will secure an equitable distribution. It will solve the labor problem and dispel the darkening clouds which are now gathering over the horizon of our civilization. It will make undeserved poverty an unknown thing.

Index